THE NORTON MIX:
SOCIOLOGY

GENERAL EDITORS

Nathan Palmer
COORDINATING EDITOR
Georgia Southern University

Tanya Gladney
University of St. Thomas

Erica Hunter
State University of New York–Albany

Fernando I. Rivera
University of Central Florida

THE NORTON MIX:
SOCIOLOGY

A CUSTOM TEXTBOOK AND READER

Introduction To Sociology Reader

Instructor Maristella H. Tapia

De Anza College

Spring Quarter 2013

NORTON
CUSTOM
W. W. NORTON & COMPANY, INC.
NEW YORK • LONDON

W. W. NORTON & COMPANY has been independent since its founding in 1923, when William Warder Norton and Mary D. Herter Norton first published lectures delivered at the People's Institute, the adult education division of New York City's Cooper Union. The firm soon expanded its program beyond the Institute, publishing books by celebrated academics from America and abroad. By midcentury, the two major pillars of Norton's publishing program—trade books and college texts—were firmly established. In the 1950s, the Norton family transferred control of the company to its employees, and today—with a staff of four hundred and a comparable number of trade, college, and professional titles published each year—W. W. Norton & Company stands as the largest and oldest publishing house owned wholly by its employees.

Editor: Karl Bakeman
Custom editor: Katie Hannah
Project editors: Kate Feighery and Melissa Atkin
Prodution managers, College: Ashley Horna and Diana Spiegle
Custom assistant editor: Erica Wnek
Custom editorial assistants: Elizabeth Dana and Sophie Hagen
Editorial assistant: Alicia Gonzalez-Gross
Managing editor: Marian Johnson
Copyeditor: Letta Wren Page
Design director: Rubina Yeh
Book designers: Joan Greenfield, Hope Miller Goodell, and Kiss Me I'm Polish
Text permissions manager: Megan Jackson
Text permissions editor: Nancy Rodwan
Photo permissions manager: Trish Marx
Photo permissions editor: Stephanie Romeo
Composition: Westchester Publishing Services
Manufacturing: RR Donnelley

ISBN 978-0-393-90709-4

W. W. Norton & Company, Inc., 500 Fifth Avenue, New York, N.Y. 10110
www.wwnorton.com
W. W. Norton & Company Ltd., Castle House, 75/76 Wells Street, London W1T 3QT

CONTENTS

Introduction To The Sociological Perspective

Culture, Socialization, and the Self

Social Interaction

Deviance and Crime

Class Stratification

Race and Ethnicity

Gender Inequality

Social Institutions: Education

Social Institutions: Work and Housing

Power and Social Change

C. WRIGHT MILLS

From *The Sociological Imagination*

I f you're taking an introductory **sociology** course, you're likely to hear about "the **sociological imagination**" early and often. In this excerpt, the influential sociologist C. Wright Mills describes what it means to look at the world through the eyes of a social analyst. To be truly curious about the world, Mills argues, you must consider history, biography, and **social structure**. Such curiosity will result in a new understanding of the world and your place in it. Do you think you have a sociological imagination? If not, what would it take to begin to exercise one?

NOWADAYS MEN OFTEN FEEL THAT THEIR PRIVATE LIVES ARE A series of traps. They sense that within their everyday worlds, they cannot overcome their troubles, and in this feeling, they are often quite correct: What ordinary men are directly aware of and what they try to do are bounded by the private orbits in which they live; their visions and their powers are limited to the close-up scenes of job, family, neighborhood; in other milieux, they move vicariously and remain spectators. And the more aware they become, however vaguely, of ambitions and of threats which transcend their immediate locales, the more trapped they seem to feel.

Underlying this sense of being trapped are seemingly impersonal changes in the very structure of continent-wide societies. The facts of contemporary history are also facts about the success and the failure of individual men and women. When a society is industrialized, a peasant becomes a worker; a feudal lord is liquidated or becomes a businessman. When classes rise or fall, a man is employed or unemployed; when the rate of investment goes up or down, a man takes new heart or goes broke. When wars happen, an insurance salesman becomes a rocket launcher; a store clerk, a radar man; a wife lives alone; a child grows up without a father. Neither the life of an individual nor the history of a society can be understood without understanding both.

Yet men do not usually define the troubles they endure in terms of historical change and institutional contradiction. The well-being they enjoy, they do not usually impute to the big ups and downs of the societies in which they live. Seldom aware of the intricate connection between the patterns of their own lives and the course of world history, ordinary men do not usually know what this connection means for the kinds of men they are becoming and for the kinds of history-making in which they might take part. They do not possess the quality of mind essential to grasp the interplay of man and society, of biography and history, of self and world. They cannot cope with their personal troubles in such ways as to control the structural transformations that usually lie behind them.

Surely it is no wonder. In what period have so many men been so totally exposed at so fast a pace to such earthquakes of change? That Americans have not known such catastrophic changes as have the men and women of other societies is due to historical facts that are now quickly becoming "merely history." The history that now affects every man is world history. Within this scene and this period, in the course of a single generation, one sixth of mankind is transformed from all that is feudal and backward into all that is modern, advanced, and fearful. Political colonies are freed; new and less visible forms of imperialism installed. Revolutions occur; men feel the intimate grip of new kinds of authority. Totalitarian societies rise, and are smashed to bits—or succeed fabulously. After two centuries of ascendancy, capitalism is shown up as only one way to make society into an industrial apparatus. After two centuries of hope, even formal democracy is restricted to a quite small portion of mankind. Everywhere in the underdeveloped world, ancient ways of life are broken up and vague expectations become urgent demands. Everywhere in the overdeveloped world, the means of authority and of violence become total in scope and bureaucratic in form. Humanity itself now lies before us, the super-nation at either pole concentrating its most coordinated and massive efforts upon the preparation of World War Three.

The very shaping of history now outpaces the ability of men to orient themselves in accordance with cherished values. And which values? Even when they do not panic, men often sense that older ways of feeling and thinking have collapsed and that newer beginnings are ambiguous to the point of moral stasis. Is it any wonder that ordinary men feel they cannot cope with the larger worlds with which they are so suddenly confronted? That they cannot understand the meaning of their epoch for their own lives? That—in defense of selfhood—they become morally insensible, trying to remain altogether private men? Is it any wonder that they come to be possessed by a sense of the trap?

––––––––––

It is not only information that they need—in this Age of Fact, information often dominates their attention and overwhelms their capacities to assimilate it. It is not only the skills of reason that they need—although their struggles to acquire these often exhaust their limited moral energy.

What they need, and what they feel they need, is a quality of mind that will help them to use information and to develop reason in order to achieve lucid summations of what is going on in the world and of what may be happening within themselves. It is this quality, I am going to contend, that journalists and scholars, artists and publics, scientists and editors are coming to expect of what may be called the sociological imagination.

1

The sociological imagination enables its possessor to understand the larger historical scene in terms of its meaning for the inner life and the external career of a variety of individuals. It enables him to take into account how individuals, in the welter of their daily experience, often become falsely conscious of their social positions. Within that welter, the framework of modern society is sought, and within that framework the psychologies of a variety of men and women are formulated. By such means the personal uneasiness of individuals is focused upon explicit troubles and the indifference of publics is transformed into involvement with public issues.

The first fruit of this imagination—and the first lesson of the social science that embodies it—is the idea that the individual can understand his own experience and gauge his own fate only by locating himself within his period, that he can know his own chances in life only by becoming aware of those of all individuals in his circumstances. In many ways it is a terrible lesson; in many ways a magnificent one. We do not know the limits of man's capacities for supreme effort or willing degradation, for agony or glee, for pleasurable brutality or the sweetness of reason. But in our time we have come to know that the limits of "human nature" are frighteningly broad. We have come to know that every individual lives, from one generation to the next, in some society; that he lives out a biography, and that he lives it out within some historical sequence. By the fact of his living he contributes, however minutely, to the shaping of this society and to the course of its history, even as he is made by society and by its historical push and shove.

The sociological imagination enables us to grasp history and biography and the relations between the two within society. That is its task and its promise. To recognize this task and this promise is the mark of the classic social analyst. And it is the signal of what is best in contemporary studies of man and society.

No social study that does not come back to the problems of biography, of history and of their intersections within a society has completed its intellectual journey. Whatever the specific problems of the classic social analysts, however limited or however broad the features of social reality they have examined, those who have been imaginatively aware of the promise of their work have consistently asked three sorts of questions:

1. What is the structure of this particular society as a whole? What are its essential components, and how are they related to one another? How does it differ from other varieties of social order? Within it, what is the meaning of any particular feature for its continuance and for its change?

2. Where does this society stand in human history? What are the mechanics by which it is changing? What is its place within and its meaning for the development of humanity as a whole? How does any particular feature we are examining affect, and how is it affected by, the historical period in which it moves? And this period—what are its essential features? How does it differ from other periods? What are its characteristic ways of history-making?

3. What varieties of men and women now prevail in this society and in this period? And what varieties are coming to prevail? In what ways are they selected and formed, liberated and repressed, made sensitive and blunted? What kinds of "human nature" are revealed in the conduct and character we observe in this society in this period? And what is the meaning for "human nature" of each and every feature of the society we are examining?

Whether the point of interest is a great power state or a minor literary mood, a family, a prison, a creed—these are the kinds of questions the best social analysts have asked. They are the intellectual pivots of classic studies of man in society—and they are the questions inevitably raised by any mind possessing the sociological imagination. For that imagination is the capacity to shift from one perspective to another—from the political to the psychological; from examination of a single family to comparative assessment of the national budgets of the world; from the theological school to the military establishment; from considerations of an oil industry to studies of contemporary poetry. It is the capacity to range from the most impersonal and remote transformations to the most intimate features of the human self—and to see the relations between the two. Back of its use there is always the urge to know the social and historical meaning of the individual in the society and in the period in which he has his quality and his being.

That, in brief, is why it is by means of the sociological imagination that men now hope to grasp what is going on in the world, and to understand what is happening in themselves as minute points of the intersections of biography and history within society. In large part, contemporary man's self-conscious view of himself as at least an outsider, if not a permanent stranger, rests upon an absorbed realization of social relativity and of the transformative power of history. The sociological imagination is the most fruitful form of this self-consciousness. By its use men whose mentalities have swept only a series of limited orbits often come to feel as if suddenly awakened in a house with which they had only supposed themselves to be familiar. Correctly or incorrectly, they often come to feel that they can now provide themselves with adequate summations, cohesive assessments, comprehensive orientations. Older decisions that once appeared sound now seem to them products of a mind unaccountably dense. Their capacity for astonishment is made lively again. They acquire a new way of thinking, they experience a transvaluation of values: in a word, by their reflection and by their sensibility, they realize the cultural meaning of the social sciences.

2

Perhaps the most fruitful distinction with which the sociological imagination works is between "the personal troubles of milieu" and "the public issues of social structure." This distinction is an essential tool of the sociological imagination and a feature of all classic work in social science.

Troubles occur within the character of the individual and within the range of his immediate relations with others; they have to do with his self and with those limited areas of social life of which he is directly and personally aware. Accordingly, the statement and the resolution of troubles properly lie within the individual as a biographical entity and within the scope of his immediate milieu—the social setting that is directly open to his personal experience and to some extent his willful activity. A trouble is a private matter: values cherished by an individual are felt by him to be threatened.

Issues have to do with matters that transcend these local environments of the individual and the range of his inner life. They have to do with the organization of many such milieux into the institutions of an historical society as a whole, with the ways in which various milieux overlap and interpenetrate to form the larger structure of social and historical life. An issue is a public matter: some value cherished by publics is felt to be threatened. Often there is a debate about what that value really is and about what it is that really threatens it. This debate is often without focus if only because it is the very nature of an issue, unlike even widespread trouble, that it cannot very well be defined in terms of the immediate and everyday environments of ordinary men. An issue, in fact, often involves a crisis in institutional arrangements, and often too it involves what Marxists call "contradictions" or "antagonisms."

———————

In these terms, consider unemployment. When, in a city of 100,000, only one man is unemployed, that is his personal trouble, and for its relief we properly look to the character of the man, his skills, and his immediate opportunities. But when in a nation of 50 million employees, 15 million men are unemployed, that is an issue, and we may not hope to find its solution within the range of opportunities open to any one individual. The very structure of opportunities has collapsed. Both the correct statement of the problem and the range of possible solutions require us to consider the economic and political institutions of the society, and not merely the personal situation and character of a scatter of individuals.

Consider war. The personal problem of war, when it occurs, may be how to survive it or how to die in it with honor; how to make money out of it; how to climb into the higher safety of the military apparatus; or how to contribute to the war's termination. In short, according to one's values, to find a set of milieux and within it to survive the war or make one's death in it meaningful. But the structural issues of war have to do with its causes; with what types of men it throws up into command; with its effects upon economic and political, family and religious institutions, with the unorganized irresponsibility of a world of nation-states.

Consider marriage. Inside a marriage a man and a woman may experience personal troubles, but when the divorce rate during the first four years of marriage is 250 out of every 1,000 attempts, this is an indication of a structural issue having to do with the institutions of marriage and the family and other institutions that bear upon them.

Or consider the metropolis—the horrible, beautiful, ugly, magnificent sprawl of the great city. For many upper-class people, the personal solution to 'the problem of the city' is to have an apartment with private garage under it in the heart of the city, and forty miles out, a house by Henry Hill, garden by Garrett Eckbo, on a hundred acres of private land. In these two controlled environments—with a small staff at each end and a private helicopter connection—most people could solve many of the problems of personal milieux caused by the facts of the city. But all this, however splendid, does not solve the public issues that the structural fact of the city poses. What should be done with this wonderful monstrosity? Break it all up into scattered units, combining residence and work? Refurbish it as it stands? Or, after evacuation, dynamite it and build new cities according to new plans in new places? What should those plans be? And who is to decide and to accomplish whatever choice is made? These are structural issues; to confront them and to solve them requires us to consider political and economic issues that affect innumerable milieux.

In so far as an economy is so arranged that slumps occur, the problem of unemployment becomes incapable of personal solution. In so far as war is inherent in the nation-state system and in the uneven industrialization of the world, the ordinary individual in his restricted milieu will be powerless—with or without psychiatric aid—to solve the troubles this system or lack of system imposes upon him. In so far as the family as an institution turns women into darling little slaves and men into their chief providers and unweaned dependents, the problem of a satisfactory marriage remains incapable of purely private solution. In so far as the overdeveloped megalopolis and the overdeveloped automobile are built-in features of the overdeveloped society, the issues of urban living will not be solved by personal ingenuity and private wealth.

———————

What we experience in various and specific milieux, I have noted, is often caused by structural changes. Accordingly, to understand the changes of many personal milieux we are required to look beyond them. And the number and variety of such structural changes increase as the institutions within which we live become more embracing and more intricately connected with one another. To be aware of the idea of social structure and to use it with sensibility is to be capable of tracing such linkages among a great variety of milieux. To be able to do that is to possess the sociological imagination.

STUDY QUESTIONS

1. What does the **sociological imagination** enable its possessor to do?

2. What is the difference between "troubles" and "issues"? How can knowing the difference help us analyze a situation?

3. Mills says that the "first lesson" of the sociological imagination is both "terrible" and "magnificent." What does he mean? In what ways do your own knowledge of history and your own place in the world seem both terrible and magnificent?

4. Choose a **culture** to describe (it could be your fraternity/sorority, the group of actors and other theater types you hang out with, a regional group such as Southerners or Westerners, or some other culture). With your group in mind, answer the questions Mills outlines as those asked by the "imaginatively aware." Discuss with your classmates what you learned about this culture in the process.

ANDRAÉ L. BROWN, MELINA DIMITRIOU,
AND LISA DRESSNER

Rituals as Tools of Resistance: From Survival to Liberation

Rituals help **families** mourn losses, transition through life, and mark significant moments. During times of crisis, rituals help families restore balance, reestablish a steady pace, and recommit to shared **values** and goals. Rituals are used extensively to cope with family stressors such as the death of a loved one, chronic illness, and changes in the life cycle such as **marriage**, retirement, or adjustment to the empty nest. But such rites are rarely incorporated into a family's process of adjusting to the loss of a member through incarceration. The incarceration process, from the time of arrest through sentencing, does not provide adequate time and space for family rituals to occur naturally. This paper demonstrates how a **community** ceremony that prepares a young man for prison may support his commitment to rehabilitation, facilitate the family's grieving process, and prepare the community for his reintegration.

FAMILY RITUALS

*Every family and every culture throughout time create, enact,
alter and preserve rituals. (Imber-Black, 2002, p. 455)*

WE ARE ALL RITUAL MAKERS. RITUALS HELP US STAY CONNECTED
to the past as we move toward the future. They enable us to preserve a sense of

continuity, consistency, identity and belonging, while simultaneously integrating change and marking the transitions in our lives.[1] In addition to cultivating a sense of identity and rootedness within families, rituals connect those families to a wider community.[2]

Social scientists describe rituals as formalized, symbolic performances. "Formalized" suggests that there is an accepted format for carrying out the event. "Symbolic" implies that the ritual's components might be more significant and meaningful than they appear on the surface. And "performance" indicates that the ritual's importance depends on how it is enacted by the participants. The extent to which participants follow a ritual's pre-established script is indicative of their sense of its importance.[3]

When family members participate in a ritual, it is quite common for each member to ascribe a unique meaning to the ceremony. Participation in a ritual also delivers a hidden meaning to the insiders, bolstering their sense of rightness and emotional commitment and providing members of the group with a sense of continuity and commonality across generations.[4]

Rituals frame and express family structures and relationships, reinforce roles and boundaries, and articulate family identity and belief systems. When we examine rituals critically, they can serve as a lens through which we can better understand a family's intergenerational patterns—how people relate, communicate, and articulate their needs.[5]

Often older generations are more committed to carrying on family rituals, seeing them as mechanisms that build successful families and that allow elders to demonstrate and validate their role in the family. But for traditions to be carried forward, younger family members must also become more appreciative of the rituals as they grow older and must feel that such practices are relevant to their lives.[6]

Mealtime provides an example of how rituals, viewed as patterns of interaction, can tell us a lot about family dynamics. We can deduce a great deal about how a family functions if we know how often a family eats together, how the food is prepared, who is seated at the table, and how they relate and converse at mealtime. With contemporary families spending more time sitting mutely in front of the television, the family meal may be the one time and place where members of the family share their stories and reflect on their daily experiences.[7]

Because the broader sociopolitical and cultural context influences how families organize, develop, and utilize rituals, any examination of the function of family rituals needs to take into account the social and political context of power, privilege, and oppression.[8] For example, who is allowed to participate in the ritual, who is accepted, and who is rejected? If we examine the extent to which lesbian, gay, transgendered, bisexual, queer, or unisex (LGTBQU) couples participate in family rituals, we need to know if the LGTBQU family member is invited to participate in a celebration, if her/his partner is also invited, and how they are treated during the celebration.

Because rituals can foster a sense of common identity, they can support families during difficult transitions by providing a sense of stability, which can reduce anxiety about change and incorporate it into the family system. Celebrations like birthdays, holidays, and family reunions are important in providing a sense of family togetherness, stability, and continuity. They also reinforce the family's racial, ethnic, religious, and cultural identity.[9]

TYPES OF RITUALS

Transition rituals, healing rituals, and identity-reforming rituals all have therapeutic value. Transition rituals mark changes in family relationships, membership, and boundaries that accompany exceptional life events such as marriage and birth. Family transition rituals can create unique and meaningful ways to facilitate insight and ease transformations.[10] We have also developed an additional transition ritual, explained in detail later, which we feel helps families and communities deal with impending incarceration.

Healing rituals, employed at times of profound loss, help to cope with the grieving process of survivors and promote healthy living after the loss. Healing rituals may also be created to address losses attendant to the breakup of relationships, reconciliation after an affair, losses of bodily parts or losses due to an illness, as well as losses of life roles, expectations, and dreams.

When a loss is accompanied by social stigma, such as death from AIDS or suicide, the healing process may be truncated because standard healing rituals may not address the specific circumstances of the loss. By creating their own healing rituals that address their own circumstances, families can find a safe space and time to genuinely mourn their loss, without worrying about social stigma.

Through rituals that involve redefining identity, therapists try to remove stigmatizing labels from individuals, couples, and families, especially where the larger sociopolitical context views them negatively.

RITUALS AS A MECHANISM OF RESISTANCE

To be human is to belong to the whole community, and to do so involves participating in the beliefs, ceremonies, rituals and festivals of that community. A person cannot detach himself from the religion of his group, for to do so is to be severed from his roots, his foundation, his context of security, his kinship and the entire group of those who make him aware of his own existence. (Mbiti, 1969, p. 2)

When a family faces traumatic life-cycle events like imprisonment, sudden loss, forced migration, divorce, and hospitalization, the creation or adaptation of rituals can help it cope with the crisis. When families are experiencing multiple or constant crises, they tend to operate in survival mode, focusing solely on the basic and immediate needs of family members. Their inability to maintain rituals increases the risks of intergenerational schisms, isolation, stigma, secrecy, and shame, especially if there is a lack of social support from the larger system. Conversely, when rituals are maintained, people are better adjusted and more satisfied because they feel a heightened sense of belonging, membership, and commitment to the family.

When traditional family structures and ceremonies do not fulfill the need for connection, some groups, particularly oppressed and marginalized communities, create their own rituals to mark transitions and elevate their spirits, and sometimes to confront and resist the dominant culture.[11]

Rituals are fluid and changing. Seemingly straightforward activities may be construed in different ways in different times and places. The format of a ceremony is not the only thing that determines its impact. Equally important is the involvement and investment of the participants.

A case in point is the history of marriage ceremonies in the African-American community. Enslaved Africans in America created their own secret wedding ceremony, called "jumping the broom," to mark their committed relationships. During the marriage ceremony the new couple jumped over a broom to symbolize that they were sweeping away their past and beginning new lives together. Although this ritual took place as the participants were enslaved, subjugated, and oppressed, the participants transformed it into an occasion of joy and pride.[12] Even today many contemporary African-American marriages incorporate this tradition.

Similarly, DeSilva describes how, in the face of starvation and almost certain death, Jewish women in a Nazi concentration camp in Czechoslovakia recorded their traditional recipes as a way to maintain their dignity.[13] Through this ritual, the women stayed connected to their culture, ethnic heritage, faith, and families of origin during a time of unimaginable stress.

Establishing and participating in their own rituals can help marginalized groups increase their self-esteem and challenge values promoted by institutions that look down on them. One example is the mechanism that LGBTQU communities developed to publicly honor the loss of lovers, friends, family, and community to HIV/AIDS related deaths.

It began in San Francisco in 1985, when gay rights activist Cleve Jones established the NAMES AIDS Memorial Quilt, the largest ongoing community arts project in the world. The quilt consists of hand-sewn pieces of cloth, each memorializing a person who has died of HIV and AIDS related causes. The names are read aloud in a public ceremony to symbolize breaking the silence of shame and stigma associated with HIV/AIDS. This ritual provides relief, solace, and solidarity for mourners and advocates.[14]

Another example is the Clothesline Project, a community ritual highlighting domestic violence. Hand-painted T-shirts are hung on a clothesline, accompanied by the sound of bells and horns. The ritual symbolizes how often a woman is assaulted, raped, or murdered. This public exposure of violence against women helps these women to regain power and heal.[15]

RITUALS FOR JUSTICE-INVOLVED FAMILIES

The United States incarcerates a much higher proportion of its people, and especially minorities, than other wealthy countries. A white boy born in 2001 has a one in seventeen chance of going to prison during his lifetime. But a black boy born the same year has a one in three chance and a Latino boy has a one in six chance of going to jail! Selective prosecution and punishment accounts for much of this difference. A black youth is about five times more likely to be incarcerated after a drug offense than his white peer. Latino youths are twice as likely as whites to get jail time for a drug arrest.

Minority youth, who make up 39 percent of the juvenile population, account for 60 percent of incarcerated juveniles. The majority of poor children live in working families that play by the rules. But racial disparity influences every aspect of the life of children of color, from education to health care to employment to society's tolerance for boys "acting up."[16]

The disproportionate incarceration rate of people of color tears young adults away from their families and their communities during their most productive years, when they should be building careers and families. Communities suffer when so many of their young men and women are prevented from establishing long-term personal relationships, getting or keeping jobs, and living conventional lives.

RENAMING CEREMONY: FROM SURVIVAL TO EMPOWERMENT AND LIBERATION

Because most African names have a meaning in many parts of Africa, naming children is an important occasion marked by elaborate ceremonies and rituals, during which a name is bestowed that describes personality traits, character, or a key life event.[17] It is hoped that a positive name like "strength" or "pride" might empower an individual to live up to its essence. Receiving names is an ongoing process, and by the time a person is old, he or she might have acquired a sizeable collection, including the names of dead family members in order to continue the family legacy.

At Affinity Counseling Group[18] the therapeutic team came up with a renaming ritual for "Gaston," a young black man out on bond, pending sentencing for violating probation for a drug offense. Gaston was not gang affiliated, although many in his family were, including an uncle who had recently received a life sentence for gang-related murders.

Gangs routinely give street names to their members, typically embodying violent and subhuman personality characteristics like Monster, Money, Boss, or Killer. The counseling group developed a "Renaming Ceremony" ritual to encourage Gaston to accept accountability for his actions, to help him stay in touch with his humanity and maintain his spirit under the conditions of prison life, and to empower him to shift his personal and family life in a positive direction.

Coming up with forms and structures for the ritual was a very fluid and flexible process. The therapeutic team's goal was to get the community to decide what they wanted to see in the ritual so that it would offer an opportunity and encouragement to an adolescent to take responsibility for his own future. The therapists also hoped to foster equity in the client-therapist relationship by expanding the client's choices through a collaborative process rather than imposing their own morality.

When the session began, all members of the therapeutic community (what we call the cultural circle) stood in a circle and held hands. The participants turned off their cell phones and an adolescent member of the circle was delegated to collect them in a basket and place them on a table in the center of the room. Another member of the circle led the recitation of the opening statement: "I place my hand in yours and together we can do what I cannot do alone. Peace."

Then the participants released their hands, made the peace sign, and returned to their chairs. Once seated, all the participants introduced themselves and said what they were feeling. The therapist then began to stage the room for the "Renaming Ceremony."

Gaston sat on a chair in the center while the members of the therapeutic community sat on the floor in concentric circles. His relatives and close friends sat in the closest circle. Positioning the participants in concentric circles around him symbolized the safety, support, and boundaries that the community wanted to create around Gaston to help him survive incarceration.

The therapists began by discussing the purpose of the gathering, which was to acknowledge how Gaston's actions had led to the difficult consequences that he and his family must now bear, as well as how the larger context of the judicial system does not promote rehabilitation and destroys the human spirit. The aim of the ritual, it was explained, was to create a memory for Gaston to hold onto, one that would remind him of his true identity should prison life begin to destroy his concept of self.

Then everyone was asked to sit silently and reflect while the hip-hop/rap artist DMX's spoken word/rap "Prayer" (2001) was played. After that, a member of the group read the essay "They're Playing Your Song" by Alan Cohen (2002), which describes the process of naming children in African tribes.

The piece details how a child is given a name at birth, and how during the struggles of childhood and early adulthood a child may lose his/her way and need to be reminded of the name's significance to the community he/she belongs to. The reading notes that the ritual of remembering one's name is more effective than punishment or scolding in bringing people back to their identity and life purpose.

The tribe creates a name and a song for each newborn and is responsible for remembering it throughout the child's life. The community supports the individual and sings that song, even when the person has forgotten it and has committed actions that are not in line with the spirit of the name.

After the reading, the participants shared their feelings. Family and friends usually grieve privately for the loss of the incarcerated, but here each person was encouraged to express his or her grief and hopes for the future. This can be especially meaningful for young men who are not encouraged in this culture to express their feelings and then are punished if their anger and rage finally manifests itself in acts of violence.

A reading of the poem "Be Who You Must Be" by Diarmuid Cronin (1997) followed the group's discussion. This poem emphasizes the importance of not imposing judgment on people and instead accepting and valuing each individual for who he is.

The client, Gaston, was given the opportunity to reflect and discuss his thoughts, feelings, regrets, anticipations, and wishes for the future. The ritual ended with a member of the community standing and stating on behalf or the entire cultural circle that Gaston's new name was "Hope." Finally, the community engaged in silent reflection as Tupac Shakur's (1993) song "Keep Your Head Up" played.

Participants were then asked to reconvene the circle for the closing ritual. A member of the group, Gaston's best friend, was called upon to "blow bubbles for the circle." As he blew a continuous stream of bubbles, others expressed what they would like to do better or give up in the upcoming weeks. They also expressed their commitments to Gaston and his family.

To end the ceremony, Gaston led the "Place my hands in yours . . ." recitation and everyone shook hands and hugged.

FURTHER AIMS OF THE RENAMING CEREMONY

Every component of the ritual served multiple purposes for all members of the cultural circle. Traditional norms of masculinity emphasize toughness and are adverse to expressions of emotion and activities that are perceived as feminine or hypersensitive. Holding hands, reciting the ritual statement, hugging, and blowing bubbles are behaviors that expand definitions of manhood to include softness, vulnerability, emotional closeness, and relationships with the other men. Holding hands with other men undercuts homophobia and encourages males to create nurturing relationships with other males, while holding hands with women encourages men to relate to females in nonsexualized ways.

Another goal is to encourage emotional connections among adolescents and create a safe and violence-free space, which is especially important because the adolescent participants in the sessions are often affiliated with different street gangs. Participants in this ritual commit themselves to forsaking violent action against any other member of the group. The goal is to create strong, lasting ties of friendship and connection as a way to create community bonding rather than gang bonding.

This is reinforced when adolescents, who want to present themselves as being very tough, see each other blowing bubbles and saying what they hope to do better or give up. By engaging in a very soft activity, like blowing bubbles, the adolescents are encouraged to feel safe to express their emotions and to commit to more life-affirming choices with members of the community.

So even before Gaston started his incarceration, the Renaming Ceremony marked the beginning of his reentry process. During the ritual, the community described what Gaston's process meant to them, what changes they saw in him, and offered their encouragement and support to him and his family. They also discussed plans for him after the end of his incarceration.

In turn, Gaston reflected on his own process and what this experience meant to him. At the end of the ritual, when the community gave him the name "Hope," they indicated that they expected him to live up to the meaning, expectations, and essence of the new name. The Renaming Ceremony also aimed to break the pattern of intergenerational incarceration and create a new legacy for Gaston, his family, and his community. It marked his shift from survival to empowerment and liberation.

In addition, the Renaming Ceremony served as a healing ritual by providing a safe and manageable space for community members to express and deal with emotions associated with the violence that has become a part of everyday life. The reactions of community participants in the ritual were strong and intense. This renaming ritual forced individuals to bring their emotions to the surface and to face the pain of loss that family and friends go through when they lose a loved one.

Another very important element of this ritual was to foster accountability. Participants had to consider their own responsibility in either having deterred or promoted Gaston's criminal involvement. And by connecting with the grieving family, they became more aware of the reality of the loss their own families would feel if they were incarcerated or killed. Participants begin to take responsibility for their lives.

IMPLICATIONS AND CONSIDERATIONS

The creative and flexible use of rituals holds promise for promoting the health and well-being of families. Creating and integrating rituals into the fabric of family life can be vital in a context where American society tends to underestimate the importance of spirituality and ignores the internal need to maintain individual and family health in a chaotic and complex world.

Different types of rituals provide rich sources of information about factors contributing to family dysfunction as well as to family health. Families are often less resistant to using rituals as tools to help produce healthy change than they are to accepting assignments or tasks aimed at change. As we explore strategies to help families build resiliency around normal as well as traumatic life cycle transitions, rituals can be very helpful in acknowledging family history and strengths, and fostering positive change in family interaction. In some instances, they can also be used as tools to support social and political action.

NOTES

1. Bennett, Wolin, and McCavity (1988); Fiese et al. (2002); Imber-Black (1999).
2. Imber-Black (2002).
3. Bjork (2002); Quantz (1999).
4. Fiese (2007).
5. Laird (1984); Mackey and Grief (1994); Roberts (1988).
6. Meske, Sanders, Meredith, and Abbott (1994).
7. Fiese and Marjinsky (1999).
8. Almeida, Dolan-Del Vecchio, and Parker (2008).
9. Karenga (1998).
10. van der Hart (1983).
11. Giroux (1988).
12. Dundes (1996).
13. DeSilva (1996).
14. NAMES Project Foundation (2008).
15. Clothesline Project (2008).
16. Brown (2004); Children's Defense Fund (2007); Payne (2008); Pewewardy and Severson (2003).
17. Mbiti (1969).
18. Affinity Counseling Group (ACG) is an example of a community-based mental health center that utilizes rituals to provide family therapy to youth and families involved in the criminal justice system. The therapeutic model used, the Cultural Context Model, focuses on raising clients' critical awareness of the dynamics of power, privilege, and oppression and how they manifest in their lives and perpetuate suffering.

REFERENCES

Almeida, R. V., K. Dolan-Del Vecchio, and L. Parker. 2008. *Transformative Family Therapy: Just Families in a Just Society*. Boston: Pearson.

Bennett, L. A., S. J. Wolin, and K. J. McCavity. 1988. "Family Identity, Ritual, and Myth: A Cultural Perspective on Life Cycle Transition." Pp. 211–234 in *Family Transitions: Continuity, and Change over Life Cycle*, edited by C. J. Falicov. New York: Guilford Press.

Bjork, C. 2002. "Reconstructing Rituals: Expressions of Autonomy and Resistance in a Sino-Indonesian School." *Anthropology and Education Quarterly* 33: 465–491.

Brown, A. L. 2004. "Exploring Blackness As a Site of Resilience for Street Life Oriented Young Black Men Living in the Inner-City." Ph.D. dissertation, Seton Hall University, South Orange, NJ.

Children's Defense Fund. 2007. *America's Cradle to Prison Pipeline.* Washington, DC: Children's Defense Furd.

Clothesline Project. 2008. Retrieved September 10, 2008, from http://clotheslineproject.org.

Coher., A. 2002. "They're Playing Your Song." Retrieved August 25, 2008, from www.alancohen.com/articles/Perennial/They'rePlayingYourSong.htm.

Cronin, D. 1997. "Be Who You Must Be." Retrieved August 25, 2008, from www.heartnsouls.com/stories/i/s887.shtml.

De Silva, C., ed. 1996. *In Memory's Kitchen: A Legacy from the Women of Terezin.* New York: Jason Aronson.

DMX. 2001. "The Prayer IV." *On The Great Depression* (CD). New York: Ruff Ryders Records.

Dundes, A. 1996. " 'Jumping the Broom': On the Origin and the Meaning of an African American Wedding Custom." *Journal of American Folklore Society* 109: 324–329.

Fiese, B. H. 2007. "Routines and Rituals: Opportunities for Participation in Family Health." *OTJR: Occupation, Participation and Health* 27:415–424.

Fiese, B. H., T. J. Tomcho, M. Douglas, K. Josephs, S. Poltrock, and T. Baker. 2002. "Fifty Years of Research on Naturally Occurring Family Routines and Rituals: Cause of Celebration?" *Journal of Family Psychology* 16: 381–390.

Fiese, B. H., and K. A. T. Marjinsky. 1999. "Dinnertime Stories: Connecting Relationship Beliefs and Child Behavior." In *The Stories that Families Tell: Narrative Coherence, Narrative Interaction, and Relationship Beliefs,* edited by B. H. Fiese, A. J. Sameroff, H. D. Grotevant, F. S. Wamboldt, S. Dickstein, and D. Fravel. *Monographs of the Society for Research in Child Development* 64 (2, Serial No. 257: 52–68) Malden, MA: Blackwell.

Giroux, H. A. 1988. *Schooling and the Struggle of Public Life.* Minneapolis, MN: University of Minnesota Press.

Imber-Black, E. 1999. "Creating Meaningful Rituals for New Life Cycle Transitions. Pp. 202–214 in *The Expanded Family Life Cycle: Individual, Family and Social Perspective,* edited by B. Carter and M. McGeldrick. Needham Heights, MA: Allyn & Bacon.

———. 2002. "Family Rituals: From Research to the Counseling Room and Back Again: Comment on the Special Edition." *Journal of Family Psychology* 16:445–446.

Karenga, M. 1998. *Kwanzaa: A Celebration for Family, Community and Culture.* Los Angeles: University of Sankore Press.

Laird, J. 1984. "Sorcerers, Shamans, and Social Workers: The Use of Rituals in Social Work Practice." *Social Work* 29: 123–129.

Mackey, J., and G. Grief. 1994. "Using Rituals to Help Parents in the School Setting: Lessons from Family Therapy." *Social Work in Education* 16: 171–178.

Mbiti, J. S. 1969. *African Religions and Philosophy.* Johannesburg, South Africa: Heinemann Educational Botswana.

Meske, C., G. F. Sanders, W. H. Meredith, and D. A. Abbott, 1994. "Perceptions of Rituals and Traditions among Elderly Persons." *Activities, Adaptation and Aging: The Journal of Activities Management* 18(2): 13–26.

NAMES Project Foundation. 2008. Retrieved August 29, 2008, from www.aidsquilt.org.

Payne, Y. A. 2008. "'Street Life' as a Site of Resiliency: How Street Life–Oriented, Black Men Frame Opportunity in the United States." *Journal of Black Psychology* 34(3): 3–31.

Pewewardy, N., and M. J. D. Severson. 2003. "A Threat to Liberty: White Privilege and Disproportionate Minority Incarceration." *Journal of Progressive Human Services* 14(2): 53–74.

Quantz, R. A. 1999. "School Ritual as Performance: A Reconstruction of Durkheim's and Turner's Uses of Ritual." *Educational Theory* 49: 493–513.

Roberts, J. 1988. "Setting the Frame: Definition, Functions, and Typology of Rituals." Pp.3–46 in *Rituals in Families and Family Therapy*, edited by E. Imber-Black, J. Roberts, and R. Whiting. New York: W. W. Norton.

Scott, J. C. 1990. *Domination and the Arts of Resistance*. New Haven, CT: Yale University Press.

Shakur, T. 1993. "Keep Your Head Up." On *Strictly 4 My N.I.G.G.A.Z.* (CD). Santa Monica, CA: Interscope Records.

van der Hart, O. 1983. *Rituals in Psychotherapy: Transition and Continuity*. New York: Irvington Publications.

STUDY QUESTIONS

1. What are **rituals** and what **role** do they play in families?

2. What is the goal of the renaming ceremony? Pick two parts of the ritual and describe the **symbolic** importance behind the action.

3. Think about the last ritual you participated in. What kind of ritual was it? What was the purpose of the ritual for you and your **family** and friends?

4. In small groups, create a list of rituals in American **society**. Which rituals do you believe are the most important? Compare and contrast the importance different **groups** place on these ceremonies.

GLORIA ANZALDÚA ⎰ *How to Tame a Wild Tongue*

GLORIA ANZALDÚA (1942–2004), a Chicana lesbian feminist, is a
well-known early female voice in Chicana writing. Her first work, *This
Bridge Called My Back* (1981), was co-authored with Cherríe Moraga.
Her next book, *Borderlands / La Frontera: The New Mestiza* (1987) called
attention not only to the difficulties she encountered growing up in the Rio
Grande Valley of Texas, but also to the hardships faced by other women living
along the U.S./Mexican border. Anzaldúa's other works include *Making Face,
Making Soul / Haciendo Caras* (1990) and *Prietita and the Ghost Woman*
(1996), a book for children.

In "How to Tame a Wild Tongue," an essay from *Borderlands*, Anzaldúa
explores the linguistic borders between Mexico and the United States and
the "border tongues" and ethnic identities that cross them. Her frequent use
of Spanish will challenge those who do not read the language to find a
dictionary or a Spanish speaker in order to discover the meaning not only of
the words but also of the deeper ideas and emotions that English sometimes
cannot convey for her. As you read, consider the reasons Anzaldúa might
have for insisting that editors not translate her Spanish phrases for English
readers. In this bilingual fashion, Anzaldúa allows her "wild tongue" to
express itself fully and without constraint.

"WE'RE GOING TO HAVE TO control your tongue," the dentist says,
pulling out all the metal from my mouth. Silver bits plop and tinkle into
the basin. My mouth is a motherlode.

The dentist is cleaning out my roots. I get a whiff of the stench when
I gasp. "I can't cap that tooth yet, yu're still draining," he says.

"We're going to have to do something about your tongue," I hear the anger rising in his voice. My tongue keeps pushing out the wads of cotton, pushing back the drills, the long thin needles. "I've never seen anything as strong or as stubborn," he says. And I think, how do you tame a wild tongue, train it to be quiet, how do you bridle and saddle it? How do you make it lie down?

> *"Who is to say that robbing a people of its language is less violent than war?"*
>
> —RAY GWYN SMITH[1]

I remember being caught speaking Spanish at recess—that was good for three licks on the knuckles with a sharp ruler. I remember being sent to the corner of the classroom for "talking back" to the Anglo teacher when all I was trying to do was tell her how to pronounce my name. "If you want to be American, speak 'American.' If you don't like it, go back to Mexico where you belong."

"I want you to speak English. *Pa' hallar buen trabajo tienes que saber hablar el inglés bien. Qué vale toda tu educación si todavía hablas inglés con un* 'accent,' " my mother would say, mortified that I spoke English like a Mexican. At Pan American University, I, and all Chicano students were required to take two speech classes. Their purpose: to get rid of our accents. 5

Attacks on one's form of expression with the intent to censor are a violation of the First Amendment. *El Anglo con cara de inocente nos arrancó la lengua.* Wild tongues can't be tamed, they can only be cut out.

OVERCOMING THE TRADITION OF SILENCE

> *Ahogadas, escupimos el oscuro.*
> *Peleando con nuestra propia sombra*
> *el silencio nos sepulta.*

En boca cerrada no entran moscas. "Flies don't enter a closed mouth" is a saying I kept hearing when I was a child. *Ser habladora* was to be

[1] Ray Gwyn Smith, *Moorland Is Cold Country*, unpublished book.

a gossip and a liar, to talk too much. *Muchachitas bien criadas,* well-bred girls don't answer back. *Es una falta de respeto* to talk back to one's mother or father. I remember one of the sins I'd recite to the priest in the confession box the few times I went to confession: talking back to my mother, *hablar pa' 'trás, repelar. Hocicona, repelona, chismosa,* having a big mouth, questioning, carrying tales are all signs of being *mal criada.* In my culture they are all words that are derogatory if applied to women—I've never heard them applied to men.

The first time I heard two women, a Puerto Rican and a Cuban, say the word *"nosotras,"* I was shocked. I had not known the word existed. Chicanas use *nosotros* whether we're male or female. We are robbed of our female being by the masculine plural. Language is a male discourse.

> And our tongues have become
> dry   the wilderness has
> dried out our tongues   and
> we have forgotten speech.
> —IRENA KLEPFISZ[2]

Even our own people, other Spanish speakers *nos quieren poner candados en la boca.* They would hold us back with their bag of *reglas de academia.*

OYÉ COMO LADRA: EL LENGUAJE DE LA FRONTERA

> *Quien tiene boca se equivoca.*
> —MEXICAN SAYING

"*Pocho,* cultural traitor, you're speaking the oppressor's language by speaking English, you're ruining the Spanish language," I have been accused by various Latinos and Latinas. Chicano Spanish is considered by the purist and by most Latinos deficient, a mutilation of Spanish.   10

[2]Irena Klepfisz, "*Di rayze aheym*/The Journey Home," in *The Tribe of Dina: A Jewish Women's Anthology*, Melanie Kaye/Kantrowitz and Irena Klepfisz, eds. (Montpelier, VT: Sinister Wisdom Books, 1986), 49.

But Chicano Spanish is a border tongue which developed naturally. Change, *evolución, enriquecimiento de palabras nuevas por invención o adopción* have created variants of Chicano Spanish, *un nuevo lenguaje. Un lenguaje que corresponde a un modo de vivir.* Chicano Spanish is not incorrect, it is a living language.

For a people who are neither Spanish nor live in a country in which Spanish is the first language; for a people who live in a country in which English is the reigning tongue but who are not Anglo; for a people who cannot entirely identify with either standard (formal, Castillian) Spanish nor standard English, what recourse is left to them but to create their own language? A language which they can connect their identity to, one capable of communicating the realities and values true to themselves—a language with terms that are neither *español ni inglés,* but both. We speak a patois, a forked tongue, a variation of two languages.

Chicano Spanish sprang out of the Chicanos' need to identify ourselves as a distinct people. We needed a language with which we could communicate with ourselves, a secret language. For some of us, language is a homeland closer than the Southwest—for many Chicanos today live in the Midwest and the East. And because we are a complex, heterogeneous people, we speak many languages. Some of the languages we speak are:

1. Standard English
2. Working-class and slang English
3. Standard Spanish
4. Standard Mexican Spanish
5. North Mexican Spanish dialect
6. Chicano Spanish (Texas, New Mexico, Arizona and California have regional variations)
7. Tex-Mex
8. *Pachuco* (called *caló*)

My "home" tongues are the languages I speak with my sister and brothers, with my friends. They are the last five listed, with 6 and 7 being closest to my heart. From school, the media and job situations, I've picked up standard and working class English. From Mamagrande Locha and from reading Spanish and Mexican literature, I've picked up Standard Spanish and Standard Mexican Spanish. From *los recién llega-*

dos, Mexican immigrants, and *braceros,* I learned the North Mexican dialect. With Mexicans I'll try to speak either Standard Mexican Spanish or the North Mexican dialect. From my parents and Chicanos living in the Valley, I picked up Chicano Texas Spanish, and I speak it with my mom, younger brother (who married a Mexican and who rarely mixes Spanish with English), aunts and older relatives.

With Chicanas from *Nuevo México* or *Arizona* I will speak Chicano   15
Spanish a little, but often they don't undrstand what I'm saying. With most California Chicanas I speak entirely in English (unless I forget). When I first moved to San Francisco, I'd rattle off something in Spanish, unintentionally embarrassing them. Often it is only with another Chicana *tejana* that I can talk freely.

Words distorted by English are known as anglicisms or *pochismos.* The *pocho* is an anglicized Mexican or American of Mexican origin who speaks Spanish with an accent characteristic of North Americans and who distorts and reconstructs the language according to the influence of English.[3] Tex-Mex, or Spanglish, comes most naturally to me. I may switch back and forth from English to Spanish in the same sentence or in the same word. With my sister and my brother Nune and with Chicano *tejano* contemporaries I speak in Tex-Mex.

From kids and people my own age I picked up *Pachuco. Pachuco* (the language of the zoot suiters) is a language of rebellion, both against Standard Spanish and Standard English. It is a secret language. Adults of the culture and outsiders cannot understand it. It is mad up of slang words from both English and Spanish. *Ruca* means girl or women, *vato* means guy or dude, *chale* means no, *simón* means yes, *churo* is sure, talk is *periquiar, pigionear* means petting, *que gacho* means how nerdy, *ponte águila* means watch out, death is called *la pelona.* Through lack of practice and not having others who can speak it, I've lost most of the *Pachuco* tongue.

[3]R. C. Ortega *Dialectología Del Barrio,* trans. Hortencia S. Alwan (Los Angeles, CA: R. C. Ortega Publisher & Bookseller, 1977), 132.

CHICANO SPANISH

Chicanos, after 250 years of Spanish/Anglo colonization have developed significant differences in the Spanish we speak. We collapse two adjacent vowels into a single syllable and sometimes shift the stress in certain words such as *maíz/maiz, cohete/cuete.* We leave out certain consonants when they appear between vowels: *lado/lao, mojado/mojao.* Chicanos from South Texas pronounce *f* as *j* as in *jue (fue).* Chicanos use "archaisms," words that are no longer in the Spanish language, words that have been evolved out. We say *semos, truje, haiga, ansina,* and *naiden.* We retain the "archaic" *j,* as in *jalar,* that derives from an earlier *h,* (the French *halar* or the Germanic *halon* which was lost to standard Spanish in the 16th century), but which is still found in several regional dialects such as the one spoken in South Texas. (Due to geography, Chicanos from the Valley of South Texas were cut off linguistically from other Spanish speakers. We tend to use words that the Spaniards brought over from Medieval Spain. The majority of the Spanish colonizers in Mexico and the Southwest came from Extremadura[4]—Hernán Cortés was one of them—and Andalucía. Andalucians pronounce *ll* like a *y,* and their *d*'s tend to be absorbed by adjacent vowels: *tirado* becomes *tirao.* They brought *el lenguaje popular, dialectos y regionalismos.*[5])

Chicanos and other Spanish speakers also shift *ll* to *y* and *z* to *s.*[6] We leave out initial syllables, saying *tar* for *estar, toy* for *estoy, hora* for *ahora (cubanos* and *puertorriqueños* also leave out initial letters of some words.) We also leave out the final syllable such as *pa* for *para.* The intervocalic *y,* the *ll* as in *tortilla, ella, botella,* gets replaced by *tortia* or *tortiya, ea, botea.* We add an additional syllable at the beginning of certain words: *atocar* for *tocar, agastar* for *gastar.* Sometimes we'll

[4]Large region of southern Spain. *Hernán Cortés*: Spanish conquistador (1485–1547) who defeated the Aztec empire and claimed Mexico for Spain. [Ed.]

[5]Eduardo Hernandéz-Chávez, Andrew D. Cohen, and Anthony F. Beltramo, *El Lenguaje de Chicanos: Regional and Social Characteristics of Language Used by Mexican Americans* (Arlington, VA: Center for Applied Linguistics, 1975), 39.

[6]Hernandéz-Chávez, xvii.

say *lavaste las vacijas,* other times *lavates* (substituting the *ates* verb endings for the *aste*).

We use angliciams, words borrowed from English: *bola* from ball, 20 *carpeta* from carpet, *máchina de lavar* (instead of *lavadora*) from washing machine. Tex-Mex argot, created by adding a Spanish sound at the beginning or end of an English word such as *cookiar* for cook, *watchar* for watch, *parkiar* for park, and *rapiar* for rape, is the result of the pressures on Spanish speakers to adapt to English.

We don't use the word *vosotros/as* or its accompanying verb form. We don't say *claro* (to mean yes), *imagínate,* or *me emociona,* unless we picked up Spanish from Latinas[7], out of a book, or in a classroom. Other Spanish-speaking groups are going through the same, or similar, development in their Spanish.

LINGUISTIC TERRORISM

> *Deslenguadas. Somos los del español deficiente. We are your linguistic nightmare, your linguistic aberration, your linguistic* mestizaje, *the subject of your* burla. *Because we speak with tongues of fire we are culturally crucified. Racially, culturally and linguistically* somos huérfanos—*we speak an orphan tongue.*

Chicanas who grew up speaking Chicano Spanish have internalized the belief that we speak poor Spanish. It is illegitimate, a bastard language. And because we internalize how our language has been used against us by the dominant culture, we use our language differences against each other.

Chicana feminists often skirt around each other with suspicion and hesitation. For the longest time I couldn't figure it out. Then it dawned on me. To be close to another Chicana is like looking into the mirror. We are afraid of what we'll see there. *Pena.* Shame. Low estimation of self. In childhood we are told that our language is wrong. Repeated attacks on our native tongue diminish our sense of self. The attacks continue throughout our lives.

[7]That is, natives of Central and South America. [Ed.]

Chicanas feel uncomfortable talking in Spanish to Latinas, afraid of their censure. Their language was not outlawed in their countries. They had a whole lifetime of being immersed in their native tongue; generations, centuries in which Spanish was a first language, taught in school, heard on radio and TV, and read in the newspaper.

If a person, Chicana or Latina, has a low estimation of my native tongue, she also has a low estimation of me. Often with *mexicanas y latinas* we'll speak English as a neutral language. Even among Chicanas we tend to speak English at parties or conferences. Yet, at the same time, we're afraid the other will think we're *agringadas* because we don't speak Chicano Spanish. We oppress each other trying to out-Chicano each other, vying to be the "real" Chicanas, to speak like Chicanos. There is no one Chicano language just as there is no one Chicano experience. A monolingual Chicana whose first language is English or Spanish is just as much a Chicana as one who speaks several variants of Spanish. A Chicana from Michigan or Chicago or Detroit is just as much a Chicana as one from the Southwest. Chicano Spanish is as diverse linguistically as it is regionally.

By the end of this century, Spanish speakers will comprise the biggest minority group in the U.S., a country where students in high schools and colleges are encouraged to take French classes because French is considered more "cultured." But for a language to remain alive it must be used.[8] By the end of this century English, and not Spanish, will be the mother tongue of most Chicanos and Latinos.

So, if you want to really hurt me, talk badly about my language. Ethnic identity is twin skin to linguistic identity—I am my language. Until I can take pride in my language, I cannot take pride in myself. Until I can accept as legitimate Chicano Texas Spanish, Tex-Mex and all the other languages I speak, I cannot accept the legitimacy of myself. Until I am free to write bilingually and to switch codes without having always to translate, while I still have to speak English or Spanish when I would rather speak Spanglish, and as long as I have to accommodate the English

25

[8]Irena Klepfisz, "Secular Jewish Identity: Yidishkayt in America," in *The Tribe of Dina,* Kaye/Kantrowitz and Klepfisz, eds., 43.

speakers rather than having them accommodate me, my tongue will be illegitimate.

I will no longer be made to feel ashamed of existing. I will have my voice: Indian, Spanish, white. I will have my serpent's tongue—my woman's voice, my sexual voice, my poet's voice. I will overcome the tradition of silence.

> *My fingers*
> *move sly against your palm.*
> *Like women everywhere, we speak in code. . . .*
> —MELANIE KAYE/KANTROWITZ[9]

"VISTAS," CORRIDOS, Y COMIDA: MY NATIVE TONGUE

In the 1960s, I read my first Chicano novel. It was *City of Night* by John Rechy, a gay Texan, son of a Scottish father and a Mexican mother. For days I walked around in stunned amazement that a Chicano could write and could get published. When I read *I Am Joaquin*[1] I was surprised to see a bilingual book by a Chicano in print. When I saw poetry written in Tex-Mex for the first time, a feeling of pure joy flashed through me. I felt like we really existed as a people. In 1971, when I started teaching High School English to Chicano students, I tried to supplement the required texts with works by Chicanos, only to be reprimanded and forbidden to do so by the principal. He claimed that I was supposed to teach "American" and English literature. At the risk of being fired, I swore my students to secrecy and slipped in Chicano short stories, poems, a play. In graduate school, while working toward a Ph.D., I had to "argue" with one advisor after the other, semester after semester, before I was allowed to make Chicano literature an area of focus.

Even before I read books by Chicanos or Mexicans, it was the 30

[9]Melanie Kaye/Kantrowitz, "Sign," in *We Speak in Code: Poems and Other Writings* (Pittsburgh, PA: Motheroot Publications, Inc., 1980), 85.
[1]Rodolfo Gonzales, *I Am Joaquín/Yo Soy Joaquín* (New York, NY: Bantam Books, 1972). It was first published in 1967.

Mexican movies I saw at the drive-in—the Thursday night special of $1.00 a carload—that gave me a sense of belonging. *"Vámonos a las vistas,"* my mother would call out and we'd all—grandmother, brothers, sister and cousins—squeeze into the car. We'd wolf down cheese and bologna white bread sandwiches while watching Pedro Infante in melodramatic tear-jerkers like *Nosotros los pobres,* the first "real" Mexican movie (that was not an imitation of European movies). I remember seeing *Cuando los hijos se van* and surmising that all Mexican movies played up the love a mother has for her children and what ungrateful sons and daughters suffer when they are not devoted to their mothers. I remember the singing-type "westerns" of Jorge Negrete and Miguel Aceves Mejía. When watching Mexican movies, I felt a sense of homecoming as well as alienation. People who were to amount to something didn't go to Mexican movies, or *bailes* or tune their radios to *bolero, rancherita,* and *corrido* music.

The whole time I was growing up, there was *norteño* music sometimes called North Mexican border music, or Tex-Mex music, or Chicano music, or *cantina* (bar) music. I grew up listening to *conjuntos,* three- or four-piece bands made up of folk musicians playing guitar, *bajo sexto,* drums and button accordion, which Chicanos had borrowed from the German immigrants who had come to Central Texas and Mexico to farm and build breweries. In the Rio Grande Valley, Steve Jordan and Little Joe Hernández were popular, and Flaco Jiménez was the accordion king. The rhythms of Tex-Mex music are those of the polka, also adapted from the Germans, who in turn had borrowed the polka from the Czechs and Bohemians.

I remember the hot, sultry evenings when *corridos*—songs of love and death on the Texas-Mexican borderlands—reverberated out of cheap amplifiers from the local *cantinas* and wafted in through my bedroom window.

Corridos first became widely used along the South Texas/Mexican border during the early conflict between Chicanos and Anglos. The *corridos* are usually about Mexican heroes who do valiant deeds against the Anglo oppressors. Pancho Villa's song, *"La cucaracha,"* is the most famous one. *Corridos* of John F. Kennedy and hsi death are still very popular in the Valley. Older Chicanos remember Lydia Mendoza, one of the great border *corrido* singers who was called *la Gloria de Tejas*. Her *"El tango negro,"* sung during the Great Depression, made her a singer of the people. The everpresent *corridos* narrated one hundred years of border history, bringing news of events as well as entertaining. These folk musicians and folk songs are our chief cultural mythmakers, and they made our hard lives seem bearable.

I grew up feeling ambivalent about our music. Country-western and rock-and-roll had more status. In the 50s and 60s, for the slightly educated and *agringado* Chicanos, there existed a sense of shame at being caught listening to our music. Yet I couldn't stop my feet from thumping to the music, could not stop humming the words, nor hide from myself the exhilaration I felt when I heard it.

There are more subtle ways that we internalize identification, especially in the forms of images and emotions. For me food and certain smells are tied to my identity, to my homeland. Woodsmoke curling up to an immense blue sky; woodsmoke perfuming my grandmother's clothes, her skin. The stench of cow manure and the yellow patches on the ground; the crack of a .22 rifle and the reek of cordite. Homemade white cheese sizzling in a pan, melting inside a folded *tortilla*. My sister Hilda's hot, spicy *menudo, chile colorado* making it deep red, pieces of *panza* and hominy floating on top. My brother Carito barbecuing *fajitas* in the backyard. Even now and 3,000 miles away, I can see my mother spicing the ground beef, pork and venison with *chile*. My mouth salivates at the thought of the hot steaming *tamales* I would be eating if I were home.

SI LE PREGUNTAS A MI MAMÁ, "¿QUÉ ERES?"

> *"Identity is the essential core of who we are as individuals,*
> *the conscious experience of the self inside."*
>
> —KAUFMAN[2]

---

[2]Kaufman, 68.

Nosotros los Chicanos straddle the borderlands. On one side of us, we are constantly exposed to the Spanish of the Mexicans, on the other side we hear the Anglos' incessant clamoring so that we forget our language. Among ourselves we don't say *nosotros los americanos, o nosotros los españoles, o nosotros los hispanos.* We say *nosotros los mexicanos* (by *mexicanos* we do not mean citizens of Mexico; we do not mean a national identity, but a racial one). We distinguish between *mexicanos del otro lado* and *mexicanos de este lado.* Deep in our hearts we believe that being Mexican has nothing to do with which country one lives in. Being Mexican is a state of soul—not one of mind, not one of citizenship. Neither eagle nor serpent, but both. And like the ocean, neither animal respects borders.

> Dime con quien andas y te diré quien eres. *(Tell me who your friends are and I'll tell you who you are.)*
> —MEXICAN SAYING

Si le preguntas a mi mamá, "¿Qué eres?" te dirá, "Soy mexicana." My brothers and sister say the same. I sometimes will answer *"soy mexicana"* and at others will say *"soy Chicana" o "soy tejana."* But I identified as *"Raza"* before I ever identified as *"mexicana"* or "Chicana."

As a culture, we call ourselves Spanish when referring to ourselves as a linguistic group and when copping out. It is then that we forget our predominant Indian genes. We are 70 to 80% Indian.[3] We call ourselves Hispanic[4] or Spanish-American or Latin American or Latin when linking ourselves to other Spanish-speaking peoples of the Western hemisphere and when copping out. We call ourselves Mexican-American[5] to signify we are neither Mexican nor American, but more the noun "American" than the adjective "Mexican" (and when copping out).

Chicanos and other people of color suffer economically for not

---

[3]Chávez, 88–90.

[4]"Hispanic" is derived from *Hispanis* (*España*, a name given to the Iberian Peninsula in ancient times when it was a part of the Roman Empire) and is a term designated by the U.S. government to make it easier to handle us on paper.

[5]The treaty of Guadalupe Hidalgo created the Mexican-American in 1848.

acculturating. This voluntary (yet forced) alienation makes for psycho-logical conflict, a kind of dual identity—we don't identify with the Anglo-American cultural values and we don't totally identify with the Mexican cultural values. We are a synergy of two cultures with various degrees of Mexicanness or Angloness. I have so internalized the bor-derland conflict that sometimes I feel like one cancels out the other and we are zero, nothing, no one. *A veces no soy nada ni nadie. Pero hasta cuando no lo soy, lo soy.*

When not copping out, when we know we are more than nothing, we call ourselves Mexican, referring to race and ancestry; *mestizo* when affirming both our Indian and Spanish (but we hardly ever own our Black ancestry); Chicano when referring to a politically aware people born and/or raised in the U.S.; *Raza* when referring to Chicanos; *tejanos* when we are Chicanos from Texas. 40

Chicanos did not know we were a people until 1965 when Cesar Chavez and the farmworkers united and *I Am Joaquín* was published and *la Raza Unida* party was formed in Texas. With that recognition, we became a distinct people. Something momentous happened to the Chicano soul—we became aware of our reality and acquired a name and a language (Chicano Spanish) that reflected that reality. Now that we had a name, some of the fragmented pieces began to fall together—who we were, what we were, how we had evolved. We began to get glimpses of what we might eventually become.

Yet the struggle of identities continues, the struggle of borders is our reality still. One day the inner struggle will cease and a true integration take place. In the meantime, *tenemos que hacerla lucha, ¿Quién está protegiendo los ranchos de mi gente? ¿Quién está tratando de cerrar la fisura entre la india y el blanco en nuestra sangre? El Chicano, sí, el Chicano que anda como un ladron en su propia casa.*

Los Chicanos how patient we seem, how very patient. There is the quiet of the Indian about us.[6] We know how to survive. When other

---

[6]Anglos, in order to alleviate their guilt for dispossessing the Chicano, stressed the Spanish part of us and perpetrated the myth of the Spanish Southwest. We have accepted the fiction that we are Hispanic, that is Spanish, in order to accommoadate ourselves to the dominant culture and its abhorrence of Indians. Chávez, 88–91.

races have given up their tongue, we've kept ours. We know what it is to live under the hammer blow of the dominant *norteamericano* culture. But more than we count the blows, we count the days the weeks the years the centuries the eons until the white laws and commerce and customs will rot in the deserts they've created, lie bleached. *Humildes* yet proud, *quietos* yet wild, *nosotros los mexicanos*-Chicanos will walk by the crumbling ashes as we go about our business. Stubborn, persevering, impenetrable as stone, yet possessing a malleability that renders us unbreakable, we, the *mestizas* and *mestizos,* will remain.

PO BRONSON AND ASHLEY MERRYMAN

Why White Parents Don't Talk about Race

from NurtureShock: New Thinking about Children

Are kids born "color blind"? Does talking about **race** to kids "make it an issue" where it otherwise wouldn't be? Does growing up in a diverse daycare, neighborhood, or school mean you are automatically not prone to **prejudice** and **discrimination**? In this essay the authors delve into these questions and explore the connection between how we parent and what our children learn about **racism**. As you read, think about if and how your parents discussed race with you and compare and contrast it to the approaches discussed.

AT THE CHILDREN'S RESEARCH LAB AT THE UNIVERSITY OF Texas, a database is kept of thousands of families in the Austin area who have volunteered to be available for scholarly research. In 2006, doctoral student Birgitte Vittrup recruited from the database about a hundred of these families, all of whom were Caucasian with a child five to seven years old. This project was her Ph.D. dissertation. The goal of Vittrup's study was to learn if typical children's videos with multicultural story lines actually have any beneficial effect on children's racial attitudes.

Her first step was to test the children, and their parents, with a Racial Attitude Measure designed by one of her mentors at the university, Dr. Rebecca Bigler. Using this measure, Vittrup asked the child a series of questions, such as:

"How many White people are nice?"
(Almost all) (A lot) (Some) (Not many) (None)

"How many Black people are nice?"
(Almost all) (A lot) (Some) (Not many) (None)

Over the test, the descriptive adjective "nice" was replaced with over twenty other adjectives like "Dishonest," "Pretty," "Curious," and "Snobby." If the kid was too shy to answer, he could point to a picture that corresponded to each of the possible answers.

Of the families, Vittrup sent a third of them home with typical multiculturally-themed videos for a week, such as an episode of *Sesame Street* where the characters visit an African American family's home, and an episode of *Little Bill*, where the entire neighborhood comes together to clean the local park.

In truth, Vittrup didn't expect that children's racial attitudes would change very much from just watching these videos. Prior research by Bigler had shown that multi-cultural curriculum in schools has far less impact than we intend it to—largely because the implicit message "We're all friends" is too vague for children to under-stand it refers to skin color.

Yet Vittrup figured that if the educational videos were supplemented with explicit conversations from parents, there would be a significant impact. So a second group of families got the videos, and Vittrup told these parents to use the videos as the jumping-off point for a conversation about interracial friendship. She gave these sets of parents a checklist of points to make, echoing the theme of the shows. "I really believed it was going to work," Vittrup recalled. Her Ph.D. depended upon it.

The last third were also given the checklist of topics, but no videos. These parents were supposed to bring up racial equality on their own, every night for five nights. This was a bit tricky, especially if the parents had never put names to kids' races before. The parents were to say things like:

> Some people on TV or at school have different skin color than us. White children and Black children and Mexican children often like the same things even though they come from different backgrounds. They are still good people and you can be their friend. If a child of a different skin color lived in our neighborhood, would you like to be his friend?

At this point, something interesting happened. Five of the families in the last group abruptly quit the study. Two directly told Vittrup, "We don't want to have these conversations with our child. We don't want to point out skin color."

Vittrup was taken aback—these families had volunteered knowing full-well it was a study of children's racial attitudes. Yet once told this required talking openly about race, they started dropping out. Three others refused to say why they were quitting, but their silence made Vittrup suspect they were withdrawing for the same reason.

This avoidance of talking about race was something Vittrup also picked up in her initial test of parents' racial attitudes. It was no surprise that in a liberal city like Austin, every parent was a welcoming multiculturalist, embracing diversity. But Vittrup had also noticed, in the original surveys, that hardly any of these white parents had ever talked to their children directly about race. They might have asserted vague principles in the home—like "Everybody's equal" or "God made all of us" or "Under the skin, we're all the same"—but they had almost never called attention to racial differences.

They wanted their children to grow up color-blind. But Vittrup could also see from her first test of the kids that they weren't color-blind at all. Asked how many white people are mean, these children commonly answered "Almost none." Asked how many blacks are mean, many answered "Some" or "A lot." Even kids who attended diverse schools answered some of the questions this way.

More disturbingly, Vittrup had also asked all the kids a very blunt question: "Do your parents like black people?" If the white parents never talked about race explicitly, did the kids know that their parents liked black people?

Apparently not: 14% said, outright, "No, my parents don't like black people"; 38% of the kids answered, "I don't know." In this supposed race-free vacuum being created by parents, kids were left to improvise their own conclusions—many of which would be abhorrent to their parents.

Vittrup hoped the families she'd instructed to talk about race would follow through.

After watching the videos, the families returned to the Children's Research Lab for retesting. As Vittrup expected, for the families who had watched the videos without any parental reinforcement and conversation, there was no improvement over their scores from a week before. The message of multicultural harmony—seemingly so apparent in the episodes—wasn't affecting the kids at all.

But to her surprise, after she crunched the numbers, Vittrup learned that neither of the other two groups of children (whose parents talked to them about interracial friendship) had improved their racial attitudes. At first look, the study was a failure. She felt like she was watching her promising career vanish before her own eyes. She'd had visions of her findings published in a major journal—but now she was just wondering if she'd even make it through her dissertation defense and get her Ph.D.

Scrambling, Vittrup consulted her dissertation advisors until she eventually sought out Bigler.

"Whether the study worked or not," Bigler replied, "it's still telling you something." Maybe there was something interesting in why it had no effect?

Combing through the parents' study diaries, Vittrup noticed an aberration. When she'd given the parents the checklist of race topics to discuss with their kindergartners, she had also asked them to record whether this had been a meaningful interaction. Did the parents merely mention the item on the checklist? Did they expand on the checklist item? Did it lead to a true discussion?

Almost all the parents reported merely mentioning the checklist items, briefly, in passing. Many just couldn't talk about race, and they quickly reverted to the vague "Everybody's equal" phrasing.

Of all the parents who were told to talk openly about interracial friendship, only six managed to do so. All of those six kids greatly improved their racial attitudes.

Vittrup sailed through her dissertation and is now an assistant professor at Texas Woman's University in Dallas. Reflecting later about the study, Vittrup realized how challenging it had been for the families: "A lot of parents came to me afterwards and admitted they just didn't know what to say to their kids, and they didn't want the wrong thing coming out of the mouth of their kids."

We all want our children to be unintimidated by differences and have the social skills to integrate in a diverse world. The question is, do we make it worse, or do we make it better, by calling attention to race?

Of course, the election of President Barack Obama has marked the beginning of a new era in race relations in the United States—but it hasn't resolved the question as to what we should tell children about race. If anything, it's pushed that issue to the forefront. Many parents have explicitly pointed out Obama's brown skin to their young children, to reinforce the message that anyone can rise to become a leader, and anyone—regardless of skin color—can be a friend, be loved, and be admired.

But still others are thinking it's better to say nothing at all about the president's race or ethnicity—because saying something about it unavoidably teaches a child a racial construct. They worry that even a positive statement ("It's wonderful that a black person can be president") will still encourage the child to see divisions within society. For them, the better course is just to let a young child learn by the example; what kids see is what they'll think is normal. For their early formative years, at least, let the children know a time when skin color does not matter.

A 2007 study in the *Journal of Marriage and Family* found that out of 17,000 families with kindergartners, 45% said they'd never, or almost never, discussed race issues with their children. But that was for all ethnicities. Nonwhite parents are about three times more likely to discuss race than white parents; 75% of the latter never, or almost never, talk about race.

For decades, we assumed that children will only see race when society points it out to them. That approach was shared by much of the scientific community—the view was that race was a societal issue best left to sociologists and demographers to figure out. However, child development researchers have increasingly begun to question that presumption. They argue that children see racial differences as much as they see the difference between pink and blue—but we tell kids that "pink" means for girls and "blue" is for boys. "White" and "black" are mysteries we leave them to figure out on their own.

———————

It takes remarkably little for children to develop in-group preferences once a difference has been recognized. Bigler ran an experiment in three preschool classrooms, where four- and five-year-olds were lined up and given T-shirts. Half the kids were given blue T-shirts, half red. The children wore the shirts for three weeks. During that time, the teachers never mentioned their colors and never again grouped the kids by shirt color. The teachers never referred to the "Blues" or the "Reds." Bigler wanted to see what would happen to the children naturally, once color groupings had been established.

The kids didn't segregate in their behavior. They played with each other freely at recess. But when asked which color team was better to belong to, or which team might win a race, they chose their own color. They liked the kids in their own group more and believed they were smarter than the other color. "The Reds never showed hatred for Blues," Bigler observed. "It was more like, 'Blues are fine, but not as good as us.'" When Reds were asked how many Reds were nice, they'd answer "All of us." Asked how many Blues were nice, they'd answer "Some." Some of the Blues were mean, and some were dumb—but not the Reds.

Bigler's experiment seems to show how children will use whatever you give them to create divisions—seeming to confirm that race becomes an issue only if we make it an issue. So why does Bigler think it's important to talk to children about race, as early as age three?

Her reasoning is that kids are *developmentally* prone to in-group favoritism; they're going to form these preferences on their own. Children categorize everything from food to toys to people at a young age. However, it takes years before their cognitive abilities allow them to successfully use more than one attribute to categorize anything. In the meantime, the attribute they rely on is that which is the most clearly visible.

Bigler contends that once a child identifies someone as most closely resembling himself, the child likes that person the most. And the child extends their shared appearances much further—believing that everything else he likes, those who look similar to him like as well. Anything he doesn't like thus belongs to those who look the least similar to him. The spontaneous tendency to assume your group shares characteristics—such as niceness, or smarts—is called *essentialism*. Kids never think groups are random.

We might imagine we're creating color-blind environments for children, but differences in skin color or hair or weight are like differences in gender—they're plainly visible. We don't have to label them for them to become salient. Even if no teacher or parent mentions race, kids will use skin color on their own, the same way they use T-shirt colors.

Within the past decade or so, developmental psychologists have begun a handful of longitudinal studies to determine exactly when children develop bias—the general premise being that the earlier the bias manifests itself, the more likely it is driven by developmental processes.

Dr. Phyllis Katz, then a professor at the University of Colorado, led one such study—following 100 black children and 100 white children for their first six years.

She tested these children and their parents nine times during those six years, with the first test at six months old.

How do researchers test a six-month-old? It's actually a common test in child development research. They show babies photographs of faces, measuring how long the child's attention remains on the photographs. Looking at a photograph longer does not indicate a preference for that photo, or for that face. Rather, looking longer means the child's brain finds the face to be out of the ordinary; she stares at it longer because her brain is trying to make sense of it. So faces that are familiar actually get shorter visual attention. Children will stare significantly longer at photographs of faces that are a different race from their parents. Race itself has no ethnic meaning, per se—but children's brains are noticing skin color differences and trying to understand their meaning.

When the kids turned three, Katz showed them photographs of other children and asked them to choose whom they'd like to have as friends. Of the white children 86% picked children of their own race. When the kids were five and six, Katz gave these children a small deck of cards, with drawings of people on them. Katz told the children to sort the cards into two piles any way they wanted. Only 16% of the kids used gender to split the piles. Another 16% used a variety of other factors, like the age or the mood of the people depicted. But 68% of the kids used race to split the cards, without any prompting.

In reporting her findings, Katz concluded: "I think it is fair to say that at no point in the study did the children exhibit the Rousseau-type of color-blindness that many adults expect."

The point Katz emphasizes is that during this period of our children's lives when we imagine it's most important to *not* talk about race is the very developmental period when children's minds are forming their first conclusions about race.

Several studies point to the possibility of developmental windows—stages when children's attitudes might be most amenable to change. During one experiment, teachers divided their students into groups of six kids, making sure each child was in a racially diverse group. Twice a week, for eight weeks, the groups met. Each child in a group had to learn a piece of the lesson and then turn around and teach it to the other five. The groups received a grade collectively. Then, the scholars watched the kids on the playground, to see if it led to more interaction cross-race. Every time a child played with another child at recess, it was noted—as was the race of the other child.

The researchers found this worked wonders on the first-grade children. Having been in the cross-race study groups led to significantly more cross-race play. But it made no difference on the third-grade children. It's possible that by third grade, when parents usually recognize it's safe to start talking a little about race, the developmental window has already closed.

––––––––––

The other deeply held assumption modern parents have is what Ashley and I have come to call the Diverse Environment Theory. If you raise a child with a fair amount of exposure to people of other races and cultures, the environment becomes the message. You don't have to talk about race—in fact, it's better to *not* talk about race. Just expose the child to diverse environments and he'll think it's entirely normal.

I know this mindset, because it perfectly describes the approach my wife and I took when our son, Luke, was born. When he was four months old, we enrolled him in a preschool located in San Francisco's Fillmore/Western Addition neighborhood. One of the many benefits of the school was its great racial diversity. For years he never once mentioned the color of anyone's skin—not at school or while watching television. We never once mentioned skin color either. We thought it was working perfectly.

Then came Martin Luther King Jr. Day at school, two months before his fifth birthday. Luke walked out of class that Friday before the weekend and started pointing at everyone, proudly announcing, "That guy comes from Africa. And she comes from Africa, too!" It was embarrassing how loudly he did this. Clearly, he had been taught to categorize skin color, and he was enchanted with his skill at doing so. "People with brown skin are from Africa," he'd repeat. He had not been taught the names for races—he had not heard the term "black" and he called us "people with pinkish-whitish skin." He named every kid in his schoolroom with brown skin, which was about half his class.

I was uncomfortable that the school hadn't warned us about the race-themed lesson. But my son's eagerness was revealing. It was obvious this was something he'd been wondering about for a while. He was relieved to have been finally given the key. Skin color was a sign of ancestral roots.

Over the next year, we started to overhear one of his white friends talking about the color of their skin. They still didn't know what to call their skin, so they used the phrase "skin like ours." And this notion of *ours versus theirs* started to take on a meaning of its own. As these kids searched for their identities, skin color had become salient. Soon, I overheard this particular white boy telling my son, "Parents don't like us to talk about our skin, so don't let them hear you."

Yet our son did mention it. When he watched basketball with us, he would say, "That guy's my favorite," and put his finger up to the screen to point the player out. "The guy with skin like ours," he would add. I questioned him at length, and I came to understand what was really going on. My young son had become self-conscious about his curly blond-brown hair. His hair would never look like the black players' hairstyles. The one white, Latvian player on the Golden State Warriors had cool hair the same color as my son's. That was the guy to root for. My son was looking for his own identity, and looking for role models. Race and hairstyle had both become part of the identity formula. Making free throws and playing tough defense hadn't.

I kept being surprised. As a parent, I dealt with these moments explicitly, telling my son it was wrong to choose anyone as his friend, or his "favorite," on the basis of their skin color or even their hairstyle. We pointed out how certain friends wouldn't be in our lives if we picked friends for their color. He got the message, and over time he not only accepted but embraced this lesson. Now he talks openly about equality and the wrongfulness of discrimination.

Not knowing then what I do now, I had a hard time understanding my son's initial impulses. I'd always thought racism was taught. If a child grows up in a non-racist world, why was he spontaneously showing race-based preferences? When did the environment that we were so proud of no longer become the message he listened to?

The Diverse Environment Theory is the core principle behind school desegregation today. Like most people, I assumed that after thirty years of school desegregation, it would have a long track record of scientific research proving that the Diverse Environment Theory works. Then Ashley and I began talking to the scholars who've compiled that very research.

For instance, Dr. Gary Orfield runs the Civil Rights Project, a think tank that was long based at Harvard but has moved to UCLA. In the summer of 2007, Orfield and a dozen top scholars wrote an amicus brief to the United States Supreme Court supporting school desegregation in Louisville, Kentucky, and Seattle, Washington. After completing the 86-page document, Orfield e-mailed it to all the social scientists on his mailing list, and he received 553 signatures of support. No fancy law firms put their stamp on it. Orfield was very proud that the brief was the work of scientists, not lawyers, thereby preserving its integrity and impartiality. "It was the authentic voice of social science," he recalled.

Privately, though, Orfield felt some frustration—even anger. He admitted the science available to make their case "wasn't what we really wanted." Despite having at their disposal at least a thousand research studies on desegregation's effects, "I was surprised none were longitudinal. It really has a substantial effect, but it has to be done the right way." Just throwing kids of different races into a school together isn't the right way, because they can self-segregate within the school. Orfield lamented the lack of funding to train teachers. Looking at the science available to make their case, Orfield recalled, "It depressed me that we've invested so little in finding the benefits of integration."

This ambiguity is visible in the text of the amicus brief. Scientists don't like to overstate their case. So the benefits of desegregation are qualified with words like "may lead" and "can improve." "Mere school integration is not a panacea," the brief warns.

UT's Bigler was one of the scholars who contributed to the brief, and she was heavily involved in the process of its creation. Her estimation of what they found is more candid than Orfield's. "In the end, I was disappointed with the amount of evidence social psychology could muster," she said. "Going to integrated schools gives you just as many chances to learn stereotypes as to unlearn them."

Calling attention to this can feel taboo. Bigler is an adamant proponent of desegregation in schools, on moral grounds. "It's an enormous step backward to increase social segregation," she commented. But it's important for parents to know that merely sending your child to a diverse school is no guarantee they'll have better racial attitudes than children at homogenous schools.

Race appears to be especially complex, compared to other objects of bias and discrimination. Dr. Thomas Pettigrew of the University of California at Santa Cruz analyzed over 500 research studies, all of which were examples of how exposure to others can potentially reduce bias. The studies that were most successful weren't about racial bias—rather, they were about bias toward the disabled, the elderly, and gays. Studies in other countries show success—such as a reduction in bias among Jews and Palestinians, or whites and blacks in South Africa. When it comes to race in America, the studies show only consistent, modest benefit among college-aged students. In high schools and elementary schools, it's a different story.

Recently, the Civil Rights Project studied high school juniors in six school districts around the country. One of those was Louisville, which appears to be a place where desegregation has had the intended benefits. Surveys of high school juniors there show that over 80% of students (of all races) feel their school experience has helped them work with and get along with members of other races and ethnic groups. Over 85% feel their school's diversity has prepared them to work in a diverse job setting.

But other districts didn't look so great. Lynn, Massachusetts, which is ten miles northeast of Boston, is generally regarded as another model of diversity and successful school desegregation. When its students were polled if they'd like to live in a diverse neighborhood when they grow up, about 70% of the nonwhite high school juniors said they wanted to. But only 35% of whites wanted to.

Dr. Walter Stephan, a professor emeritus at New Mexico State University, made it his life's work to survey students' racial attitudes after their first year of desegregation. He found that in 16% of the desegregated schools examined, the attitudes of whites toward African Americans became more favorable. In 36% of the schools, there was no difference. In 48% of the schools, white students' attitudes toward blacks became *worse*. Stephan is no segregationist—he signed the amicus brief, and he is one of the most respected scholars in the field.

The unfortunate twist of diverse schools is that they don't necessarily lead to more cross-race friendships. Often it's the opposite.

Duke University's Dr. James Moody—an expert on how adolescents form and maintain social networks—analyzed data on over 90,000 teenagers at 112 different schools from every region of the country. The students had been asked to name their five best male friends and their five best female friends. Moody matched the ethnicity of the student with the race of each of her named friends, then Moody compared the number of each student's cross-racial friendships with the school's overall diversity.

Moody found that the more diverse the school, the more the kids self-segregate by race and ethnicity within the school, and thus the likelihood that any two kids of different races have a friendship goes *down*.

As a result, junior high and high school children in diverse schools experience two completely-contrasting social cues on a daily basis. The first cue is inspiring—that many students have a friend of another race. The second cue is tragic—that far *more* kids just like to hang with their own. It's this second dynamic that becomes more and more visible as overall school diversity goes up. As a child circulates through school, she sees more groups that her race disqualifies her from, more tables in the lunchroom she can't sit at, and more implicit lines that are taboo to cross. This is unmissable even if she, personally, has friends of other races.

It's true that, for every extracurricular one kid has in common with a child of another race, the likelihood that they will be friends increases. But what's stunning about Moody's analysis is that he's taken that into account: Moody included statistical controls for activities, sports, academic tracking, and other school-structural conditions that tend to desegregate (or segregate) students within the school. And the rule still holds true: more diversity translates into more division between students.

Having done its own analysis of teen friendships, a team from the University of North Carolina, Chapel Hill, confirmed Moody's assessment. "More diverse schools have, overall, more potential interracial contact and hence more interracial dyads of 'potential' friends," these researchers explained—but this opportunity was being squandered: "The probability of interracial dyads being friends decreases in more diverse schools."

Those increased opportunities to interact are *also*, effectively, increased opportunities to reject each other. And that is what's happening.

"There has been a new resegregation among youth in primary and secondary schools and on college campuses across the country," wrote Dr. Brendesha Tynes of the University of Illinois, Urbana-Champaign. Tynes concluded, "Even in multiracial schools, once young people leave the classroom very little interracial discussion takes place because a desire to associate with one's own ethnic group often discourages interaction between groups."

All told, the odds of a white high-schooler in America having a best friend of another race is only 8%. Those odds barely improve for the second-best friend, or the third best, or the fifth. For blacks, the odds aren't much better: 85% of black kids' best friends are also black. Cross-race friends also tend to share a single activity, rather than multiple activities; as a result, these friendships are more likely to be lost over time, as children transition from middle school to high school.

It is tempting to believe that because their generation is so diverse, today's children grow up knowing how to get along with people of every race. But numerous studies suggest that this is more of a fantasy than a fact.

I can't help but wonder—would the track record of desegregation be so mixed if parents reinforced it, rather than remaining silent?

———————

Is it really so difficult to talk with children about race when they're very young? What jumped out at Phyllis Katz, in her study of 200 black and white children, was that parents are very comfortable talking to their children about gender, and they work very hard to counterprogram against boy-girl stereotypes. That ought to be our model for talking about race. The same way we remind our daughters, "Mommies can be doctors just like daddies," we ought to be telling all children that doctors can be any skin color. It's not complicated *what to say*. It's only a matter of how often we reinforce it.

Shushing children when they make an improper remark is an instinctive reflex, but often the wrong move. Prone to categorization, children's brains can't help but attempt to generalize rules from the examples they see. It's the worst kind of embarrassment when a child blurts out, "Only brown people can have breakfast at school," or "You can't play basketball, you're white, so you have to play baseball." But shushing them only sends the message that this topic is unspeakable, which makes race more loaded, and more intimidating.

Young children draw conclusions that may make parents cringe, even if they've seen a few counterexamples. Children are not passive absorbers of knowledge; rather, they are active constructors of concepts. Bigler has seen many examples where children distort their recollections of facts to fit the categories they've already formed in their minds. The brain's need for categories to fit perfectly is even stronger at age seven than at age five, so a second grader might make more distortions than a kindergartner to defend his categories. To a parent, it can seem as if the child is getting worse at understanding a diverse world, not better.

To be effective, researchers have found, conversations about race have to be explicit, in unmistakeable terms that children understand. A friend of mine repeatedly told her five-year-old son, "Remember, everybody's equal." She thought she was getting the message across. Finally, after seven months of this, her boy asked, "Mommy, what's 'equal' mean?"

Bigler ran a study where children read brief historical biographies of famous African Americans. For instance, in a biography of Jackie Robinson, they read that he was the first African American in the major leagues. But only half heard about how he'd previously been relegated to the Negro leagues, and how he suffered taunts from white fans. Those facts—in five brief sentences—were omitted in the version given to the other half of the children.

After the two-week history class, the children were surveyed on their racial attitudes. White children who got the full story about historical discrimination had significantly better attitudes toward blacks than those who got the neutered version. Explicitness works.

"It also made them feel some guilt," Bigler added. "It knocked down their glorified view of white people." They couldn't justify in-group superiority.

Bigler is very cautious about taking the conclusion of her Jackie Robinson study too far. She notes the bios were explicit, but about *historical* discrimination. "If we'd had them read stories of contemporary discrimination from today's newspapers, it's quite possible it would have made the whites defensive, and only made the blacks angry at whites."

Another scholar has something close to an answer on that. Dr. April Harris-Britt, a clinical psychologist and professor at University of North Carolina at Chapel Hill, studies how minority parents help their children develop a racial identity from a young age. All minority parents at some point tell their children that discrimination is out there, but they shouldn't let it stop them. However, these conversations are not triggered by their children bringing it up. Rather, the parent often suffers a discriminatory incident, and it pushes him to decide, "It's time I prepared my child for this."

Is it good for them? Harris-Britt found that some preparation for bias was beneficial to children, and that it was necessary—94% of African American eighth graders reported to Harris-Britt that they'd felt discriminated against in the prior three months. But if children heard these preparation-for-bias warnings often (rather than just occasionally), they were significantly less likely to connect their successes to effort, and much more likely to blame their failures on their teachers—whom they saw as biased against them.

Harris-Britt warns that frequent predictions of future discrimination ironically become as destructive as experiences of actual discrimination: "If you overfocus on those types of events, you give the children the message that the world is going to be hostile—you're just not valued and that's just the way the world is."

Preparation-for-bias is not, however, the only way minorities talk to their children about race. The other broad category of conversation, in Harris-Britt's analysis, is ethnic pride. From a very young age, minority children are coached to be proud of their ethnic history. She found that this was exceedingly good for children's self-confidence; in one study, black children who'd heard messages of ethnic pride were more engaged in school and more likely to attribute their success to their effort and ability.

That leads to the question that everyone wonders but rarely dares to ask. If "black pride" is good for African American children, where does that leave white children? It's horrifying to imagine kids being "proud to be white." Yet many scholars argue that's exactly what children's brains are already computing. Just as minority children are aware that they belong to an ethnic group with less status and wealth, most white children naturally decipher that they belong to the race that has more power, wealth, and control in society; this provides security, if not confidence. So a pride message would not just be abhorrent—it'd be redundant.

When talking to teens, it's helpful to understand how their tendency to form groups and cliques is partly a consequence of American culture. In America, we encourage individuality. Children freely and openly develop strong preferences—defining their self-identity by the things they like and dislike. They learn to see differences. Though singular identity is the long-term goal, in high school this identity-quest is satisfied by forming and joining distinctive subgroups. So, in an ironic twist, the more a culture emphasizes individualism, the more the high school years will be marked by subgroupism. Japan, for instance, values social harmony over individualism, and children are discouraged from asserting personal preferences. Thus, less groupism is observed in their high schools.

The security that comes from belonging to a group, especially for teens, is palpable. Traits that mark this membership are—whether we like it or not—central to this developmental period. University of Michigan researchers did a study that shows just how powerful this need to belong is, and how much it can affect a teen.

The researchers brought 100 Detroit black high school students in for one-on-one interviews. They asked each teen to rate himself on how light or dark he considered his skin tone to be. Then the scholars asked about the teens' confidence levels in social circles and school. From the high schools, the researchers obtained the teens' grade point averages.

Particularly for the boys, those who rated themselves as dark-skinned blacks had the highest GPAs. They also had the highest ratings for social acceptance and academic confidence. The boys with lighter skin tones were less secure socially and academically.

The researchers subsequently replicated these results with students who "looked Latino."

The researchers concluded that doing well in school could get a minority teen labeled as "acting white." Teens who were visibly sure of membership within the minority community were protected from this insult and thus more willing to act outside the group norm. But the light-skinned blacks and the Anglo-appearing Hispanics— their status within the minority felt more precarious. So they acted more in keeping with their image of the minority identity—even if it was a negative stereotype—in order to solidify their status within the group.

Over the course of our research, we heard many stories of how people—from parents to teachers—were struggling to talk about race with their children. For some, the conversations came up after a child had made an embarrassing comment in public. A number had the issue thrust on them, because of an interracial marriage or an international adoption. Still others were just introducing children into a diverse environment, wondering when and if the timing was right.

But the story that most affected us came from a small town in rural Ohio. Two first-grade teachers, Joy Bowman and Angela Johnson, had agreed to let a professor from Ohio State University, Dr. Jeane Copenhaver-Johnson, observe their classrooms for the year. Of the 33 children, about two-thirds identified themselves as "white" or even "hillbilly," while the others were black or of mixed-race descent.

It being December—just one month after Copenhaver's project had begun—the teachers both decided to follow up a few other Santa stories they'd read to their classes with *Twas the Night B'fore Christmas*, Melodye Rosales' retelling of the Clement C. Moore classic.

The room already dotted with holiday paraphernalia, Johnson had all of her first graders gather around the carpet for story time. As she began reading, the kids were excited by the book's depiction of a family waiting for Santa to come. A couple children burst out with stories of planned Christmas decorations and expectations for Santa's arrival to their own houses. A few of the children, however, quietly fidgeted. They seemed puzzled that this storybook was different: in this one, it was a black family all snug in their beds.

Then, there was the famed clatter on the roof. The children leaned in to get their first view of Santa and the sleigh as Johnson turned the page—

And they saw that Santa was black.

"He's black!" gasped a white little girl.

Another white boy exclaimed, "I thought he was white!"

Immediately, the children began to chatter about the stunning development.

At the ripe old ages of six and seven, the children had no doubt that there was a Real Santa. Of that fact, they were absolutely sure. But suddenly—there was this huge question mark. Could Santa be black? And if so, what did that mean?

While some of the black children were delighted with the idea that Santa could be black, still others were unsure. Some of the white children initially rejected this idea out of hand: a black Santa couldn't be real. But even the little girl who was the most adamant that the Real Santa must be white considered the possibility that a black Santa could fill in for White Santa if he was hurt. And she still gleefully yelled along with the black Santa's final "Merry Christmas to All! Y'all Sleep Tight." Still another of the white girls progressed from initially rejecting a black Santa outright to conceding that maybe Black Santa was a "Helper Santa." By the end of the story, she was asking if this black Santa couldn't somehow be a cousin or brother to the white Santa they already knew about. Her strong need that it was a white Santa who came to her house was clearly still intact—but those concessions were quite a switch in about ten pages.

Later that week, Copenhaver returned to see this play out again in another teacher's class. Similar debates ensued. A couple of the children offered the idea that perhaps Santa's "mixed with black and white"—perhaps Santa was something in the middle, like an Indian. One boy went with a Two-Santa Hypothesis: White Santa and Black Santa must be friends who take turns visiting children, he concluded. When Bowman made the apparently huge mistake of saying that she'd never seen Santa, the children all quickly corrected her: they knew everyone had seen Santa at the mall. Not that that clarified the situation any.

In both classes, the debate raged off-and-on for a week, until a school party. Santa was coming. And they were all sure it was the Real Santa who was coming.

Then Santa arrived at the party—and he was black. Just like in the picture book.

The black children were exultant—since this proved that Santa was black. Some of the white children said that this black Santa was too thin, and that meant that the Real Santa was the fat white one at Kmart. But one of the white girls retorted that she had met the man and was convinced. Santa was brown.

Amy, one of the white children who'd come up with the mixed-race Santa theory, abandoned that idea upon meeting Black Santa. But she wondered if maybe Black Santa went to the black kids' houses while White Santa delivered the white kids' presents. A black child also wondered if this Santa would take care of the white kids himself, or if perhaps he would pass along their toy requests to a white Santa hidden somewhere else.

Another black child, Brent, still doubted. He really wanted a black Santa to be true, but he wasn't convinced. So he bravely confronted Santa. "There ain't no black Santas!" Brent insisted.

"Son, what color do you see?" Santa replied.

"Black—but under your socks you might not be!"

"Lookit here." Santa pulled up a pant leg, to let Brent see the skin underneath.

A thrilled Brent was sold. "This is a black Santa!" he yelled. "He's got black skin and his black boots are like the white Santa's boots."

A black Santa storybook wasn't enough to change the children's mindsets. It didn't crush every stereotype. Even the black kids who were excited about a black Santa—when Johnson asked them to draw Santa—they still depicted a Santa whose skin was as snowy-white as his beard.

But the shock of the Santa storybook did allow the children to start talking about race in a way that had never before occurred to them. And their questions started a year-long dialogue about race issues.

By the end of the year, the teachers were regularly incorporating books that dealt directly with issues of racism into their reading. Both black and white children were collaborating on book projects on Martin Luther King Jr. And when the kids read one book about the civil rights movement, both a black and a white child noticed that white people were nowhere to be found in the story, and, troubled, they decided to find out just where in history both peoples were.

STUDY QUESTIONS

1. Why do most white parents not talk about **race** with their children? And why do most families of color teach their children about race?

2. What is the diverse environment theory and why do the authors believe that it alone cannot instill tolerance and acceptance into our children?

3. Did your parents talk to you about **gender**? Did they tell you that boys and girls are equal and can achieve anything? Did your parents talk to you about race in the

same way? If there were differences, why do you think your parents approached race differently from gender?

4. Research done with red and blue T-shirts suggests that kids are "developmentally prone to in-group favoritism." Does this make **racism** biological? Should parents explicitly teach their children to value others who are different from themselves?

ERVING GOFFMAN

Performances

from The Presentation of Self in Everyday Life

J ust who do you think you are? And, who do you want other people to think you are? As Erving Goffman notes, each of us performs as we want to be seen. That is, we are acting in a way that reflects how we see ourselves and how we think others see us. Goffman explores how our sense of **self** is constructed by the performances we give and by the **fronts** we wear like masks. As you read be thinking of what you do to construct in the minds of others the perception of who you are.

BELIEF IN THE PART ONE IS PLAYING

WHEN AN INDIVIDUAL PLAYS A PART HE IMPLICITLY REQUESTS his observers to take seriously the impression that is fostered before them. They are asked to believe that the character they see actually possesses the attributes he appears to possess, that the task he performs will have the consequences that are implicitly claimed for it, and that, in general, matters are what they appear to be. In line with this, there is the popular view that the individual offers his performance and puts on his show "for the benefit of other people." It will be convenient to begin a consideration of performances by turning the question around and looking at the individual's own belief in the impression of reality that he attempts to engender in those among whom he finds himself.

At one extreme, one finds that the performer can be fully taken in by his own act; he can be sincerely convinced that the impression of reality which he stages is the real reality. When his audience is also convinced in this way about the show he puts on—and this seems to be the typical case—then for the moment at least, only the sociologist or the socially disgruntled will have any doubts about the "realness" of what is presented.

At the other extreme, we find that the performer may not be taken in at all by his own routine. This possibility is understandable, since no one is in quite as good an observational position to see through the act as the person who puts it on. Coupled with this, the performer may be moved to guide the conviction of his audience only as a means to other ends, having no ultimate concern in the conception that they have of him or of the situation. When the individual has no belief in his own act and no ultimate concern with the beliefs of his audience, we may call him cynical, reserving the term "sincere" for individuals who believe in the impression fostered by their own performance. It should be understood that the cynic, with all his professional disinvolvement, may obtain unprofessional pleasures from his masquerade, experiencing a kind of gleeful spiritual aggression from the fact that he can toy at will with something his audience must take seriously.[1]

It is not assumed, of course, that all cynical performers are interested in deluding their audiences for purposes of what is called "self-interest" or private gain. A cynical individual may delude his audience for what he considers to be their own good, or for the good of the community, etc. For illustrations of this we need not appeal to sadly enlightened showmen such as Marcus Aurelius or Hsun Tzǔ.[2] We know that in service occupations practitioners who may otherwise be sincere are sometimes forced to delude their customers because their customers show such a heartfelt demand for it. Doctors who are led into giving placebos, filling station attendants who resignedly check and recheck tire pressures for anxious women motorists, shoe clerks who sell a shoe that fits but tell the customer it is the size she wants to hear—these are cynical performers whose audiences will not allow them to be sincere. Similarly, it seems that sympathetic patients in mental wards will sometimes feign bizarre symptoms so that student nurses will not be subjected to a disappointingly sane performance.[3] So also,

---

[1] Perhaps the real crime of the confidence man is not that he takes money from his victims but that he robs all of us of the belief that middle-class manners and appearance can be sustained only by middle class people. A disabused professional can be cynically hostile to the service relation his clients expect him to extend to them, the confidence man is in a position to hold the whole "legit" world in this contempt. [All notes are those of the author unless otherwise indicated.]

[2] Marcus Aurelius Antoninus (121–180 C.E.) was a Roman emperor and Stoic philosopher. Hsun Tzǔ (312–230 B.C.E.) was a Chinese philosopher. [Ed.]

[3] See Taxel, p. 4. Harry Stack Sullivan has suggested that the tact of institutionalized performers can operate in the other direction, resulting in a kind of *noblesse-oblige* sanity. See his "Socio-Psychiatric Research," *American Journal of Psychiatry*, X, pp. 987–88. "A study of 'social recoveries'

when inferiors extend their most lavish reception for visiting superiors, the selfish desire to win favor may not be the chief motive; the inferior may be tactfully attempting to put the superior at ease by simulating the kind of world the superior is thought to take for granted.

I have suggested two extremes: an individual may be taken in by his own act or be cynical about it. These extremes are something a little more than just the ends of a continuum. Each provides the individual with a position which has its own particular securities and defenses, so there will be a tendency for those who have traveled close to one of these poles to complete the voyage. Starting with lack of inward belief in one's role, the individual may follow the natural movement described by Park:

> It is probably no mere historical accident that the word person, in its first meaning, is a mask. It is rather a recognition of the fact that everyone is always and everywhere, more or less consciously, playing a role . . . It is in these roles that we know each other; it is in these roles that we know ourselves.[4]

> In a sense, and in so far as this mask represents the conception we have formed of ourselves—the role we are striving to live up to—this mask is our truer self, the self we would like to be. In the end, our conception of our role becomes second nature and an integral part of our personality. We come into the world as individuals, achieve character, and become persons.[5]

This may be illustrated from the community life of Shetland.[6] For the last four or five years the island's tourist hotel has been owned and operated by a married couple of crofter origins. From the beginning, the owners were forced to set aside their own conceptions as to how life ought to be led, displaying in the hotel a full round of middle-class services and amenities. Lately, however, it appears that the managers have become less cynical about the performance that they stage; they themselves are becoming middle class and more and more enamored of the selves their clients impute to them.

Another illustration may be found in the raw recruit who initially follows army etiquette in order to avoid physical punishment and eventually comes to follow the

---

in one of our large mental hospitals some years ago taught me that patients were often released from care because they had learned not to manifest symptoms to the environing persons; in other words, had integrated enough of the personal environment to realize the prejudice opposed to their delusions. It seemed almost as if they grew wise enough to be tolerant of the imbecility surrounding them, having finally discovered that it was stupidity and not malice. They could then secure satisfaction from contact with others, while discharging a part of their cravings by psychotic means."

[4] Robert Ezra Park, *Race and Culture* (Glencoe, Ill.: The Free Press, 1950), p. 249.

[5] *Ibid.*, p. 250.

[6] Shetland Isle study.

rules so that his organization will not be shamed and his officers and fellow soldiers will respect him.

As suggested, the cycle of disbelief-to-belief can be followed in the other direction, starting with conviction or insecure aspiration and ending in cynicism. Professions which the public holds in religious awe often allow their recruits to follow the cycle in this direction, and often recruits follow it in this direction not because of a slow realization that they are deluding their audience—for by ordinary social standards the claims they make may be quite valid—but because they can use this cynicism as a means of insulating their inner selves from contact with the audience. And we may even expect to find typical careers of faith, with the individual starting out with one kind of involvement in the performance he is required to give, then moving back and forth several times between sincerity and cynicism before completing all the phases and turning-points of self-belief for a person of his station. Thus, students of medical schools suggest that idealistically oriented beginners in medical school typically lay aside their holy aspirations for a period of time. During the first two years the students find that their interest in medicine must be dropped that they may give all their time to the task of learning how to get through examinations. During the next two years they are too busy learning about diseases to show much concern for the persons who are diseased. It is only after their medical schooling has ended that their original ideals about medical service may be reasserted.[7]

While we can expect to find natural movement back and forth between cynicism and sincerity, still we must not rule out the kind of transitional point that can be sustained on the strength of a little self-illusion. We find that the individual may attempt to induce the audience to judge him and the situation in a particular way, and he may seek this judgment as an ultimate end in itself, and yet he may not completely believe that he deserves the valuation of self which he asks for or that the impression of reality which he fosters is valid. Another mixture of cynicism and belief is suggested in Kroeber's discussion of shamanism:

> Next, there is the old question of deception. Probably most shamans or medicine men, the world over, help along with sleight-of-hand in curing and especially in exhibitions of power. This sleight-of-hand is sometimes deliberate; in many cases awareness is perhaps not deeper than the foreconscious. The attitude, whether there has been repression or not, seems to be as toward a pious fraud. Field ethnographers seem quite generally convinced that even shamans who know that they add fraud nevertheless also believe in their powers, and especially in those of other shamans: they consult them when they themselves or their children are ill.[8]

---

[7] H. S. Becker and Blanche Greer, "The Fate of Idealism in Medical School," *American Sociological Review*, 23, pp. 50–56.

[8] A. L. Kroeber, *The Nature of Culture* (Chicago: University of Chicago Press, 1952), p. 311.

FRONT

I have been using the term "performance" to refer to all the activity of an individual which occurs during a period marked by his continuous presence before a particular set of observers and which has some influence on the observers. It will be convenient to label as "front" that part of the individual's performance which regularly functions in a general and fixed fashion to define the situation for those who observe the performance. Front, then, is the expressive equipment of a standard kind intentionally or unwittingly employed by the individual during his performance. For preliminary purposes, it will be convenient to distinguish and label what seem to be the standard parts of front.

First, there is the "setting," involving furniture, décor, physical layout, and other background items which supply the scenery and stage props for the spate of human action played out before, within, or upon it. A setting tends to stay put, geographically speaking, so that those who would use a particular setting as part of their performance cannot begin their act until they have brought themselves to the appropriate place and must terminate their performance when they leave it. It is only in exceptional circumstances that the setting follows along with the performers; we see this in the funeral cortège, the civic parade, and the dreamlike processions that kings and queens are made of. In the main, these exceptions seem to offer some kind of extra protection for performers who are, or who have momentarily become, highly sacred. These worthies are to be distinguished, of course, from quite profane performers of the peddler class who move their place of work between performances, often being forced to do so. In the matter of having one fixed place for one's setting, a ruler may be too sacred, a peddler too profane.

In thinking about the scenic aspects of front, we tend to think of the living room in a particular house and the small number of performers who can thoroughly identify themselves with it. We have given insufficient attention to assemblages of sign-equipment which large numbers of performers can call their own for short periods of time. It is characteristic of Western European countries, and no doubt a source of stability for them, that a large number of luxurious settings are available for hire to anyone of the right kind who can afford them. One illustration of this may be cited from a study of the higher civil servant in Britain:

> The question how far the men who rise to the top in the Civil Service take on the "tone" or "color" of a class other than that to which they belong by birth is delicate and difficult. The only definite information bearing on the question is the figures relating to the membership of the great London clubs. More than three-quarters of our high administrative officials belong to one or more clubs of high status and considerable luxury, where the entrance fee might be twenty guineas or more, and the annual subscription from twelve to twenty guineas. These institutions are of the upper class (not even of the upper-middle) in their premises, their equipment, the style of living practiced

there, their whole atmosphere. Though many of the members would not be described as wealthy, only a wealthy man would unaided provide for himself and his family space, food and drink, service, and other amenities of life to the same standard as he will find at the Union, the Travellers', or the Reform.[9]

Another example can be found in the recent development of the medical profession where we find that it is increasingly important for a doctor to have access to the elaborate scientific stage provided by large hospitals, so that fewer and fewer doctors are able to feel that their setting is a place that they can lock up at night.[1]

If we take the term "setting" to refer to the scenic parts of expressive equipment, one may take the term "personal front" to refer to the other items of expressive equipment, the items that we most intimately identify with the performer himself and that we naturally expect will follow the performer wherever he goes. As part of personal front we may include: insignia of office or rank; clothing; sex, age, and racial characteristics; size and looks; posture; speech patterns; facial expressions; bodily gestures; and the like. Some of these vehicles for conveying signs, such as racial characteristics, are relatively fixed and over a span of time do not vary for the individual from one situation to another. On the other hand, some of these sign vehicles are relatively mobile or transitory, such as facial expression, and can vary during a performance from one moment to the next.

It is sometimes convenient to divide the stimuli which make up personal front into "appearance" and "manner," according to the function performed by the information that these stimuli convey. "Appearance" may be taken to refer to those stimuli which function at the time to tell us of the performer's social statuses. These stimuli also tell us of the individual's temporary ritual state, that is, whether he is engaging in formal social activity, work, or informal recreation, whether or not he is celebrating a new phase in the season cycle or in his life-cycle. "Manner" may be taken to refer to those stimuli which function at the time to warn us of the interaction role the performer will expect to play in the oncoming situation. Thus a haughty, aggressive manner may give the impression that the performer expects to be the one who will initiate the verbal interaction and direct its course. A meek, apologetic manner may give the impression that the performer expects to follow the lead of others, or at least that he can be led to do so.

We often expect, of course, a confirming consistency between appearance and manner; we expect that the differences in social statuses among the interactants will be expressed in some way by congruent differences in the indications that are made of an expected interaction role. This type of coherence of front may be illustrated by the following description of the procession of a mandarin through a Chinese city:

---

[9] H. E. Dale, *The Higher Civil Service of Great Britain* (Oxford: Oxford University Press, 1941), p. 50.
[1] David Solomon, "Career Contingencies of Chicago Physicians" (unpublished Ph.D. dissertation, Department of Sociology, University of Chicago, 1952), p. 74.

Coming closely behind . . . the luxurious chair of the mandarin, carried by eight bearers, fills the vacant space in the street. He is mayor of the town, and for all practical purposes the supreme power in it. He is an ideal-looking official, for he is large and massive in appearance, whilst he has that stern and uncompromising look that is supposed to be necessary in any magistrate who would hope to keep his subjects in order. He has a stern and forbidding aspect, as though he were on his way to the execution ground to have some criminal decapitated. This is the kind of air that the mandarins put on when they appear in public. In the course of many years' experience, I have never once seen any of them, from the highest to the lowest, with a smile on his face or a look of sympathy for the people whilst he was being carried officially through the streets.[2]

But, of course, appearance and manner may tend to contradict each other, as when a performer who appears to be of higher estate than his audience acts in a manner that is unexpectedly equalitarian, or intimate, or apologetic, or when a performer dressed in the garments of a high position presents himself to an individual of even higher status.

In addition to the expected consistency between appearance and manner, we expect, of course, some coherence among setting, appearance, and manner.[3] Such coherence represents an ideal type that provides us with a means of stimulating our attention to and interest in exceptions. In this the student is assisted by the journalist, for exceptions to expected consistency among setting, appearance, and manner provide the piquancy and glamor of many careers and the salable appeal of many magazine articles. For example, a *New Yorker* profile on Roger Stevens (the real estate agent who engineered the sale of the Empire State Building) comments on the startling fact that Stevens has a small house, a meager office, and no letterhead stationery.[4]

In order to explore more fully the relations among the several parts of social front, it will be convenient to consider here a significant characteristic of the information conveyed by front, namely, its abstractness and generality.

However specialized and unique a routine is, its social front, with certain exceptions, will tend to claim facts that can be equally claimed and asserted of other, somewhat different routines. For example, many service occupations offer their clients a performance that is illuminated with dramatic expressions of cleanliness, modernity, competence, and integrity. While in fact these abstract standards have a different significance in different occupational performances the observer is encouraged to stress the abstract similarities. For the observer this is a wonderful, though sometimes disastrous, convenience. Instead of having to maintain a different pattern of expectation and responsive treatment for each slightly different performer and performance,

---

[2] J. Macgowan, *Sidelights on Chinese Life* (Philadelphia: Lippincott, 1908), p. 187.

[3] Cf. Kenneth Burke's comments on the "scene-act-agent ratio," *A Grammar of Motives* (New York: Prentice-Hall, 1945), pp. 6–9.

[4] E. J. Kahn, Jr., "Closings and Openings," *The New Yorker,* February 13 and 20, 1954.

he can place the situation in a broad category around which it is easy for him to mobilize his past experience and stereo-typical thinking. Observers then need only be familiar with a small and hence manageable vocabulary of fronts, and know how to respond to them, in order to orient themselves in a wide variety of situations. Thus in London the current tendency for chimney sweeps[5] and perfume clerks to wear white lab coats tends to provide the client with an understanding that the delicate tasks performed by these persons will be performed in what has become a standardized, clinical confidential manner.

There are grounds for believing that the tendency for a large number of different acts to be presented from behind a small number of fronts is a natural development in social organization. Radcliffe-Brown has suggested this in his claim that a "descriptive" kinship system which gives each person a unique place may work for very small communities, but, as the number of persons becomes large, clan segmentation becomes necessary as a means of providing a less complicated system of identifications and treatments.[6] We see this tendency illustrated in factories, barracks, and other large social establishments. Those who organize these establishments find it impossible to provide a special cafeteria, special modes of payment, special vacation rights, and special sanitary facilities for every line and staff status category in the organization, and at the same time they feel that persons of dissimilar status ought not to be indiscriminately thrown together or classified together. As a compromise, the full range of diversity is cut at a few crucial points, and all those within a given bracket are allowed or obliged to maintain the same social front in certain situations.

In addition to the fact that different routines may employ the same front, it is to be noted that a given social front tends to become institutionalized in terms of the abstract stereotyped expectations to which it gives rise, and tends to take on a meaning and stability apart from the specific tasks which happen at the time to be performed in its name. The front becomes a "collective representation" and a fact in its own right.

When an actor takes on an established social role, usually he finds that a particular front has already been established for it. Whether his acquisition of the role was primarily motivated by a desire to perform the given task or by a desire to maintain the corresponding front, the actor will find that he must do both.

Further, if the individual takes on a task that is not only new to him but also unestablished in the society, or if he attempts to change the light in which his task is viewed, he is likely to find that there are already several well-established fronts among which he must choose. Thus, when a task is given a new front we seldom find that the front it is given is itself new.

* * *

---

[5] See Mervyn Jones, "White as a Sweep," *The New Statesman and Nation*, December 6, 1952.
[6] A. R. Radcliffe-Brown, "The Social Organization of Australian Tribes," *Oceania*, I, 440.

1. What are settings and how do we use them to communicate who we are? It may be helpful to think about how a particular profession is communicated with setting.

2. What does Goffman mean when he says that personal **fronts** can become "collective representations"?

3. How do you communicate to the world around you who you are? Discuss your personal front (in both manner and appearance) and the settings you use to present it. Your answer should demonstrate your understanding of these terms.

4. Go to a public place like a park, college student union, or shopping mall with a notebook and a pen. Watch and wait for a pair of people to meet. Write down how you see people presenting themselves when they see someone they know in public. What physical and nonphysical cues do they give one another?

ROBERT D. PUTNAM

Thinking about Social Change
in America

from *Bowling Alone: The Collapse and Revival of*
American Community

F or generations, Americans have been civic-minded. They've joined Rotary Clubs and the Shriners, softball teams and city councils. But, in this selection, Robert D. Putnam asks, "Where did everybody go?" Since the mid-1970s, Putnam argues, civic participation has steadily decreased. As the organizations in which "everyone" used to participate fade into obscurity, they also leave a real hole in the social safety net, since they provided a great deal of **social capital** for the communities they served. Without such **groups**, Putnam wonders, will **society** survive? As you read, think about whether you believe civic participation has dropped off—that is, whether people really are opting out of community service and participation—or if it is changing. If it's changing, where *have* all the people gone?

NO ONE IS LEFT FROM THE GLENN VALLEY, PENNSYLVANIA, Bridge Club who can tell us precisely when or why the group broke up, even though its forty-odd members were still playing regularly as recently as 1990, just as they had done for more than half a century. The shock in the Little Rock, Arkansas, Sertoma club, however, is still painful: in the mid-1980s, nearly fifty people had attended the weekly luncheon to plan activities to help the hearing- and speech-impaired, but a decade later only seven regulars continued to show up.

The Roanoke, Virginia, chapter of the National Association for the Advancement of Colored People (NAACP) had been an active force for civil rights since 1918, but during the 1990s membership withered from about 2,500 to a few hundred. By November 1998 even a heated contest for president drew only fifty-seven voting members. Black city councillor Carroll Swain observed ruefully, "Some people today are a wee bit complacent until something jumps up and bites them." VFW Post 2378 in Berwyn, Illinois, a blue-collar suburb of Chicago, was long a bustling "home away from home" for local veterans and a kind of working-class country club for the neighborhood, hosting wedding receptions and class reunions. By 1999, however, membership had so dwindled that it was a struggle just to pay taxes on the yellow brick post hall. Although numerous veterans of Vietnam and the post-Vietnam military lived in the area, Tom Kissell, national membership director for the VFW, observed, "Kids today just aren't joiners."[1]

The Charity League of Dallas had met every Friday morning for fifty-seven years to sew, knit, and visit, but on April 30, 1999, they held their last meeting; the average age of the group had risen to eighty, the last new member had joined two years earlier, and president Pat Dilbeck said ruefully, "I feel like this is a sinking ship." Precisely three days later and 1,200 miles to the northeast, the Vassar alumnae of Washington, D.C., closed down their fifty-first—and last—annual book sale. Even though they aimed to sell more than one hundred thousand books to benefit college scholarships in the 1999 event, co-chair Alix Myerson explained, the volunteers who ran the program "are in their sixties, seventies, and eighties. They're dying, and they're not replaceable." Meanwhile, as Tewksbury Memorial High School (TMHS), just north of Boston, opened in the fall of 1999, forty brand-new royal blue uniforms newly purchased for the marching band remained in storage, since only four students signed up to play. Roger Whittlesey, TMHS band director, recalled that twenty years earlier the band numbered more than eighty, but participation had waned ever since.[2] Somehow in the last several decades of the twentieth century all these community groups and tens of thousands like them across America began to fade.

It wasn't so much that old members dropped out—at least not any more rapidly than age and the accidents of life had always meant. But community organizations were no longer continuously revitalized, as they had been in the past, by freshets of new members. Organizational leaders were flummoxed. For years they assumed that their problem must have local roots or at least that it was peculiar to their organization, so they commissioned dozens of studies to recommend reforms.[3] The slowdown was puzzling because for as long as anyone could remember, membership rolls and activity lists had lengthened steadily.

In the 1960s, in fact, community groups across America had seemed to stand on the threshold of a new era of expanded involvement. Except for the civic drought induced by the Great Depression, their activity had shot up year after year, cultivated by assiduous civic gardeners and watered by increasing affluence and education. Each annual report registered rising membership. Churches and synagogues were packed, as more Americans worshiped together than only a few decades earlier, perhaps more than ever in American history.

Moreover, Americans seemed to have time on their hands. A 1958 study under the auspices of the newly inaugurated Center for the Study of Leisure at the University of Chicago fretted that "the most dangerous threat hanging over American society is the threat of leisure," a startling claim in the decade in which the Soviets got the bomb.[4] *Life* magazine echoed the warning about the new challenge of free time: "Americans now face a glut of leisure," ran a headline in February 1964. "The task ahead: how to take life easy."

> As a matter of fact, mankind now possesses for the first time the tools and knowledge to create whatever kind of world he wants.... Despite our Protestant ethic, there are many signs that the message is beginning to get through to some people.... Not only are Americans flocking into bowling leagues and garden clubs, they are satisfying their gregarious urges in countless neighborhood committees to improve the local roads and garbage collections and to hound their public servants into doing what the name implies.[5]

The civic-minded World War II generation was, as its own John F. Kennedy proclaimed at his inauguration, picking up the torch of leadership, not only in the nation's highest office, but in cities and towns across the land. Summarizing dozens of studies, political scientist Robert E. Lane wrote in 1959 that "the ratio of political activists to the general population, and even the ratio of male activists to the male population, has generally increased over the past fifty years." As the 1960s ended, sociologists Daniel Bell and Virginia Held reported that "there is more participation than ever before in America ... and more opportunity for the active interested person to express his personal and political concerns."[6] Even the simplest political act, voting, was becoming ever more common. From 1920, when women got the vote, through 1960, turnout in presidential elections had risen at the rate of 1.6 percent every four years, so on a simple straight-line projection it seemed reasonable, as a leading political scientist later observed, to expect turnout to be nearly 70 percent and rising on the nation's two hundredth birthday in 1976.[7]

By 1965 disrespect for public life, so endemic in our history, seemed to be waning. Gallup pollsters discovered that the number of Americans who would like to see their children "go into politics as a life's work" had nearly doubled over little more than a decade. Although this gauge of esteem for politics stood at only 36 percent, it had never before been recorded so high, nor has it since. More strikingly, Americans felt increased confidence in their neighbors. The proportion that agreed that "most people can be trusted," for example, rose from an already high 66 percent during and after World War II to a peak of 77 percent in 1964.[8]

The fifties and sixties were hardly a "golden age," especially for those Americans who were marginalized because of their race or gender or social class or sexual orientation. Segregation, by race legally and by gender socially, was the norm, and intolerance, though declining, was still disturbingly high. Environmental degradation had only just been exposed by Rachel Carson, and Betty Friedan had not yet deconstructed the feminine mystique. Grinding rural poverty had still to be discovered by the national media. Infant mortality, a standard measure of public health, stood at twenty-six per one thousand births—forty-four per one thousand for black infants—in 1960, nearly four times worse than those indexes would be at the end of the century. America in *Life* was white, straight, Christian, comfortable, and (in the public square, at least) male.[9] Social reformers had their work cut out for them. However, engagement in community affairs and the sense of shared identity and reciprocity had never been greater in modern America, so the prospects for broad-based civic mobilization to address our national failings seemed bright.

The signs of burgeoning civic vitality were also favorable among the younger generation, as the first of the baby boomers approached college. Dozens of studies confirmed that education was by far the best predictor of engagement in civic life, and universities were in the midst of the most far-reaching expansion in American history. Education seemed the key to both greater tolerance and greater social involvement. Simultaneously shamed and inspired by the quickening struggle for civil rights launched by young African Americans in the South, white colleges in the North began to awaken from the silence of the fifties. Describing the induction of this new generation into the civil rights struggles of the 1960s, sociologist Doug McAdam emphasizes their self-assurance:

> We were a "can do" people, who accomplished whatever we set out to do. We had licked the Depression, turned the tide in World War II, and rebuilt Europe after the war.... Freedom Summer was an audacious undertaking consistent with the exaggerated sense of importance and potency shared by the privileged members of America's postwar generation.[10]

The baby boom meant that America's population was unusually young, whereas civic involvement generally doesn't bloom until middle age. In the short run, therefore, our youthful demography actually tended to dampen the ebullience of civil society. But that very bulge at the bottom of the nation's demographic pyramid boded well for the future of community organizations, for they could look forward to swelling membership rolls in the 1980s, when the boomers would reach the peak "joining" years of the life cycle. And in the meantime, the bull session buzz about "participatory democracy" and "all power to the people" seemed to augur ever more widespread engagement in community affairs. One of America's most acute social observers prophesied in 1968, "Participatory democracy has all along been the political style (if not the slogan) of the American middle and upper class. It will become a more widespread style as more persons enter into those classes."[11] Never in our history had the future of civic life looked brighter.

———————

What happened next to civic and social life in American communities? In recent years social scientists have framed concerns about the changing character of American society in terms of the concept of "social capital." By analogy with notions of physical capital and human capital—tools and training that enhance individual productivity—the core idea of social capital theory is that social networks have value. Just as a screwdriver (physical capital) or a college education (human capital) can increase productivity (both individual and collective), so too social contacts affect the productivity of individuals and groups.

Whereas physical capital refers to physical objects and human capital refers to properties of individuals, social capital refers to connections among individuals—social networks and the norms of reciprocity and trustworthiness that arise from them. In that sense social capital is closely related to what some have called "civic virtue." The difference is that "social capital" calls attention to the fact that civic virtue is most powerful when embedded in a dense network of reciprocal social relations. A society of many virtuous but isolated individuals is not necessarily rich in social capital.

The term *social capital* itself turns out to have been independently invented at least six times over the twentieth century, each time to call attention to the ways in which our lives are made more productive by social ties. The first known use of the concept was not by some cloistered theoretician, but by a practical reformer of the Progressive Era—L. J. Hanifan, state supervisor of rural schools in West Virginia. Writing in 1916 to urge the importance of community involvement for successful schools, Hanifan invoked the idea of "social capital" to explain why. For Hanifan, social capital referred to

> those tangible substances [that] count for most in the daily lives of people: namely good will, fellowship, sympathy, and social intercourse among the individuals and families who make up a social unit.... The individual is helpless socially, if left to himself.... If he comes into contact with his neighbor, and they with other neighbors, there will be an accumulation of social capital, which may immediately satisfy his social needs and which may bear a social potentiality sufficient to the substantial improvement of living conditions in the whole community. The community as a whole will benefit by the coöperation of all its parts, while the individual will find in his associations the advantages of the help, the sympathy, and the fellowship of his neighbors.[12]

Hanifan's account of social capital anticipated virtually all the crucial elements in later interpretations, but his conceptual invention apparently attracted no notice from other social commentators and disappeared without a trace. But like sunken treasure recurrently revealed by shifting sands and tides, the same idea was independently rediscovered in the 1950s by Canadian sociologists to characterize the club memberships of arriviste suburbanites, in the 1960s by urbanist Jane Jacobs to laud neighborliness in the modern metropolis, in the 1970s by economist Glenn Loury to analyze the social legacy of slavery, and in the 1980s by French social theorist Pierre

Bourdieu and by German economist Ekkehart Schlicht to underline the social and economic resources embodied in social networks. Sociologist James S. Coleman put the term firmly and finally on the intellectual agenda in the late 1980s, using it (as Hanifan had originally done) to highlight the social context of education.[13]

As this array of independent coinages indicates, social capital has both an individual and a collective aspect—a private face and a public face. First, individuals form connections that benefit our own interests. One pervasive strategem of ambitious job seekers is "networking," for most of us get our jobs because of whom we know, not what we know—that is, our social capital, not our human capital. Economic sociologist Ronald Burt has shown that executives with bounteous Rolodex files enjoy faster career advancement. Nor is the private return to social capital limited to economic rewards. As Claude S. Fischer, a sociologist of friendship, has noted, "Social networks are important in all our lives, often for finding jobs, more often for finding a helping hand, companionship, or a shoulder to cry on."[14]

If individual clout and companionship were all there were to social capital, we'd expect foresighted, self-interested individuals to invest the right amount of time and energy in creating or acquiring it. However, social capital also can have "externalities" that affect the wider community, so that not all the costs and benefits of social connections accrue to the person making the contact.[15] As we shall see, a well-connected individual in a poorly connected society is not as productive as a well-connected individual in a well-connected society. And even a poorly connected individual may derive some of the spillover benefits from living in a well-connected community. If the crime rate in my neighborhood is lowered by neighbors keeping an eye on one another's homes, I benefit even if I personally spend most of my time on the road and never even nod to another resident on the street.

Social capital can thus be simultaneously a "private good" and a "public good." Some of the benefit from an investment in social capital goes to bystanders, while some of the benefit redounds to the immediate interest of the person making the investment. For example, service clubs, like Rotary or Lions, mobilize local energies to raise scholarships or fight disease at the same time that they provide members with friendships and business connections that pay off personally.

Social connections are also important for the rules of conduct that they sustain. Networks involve (almost by definition) mutual obligations; they are not interesting as mere "contacts." Networks of community engagement foster sturdy norms of reciprocity: I'll do this for you now, in the expectation that you (or perhaps someone else) will return the favor. "Social capital is akin to what Tom Wolfe called 'the favor bank' in his novel *The Bonfire of the Vanities*," notes economist Robert Frank.[16] It was, however, neither a novelist nor an economist, but Yogi Berra who offered the most succinct definition of reciprocity: "If you don't go to somebody's funeral, they won't come to yours."

Sometimes, as in these cases, reciprocity is *specific:* I'll do this for you if you do that for me. Even more valuable, however, is a norm of *generalized* reciprocity: I'll do this for you without expecting anything specific back from you, in the confident expectation that someone else will do something for me down the road. The Golden Rule is one formulation of generalized reciprocity. Equally instructive is the T-shirt slogan used by the Gold Beach, Oregon, Volunteer Fire Department to publicize their annual fund-raising effort: "Come to our breakfast, we'll come to your fire." "We act on a norm of specific reciprocity," the firefighters seem to be saying, but onlookers smile because they recognize the underlying norm of generalized reciprocity—the firefighters will come even if *you* don't. When Blanche DuBois depended on the kindness of strangers, she too was relying on generalized reciprocity.

A society characterized by generalized reciprocity is more efficient than a distrustful society, for the same reason that money is more efficient than barter. If we don't have to balance every exchange instantly, we can get a lot more accomplished. Trustworthiness lubricates social life. Frequent interaction among a diverse set of people tends to produce a norm of generalized reciprocity. Civic engagement and social capital entail mutual obligation and responsibility for action. As L. J. Hanifan and his successors recognized, social networks and norms of reciprocity can facilitate cooperation for mutual benefit. When economic and political dealing is embedded in dense networks of social interaction, incentives for opportunism and malfeasance are reduced. This is why the diamond trade, with its extreme possibilities for fraud, is concentrated within close-knit ethnic enclaves. Dense social ties facilitate gossip and other valuable ways of cultivating reputation—an essential foundation for trust in a complex society.

Physical capital is not a single "thing," and different forms of physical capital are not interchangeable. An eggbeater and an aircraft carrier both appear as physical capital in our national accounts, but the eggbeater is not much use for national defense, and the carrier would not be much help with your morning omelet. Similarly, social capital—that is, social networks and the associated norms of reciprocity—comes in many different shapes and sizes with many different uses. Your extended family represents a form of social capital, as do your Sunday school class, the regulars who play poker on your commuter train, your college roommates, the civic organizations to which you belong, the Internet chat group in which you participate, and the network of professional acquaintances recorded in your address book.

Sometimes "social capital," like its conceptual cousin "community," sounds warm and cuddly. Urban sociologist Xavier de Souza Briggs, however, properly warns us to beware of a treacly sweet, "kumbaya"* interpretation of social capital.[17] Networks and the associated norms of reciprocity are generally good for those inside the network, but the external effects of social capital are by no means always positive. It was social capital, for example, that enabled Timothy McVeigh to bomb the Alfred P. Murrah

---

* African American spiritual (from the Creole language Gullah, meaning "Come by Here") that became a popular 1960s folk song and eventually a symbol of peaceful coexistence.

Federal Building in Oklahoma City. McVeigh's network of friends, bound together by a norm of reciprocity, enabled him to do what he could not have done alone. Similarly, urban gangs, NIMBY ("not in my backyard") movements, and power elites often exploit social capital to achieve ends that are antisocial from a wider perspective. Indeed, it is rhetorically useful for such groups to obscure the difference between the pro-social and antisocial consequences of community organizations. When Floridians objected to plans by the Ku Klux Klan to "adopt a highway," Jeff Coleman, grand wizard of the Royal Knights of the KKK, protested, "Really, we're just like the Lions or the Elks. We want to be involved in the community."[18]

Social capital, in short, can be directed toward malevolent, antisocial purposes, just like any other form of capital.[19] (McVeigh also relied on physical capital, like the explosive-laden truck, and human capital, like bomb-making expertise, to achieve his purposes.) Therefore it is important to ask how the positive consequences of social capital—mutual support, cooperation, trust, institutional effectiveness—can be maximized and the negative manifestations—sectarianism, ethnocentrism, corruption—minimized. Toward this end, scholars have begun to distinguish many different forms of social capital.

Some forms involve repeated, intensive, multistranded networks—like a group of steelworkers who meet for drinks every Friday after work and see each other at mass on Sunday—and some are episodic, single stranded, and anonymous, like the faintly familiar face you see several times a month in the supermarket checkout line. Some types of social capital, like a Parent-Teacher Association, are formally organized, with incorporation papers, regular meetings, a written constitution, and connection to a national federation, whereas others, like a pickup basketball game, are more informal. Some forms of social capital, like a volunteer ambulance squad, have explicit public-regarding purposes; some, like a bridge club, exist for the private enjoyment of the members; and some, like the Rotary club mentioned earlier, serve both public and private ends.

Of all the dimensions along which forms of social capital vary, perhaps the most important is the distinction between *bridging* (or inclusive) and *bonding* (or exclusive).[20] Some forms of social capital are, by choice or necessity, inward looking and tend to reinforce exclusive identities and homogeneous groups. Examples of bonding social capital include ethnic fraternal organizations, church-based women's reading groups, and fashionable country clubs. Other networks are outward looking and encompass people across diverse social cleavages. Examples of bridging social capital include the civil rights movement, many youth service groups, and ecumenical religious organizations.

Bonding social capital is good for undergirding specific reciprocity and mobilizing solidarity. Dense networks in ethnic enclaves, for example, provide crucial social and psychological support for less fortunate members of the community, while furnishing start-up financing, markets, and reliable labor for local entrepreneurs. Bridging networks, by contrast, are better for linkage to external assets and for information diffusion. Economic sociologist Mark Granovetter has pointed out that when seeking jobs—or political allies—the "weak" ties that link me to distant acquaintances who move in different circles from mine are actually more valuable than the "strong" ties that link me to relatives and intimate friends whose sociological niche is very like my own. Bonding social capital is, as Xavier de Souza Briggs puts it, good for "getting by," but bridging social capital is crucial for "getting ahead."[21]

Moreover, bridging social capital can generate broader identities and reciprocity, whereas bonding social capital bolsters our narrower selves. In 1829 at the founding of a community lyceum in the bustling whaling port of New Bedford, Massachusetts, Thomas Greene eloquently expressed this crucial insight:

> We come from all the divisions, ranks and classes of society . . . to teach and to be taught in our turn. While we mingle together in these pursuits, we shall learn to know each other more intimately; we shall remove many of the prejudices which ignorance or partial acquaintance with each other had fostered. . . . In the parties and sects into which we are divided, we sometimes learn to love our brother at the expense of him whom we do not in so many respects regard as a brother. . . . We may return to our homes and firesides [from the lyceum] with kindlier feelings toward one another, because we have learned to know one another better.[22]

Bonding social capital constitutes a kind of sociological superglue, whereas bridging social capital provides a sociological WD-40. Bonding social capital, by creating strong in-group loyalty, may also create strong out-group antagonism, as Thomas Greene and his neighbors in New Bedford knew, and for that reason we might expect negative external effects to be more common with this form of social capital. Nevertheless, under many circumstances both bridging and bonding social capital can have powerfully positive social effects.

Many groups simultaneously bond along some social dimensions and bridge across others. The black church, for example, brings together people of the same race and religion across class lines. The Knights of Columbus was created to bridge cleavages among different ethnic communities while bonding along religious and gender lines. Internet chat groups may bridge across geography, gender, age, and religion, while being tightly homogeneous in education and ideology. In short, bonding and bridging are not "either-or" categories into which social networks can be neatly divided, but "more or less" dimensions along which we can compare different forms of social capital.

It would obviously be valuable to have distinct measures of the evolution of these various forms of social capital over time. However, like researchers on global warming, we must make do with the imperfect evidence that we can find, not merely lament its deficiencies. Exhaustive descriptions of social networks in America—even at a single point in time—do not exist. I have found no reliable, comprehensive, nationwide measures of social capital that neatly distinguish "bridgingness" and "bondingness."

In our empirical account of recent social trends, therefore, this distinction will be less prominent than I would prefer. On the other hand, we must keep this conceptual differentiation at the back of our minds as we proceed, recognizing that bridging and bonding social capital are not interchangeable.

———————

"Social capital" is to some extent merely new language for a very old debate in American intellectual circles. Community has warred incessantly with individualism for preeminence in our political hagiology. Liberation from ossified community bonds is a recurrent and honored theme in our culture, from the Pilgrims' storied escape from religious convention in the seventeenth century to the lyric nineteenth-century paeans to individualism by Emerson ("Self-Reliance"), Thoreau ("Civil Disobedience"), and Whitman ("Song of Myself") to Sherwood Anderson's twentieth-century celebration of the struggle against conformism by ordinary citizens in *Winesburg, Ohio* to the latest Clint Eastwood film. Even Alexis de Tocqueville, patron saint of American communitarians, acknowledged the uniquely democratic claim of individualism, "a calm and considered feeling which disposes each citizen to isolate himself from the mass of his fellows and withdraw into the circle of family and friends; with this little society formed to his taste, he gladly leaves the greater society to look after itself."[23]

Our national myths often exaggerate the role of individual heroes and understate the importance of collective effort. Historian David Hackett Fischer's gripping account of opening night in the American Revolution, for example, reminds us that Paul Revere's alarum was successful only because of networks of civic engagement in the Middlesex villages. Towns without well-organized local militia, no matter how patriotic their inhabitants, were AWOL from Lexington and Concord.[24] Nevertheless, the myth of rugged individualism continues to strike a powerful inner chord in the American psyche.

Debates about the waxing and waning of "community" have been endemic for at least two centuries. "Declensionist narratives"—postmodernist jargon for tales of decline and fall—have a long pedigree in our letters. We seem perennially tempted to contrast our tawdry todays with past golden ages. We apparently share this nostalgic predilection with the rest of humanity. As sociologist Barry Wellman observes,

> It is likely that pundits have worried about the impact of social change on communities ever since human beings ventured beyond their caves. . . . In the [past] two centuries many leading social commentators have been gainfully employed suggesting various ways in which large-scale social changes associated with the Industrial Revolution may have affected the structure and operation of communities. . . . This ambivalence about the consequences of large-scale changes continued well into the twentieth century. Analysts have kept asking if things have, in fact, fallen apart.[25]

At the conclusion of the twentieth century, ordinary Americans shared this sense of civic malaise. We were reasonably content about our economic prospects, hardly a surprise after an expansion of unprecedented length, but we were not equally convinced that we were on the right track morally or culturally. Of baby boomers interviewed in 1987, 53 percent thought their parents' generation was better in terms of "being a concerned citizen, involved in helping others in the community," as compared with only 21 percent who thought their own generation was better. Fully 77 percent said the nation was worse off because of "less involvement in community activities." In 1992 three-quarters of the U.S. workforce said that "the breakdown of community" and "selfishness" were "serious" or "extremely serious" problems in America. In 1996 only 8 percent of all Americans said that "the honesty and integrity of the average American" were improving, as compared with 50 percent of us who thought we were becoming less trustworthy. Those of us who said that people had become less civil over the preceding ten years outnumbered those who thought people had become more civil, 80 percent to 12 percent. In several surveys in 1999 two-thirds of Americans said that America's civic life had weakened in recent years, that social and moral values were higher when they were growing up, and that our society was focused more on the individual than the community. More than 80 percent said there should be more emphasis on community, even if that put more demands on individuals.[26] Americans' concern about weakening community bonds may be misplaced or exaggerated, but a decent respect for the opinion of our fellow citizens suggests that we should explore the issue more thoroughly.

It is emphatically not my view that community bonds in America have weakened steadily throughout our history—or even throughout the last hundred years. On the contrary, American history carefully examined is a story of ups and downs in civic engagement, *not just downs*—a story of collapse *and* of renewal. Within living memory the bonds of community in America were becoming stronger, not weaker, and it is within our power to reverse the decline of the last several decades.

Nevertheless, my argument is, at least in appearance, in the declensionist tradition, so it is important to avoid simple nostalgia. Precisely because the theme of this book might lend itself to gauzy self-deception, our methods must be transparent. Is life in communities as we enter the twenty-first century really so different after all from the reality of American communities in the 1950s and 1960s? One way of curbing nostalgia is to count things. Are club meetings really less crowded today than yesterday, or does it just seem so? Do we really know our neighbors less well than our parents did, or is our childhood recollection of neighborhood barbecues suffused with a golden glow of wishful reminiscence? Are friendly poker games less common now, or is it merely that we ourselves have outgrown poker? League bowling may be passé, but how about softball and soccer? Are strangers less trustworthy now? Are boomers and X'ers really less engaged in community life? After all, it was the preceding generation that was once scorned as "silent." Perhaps the younger generation today is no less engaged than their predecessors, but engaged in new ways.

* * *

Before October 29, 1997, John Lambert and Andy Boschma knew each other only through their local bowling league at the Ypsi-Arbor Lanes in Ypsilanti, Michigan. Lambert, a sixty-four-year-old retired employee of the University of Michigan hospital, had been on a kidney transplant waiting list for three years when Boschma, a thirty-three-year-old accountant, learned casually of Lambert's need and unexpectedly approached him to offer to donate one of his own kidneys.

"Andy saw something in me that others didn't," said Lambert. "When we were in the hospital Andy said to me, 'John, I really like you and have a lot of respect for you. I wouldn't hesitate to do this all over again.' I got choked up." Boschma returned the feeling: "I obviously feel a kinship [with Lambert]. I cared about him before, but now I'm really rooting for him." This moving story speaks for itself, but the photograph that accompanied this report in the *Ann Arbor News* reveals that in addition to their differences in profession and generation, Boschma is white and Lambert is African American. That they bowled together made all the difference.[27] In small ways like this—and in larger ways, too—we Americans need to reconnect with one another. That is the simple argument of this book.

NOTES

1. David Scott and Geoffrey Godbey, "Recreation Specialization in the Social World of Contract Bridge," *Journal of Leisure Research* 26 (1994): 275–295; Suzi Parker, "Elks, Lions May Go Way of the Dodo," *Christian Science Monitor*, August 24, 1998; John D. Cramer, "Relevance of Local NAACP Is Up for Debate," *Roanoke Times*, January 24, 1999; Dirk Johnson, "As Old Soldiers Die, V.F.W. Halls Fade Away," *New York Times*, September 6, 1999. I am grateful to Professor David Scott for information about the Glenn Valley Bridge Club; "Glenn Valley" is a pseudonym for a college town in central Pennsylvania.

2. Christine Wicker, "A Common Thread of Decency," *Dallas Morning News*, May 1, 1999; David Streitfeld, "The Last Chapter: After 50 Years, Vassar Ends Its Famed Book Sale," *Washington Post*, April 28, 1999, C1; Caroline Louise Cole, "So Many New Uniforms, but So Few Musicians," *Boston Sunday Globe Northwest Weekly*, September 5, 1999, 1.

3. Jeffrey A. Charles, *Service Clubs in American Society: Rotary, Kiwanis, and Lions* (Urbana: University of Illinois Press; 1993), 157.

4. Eric Larrabee and Rolf Meyersohn, *Mass Leisure* (Glencoe, Ill.: Free Press, 1958), 359, as quoted in Foster Rhea Dulles, *A History of Recreation: America Learns to Play*, 2nd ed. (New York: Appleton-Century-Crofts, 1965), 390.

5. *Life*, February 21, 1964, 91, 93. I am grateful to Rob Paarlberg for spotting this remarkable issue in a Maine flea market.

6. Robert E. Lane, *Political Life: Why People Get Involved in Politics* (Glencoe, Ill.: Free Press, 1959), 94; Daniel Bell and Virginia Held, "The Community Revolution," *The Public Interest*, 16 (1969): 142.

7. In fact, turnout in 1976 was 53 percent and falling. See Richard A. Brody, "The Puzzle of Political Participation in America," in *The New American Political System*, ed. Anthony King (Washington, D.C.: American Enterprise Institute for Public Policy Research, 1978).

8. George H. Gallup, *The Gallup Poll: Public Opinion 1935–1971* (New York: Random House, 1972); Karlyn Bowman, "Do You Want to Be President?," *Public Perspective* 8 (February/March 1997): 40; Robert E. Lane, "The Politics of Consensus in an Age of Affluence," *American Political Science Review* 59 (December 1965): 879; and Richard G. Niemi, John Mueller, and Tom W. Smith, *Trends in Public Opinion* (New York: Greenwood Press, 1989), 303. The version of the "trust" question used in the 1940s, 1950s, and 1960s is not directly comparable to the one that has become standard in most recent years.

9. See Thomas R. Rochon, *Culture Moves: Ideas, Activism, and Changing Values* (Princeton, N.J.: Princeton University Press, 1998), xiii–xiv.

10. Doug McAdam, *Freedom Summer* (New York: Oxford University Press, 1988), 14–15.

11. James Q. Wilson, "Why Are We Having a Wave of Violence?" *The New York Times Magazine*, May 19, 1968, 120.

12. Lyda Judson Hanifan, "The Rural School Community Center," *Annals of the American Academy of Political and Social Science* 67 (1916): 130–138, quotation at 130. Ever the practical reformer, Hanifan was self-conscious about using the term *capital* to encourage hard-nosed businessmen and economists to recognize the productive importance of social assets. Having introduced the idea of social capital, he observes, "That there is a great lack of such social capital in some rural districts need not be retold in this chapter. The important question at this time is: How can these conditions be improved? The story which follows is an account of the way a West Virginia rural community in a single year actually developed social capital and then used this capital in the improvement of its recreational, intellectual, moral, and economic conditions." His essay, which included a list of practical exercises for community-based activists, was originally prepared in 1913 for West Virginia schoolteachers as "a handbook for community meetings at rural schoolhouses," and it was subsequently incorporated in L. J. Hanifan, *The Community Center* (Boston: Silver, Burdett, 1920). I am grateful to Brad Clarke for first spotting this usage of the term *social capital*.

13. John R. Seeley, Alexander R. Sim, and Elizabeth W. Loosley, *Crestwood Heights: A Study of the Culture of Suburban Life* (New York: Basic Books, 1956); Jane Jacobs, *The Death and Life of Great American Cities* (New York: Random House, 1961); Glenn Loury, "A Dynamic Theory of Racial Income Differences," in *Women, Minorities, and Employment Discrimination,* ed. P.A. Wallace and A. LeMund (Lexington, Mass.: Lexington Books, 1977), 153–188; Pierre Bourdieu, "Forms of Capital," in *Handbook of Theory and Research for the Sociology of Education*, ed. John G. Richardson (New York: Greenwood Press, 1983), 241–258; Ekkehart Schlicht, "Cognitive Dissonance in Economics," in *Normengeleitetes Verhalten in den Sozialwissenschaften* (Berlin: Duncker and Humblot, 1984), 61–81; James S. Coleman, "Social Capital in the Creation of Human Capital," *American Journal of Sociology* 94 (1988): S95–S120; and James S. Coleman, *Foundations of Social Theory* (Cambridge, Mass.: Harvard University Press, 1990). See also George C. Homans, *Social Behavior: Its Elementary Forms* (New York: Harcourt, Brace & World, 1961), 378–98. Except for a brief acknowledgment by Coleman of Loury's work, I can find no evidence that any of these theorists were aware of any of the preceding usages. For a comprehensive overview of the conceptual history of "social capital," see Michael Woolcock, "Social Capital and Economic Development: Toward a Theoretical Synthesis and Policy Framework," *Theory and Society* 27 (1998): 151–208.

14. Ronald S. Burt, *Structural Holes: The Social Structure of Competition* (Cambridge, Mass.: Harvard University Press, 1992); Ronald S. Burt, "The Contingent Value of Social Capital,"

Administrative Science Quarterly 42 (1997): 339–365; and Ronald S. Burt, "The Gender of Social Capital," *Rationality & Society* 10 (1998): 5–46; Claude S. Fischer, "Network Analysis and Urban Studies," in *Networks and Places: Social Relations in the Urban Setting*, ed. Claude S. Fischer (New York: Free Press, 1977), 19; James D. Montgomery, "Social Networks and Labor-Market Outcomes: Toward an Economic Analysis," *American Economic Review* 81 (1991): 1408–1418, esp. table 1.

15. In earlier work I emphasized this public dimension of social capital almost to the exclusion of the private returns to social capital. See Robert D. Putnam, "The Prosperous Community: Social Capital and Public Affairs," *The American Prospect* 13 (1993): 35–42, on which the present text draws. For a literature review that highlights the private returns almost to the exclusion of the collective dimension, see Alejandro Portes, "Social Capital: Its Origins and Applications in Modern Sociology," *Annual Review of Sociology* 22 (1998): 1–24.

16. Robert Frank in private conversation.

17. Xavier de Souza Briggs, "Social Capital and the Cities: Advice to Change Agents," *National Civic Review* 86 (summer 1997): 111–117.

18. *U.S. News & World Report* (August 4, 1997): 18. Fareed Zakaria, "Bigger Than the Family, Smaller Than the State," *New York Times Book Review*, August 13, 1995: 1, pointed out that McVeigh and his co-conspirators spent evenings together in a bowling alley and concluded that "we would all have been better off if Mr. McVeigh had gone bowling alone." Sometimes, as in certain cults or clans, even the *internal* effects of social capital can be negative, but these are less common than negative *external* effects.

19. In *Making Democracy Work: Civic Traditions in Modern Italy* (Princeton, N.J.: Princeton University Press, 1993), I ignored the possibility that social capital might have antisocial effects, but I recognized this possibility explicitly in "The Prosperous Community," published that same year.

20. So far as I can tell, credit for coining these labels belongs to Ross Gittell and Avis Vidal, *Community Organizing: Building Social Capital as a Development Strategy* (Thousand Oaks, Calif.: Sage, 1998), 8.

21. Mark S. Granovetter, "The Strength of Weak Ties," *American Journal of Sociology* 78 (1973): 1360–1380; Xavier de Souza Briggs, "Doing Democracy Up Close: Culture, Power, and Communication in Community Building," *Journal of Planning Education and Research* 18 (1998): 1–13.

22. As quoted in Richard D. Brown, "The Emergence of Voluntary Associations in Massachusetts," *Journal of Voluntary Action Research* 2 (April 1973): 64–73, at 69. See also Ashutosh Varshney, *Ethnic Conflict and Civic Life: Hindus and Muslims in India* (New Haven, Conn.: Yale University Press, 2000).

23. Alexis de Tocqueville, *Democracy in America*, ed. J. P. Mayer, trans. George Lawrence (Garden City, N.Y.: Doubleday, 1969), 506. See also Wilson Carey McWilliams, *The Idea of Fraternity in America* (Berkeley: University of California Press, 1973), and Thomas Bender, *Community and Social Change in America* (Baltimore, Md.: Johns Hopkins University Press, 1978).

24. David Hackett Fischer, *Paul Revere's Ride* (New York: Oxford University Press, 1994).

25. Barry Wellman, "The Community Question Re-Evaluated," in *Power, Community, and the City*, Michael Peter Smith, ed. (New Brunswick, N.J.: Transaction 1988), 81–107, quotation at 82–83. Pamela Paxton, "Is Social Capital Declining in the United States? A Multiple Indicator Assessment," *American Journal of Sociology* 105 (1999): 88–127.

26. *The Public Perspective* 8 (December/January 1997): 64; Robert Wuthnow, "Changing Character of Social Capital in the United States," in *The Dynamics of Social Capital in Comparative Perspective*, Robert D. Putnam, ed. (2000, forthcoming); *The Public Perspective 10* (April/May 1999): 15; *Wall Street Journal*, June 24, 1999, A12; Mark J. Penn, "The Community Consensus," *Blueprint: Ideas for a New Century* (spring 1999). Respondents with no opinion are excluded.

27. Emma Jackson, "Buddy Had Kidney to Spare," *Ann Arbor News* (January 5, 1998). Thanks to Michael Dover for his elegant posting of this story in the Nonprofit and Voluntary Action listserv, www.arnova.org/arnova_1.htm, January 6, 1998.

STUDY QUESTIONS

1. What is **social capital**? It may help to compare social capital to human capital and physical capital in your answer.

2. What is the difference between the two types of social capital Putnam describes: bridging and bonding capital? Give an example of each that is *not* provided in the chapter.

3. Describe a situation in which you were able to achieve something (say, getting a job) because of a social connection. That is to say, when have you cashed in some of your social capital? Where did you get that social capital in the first place?

4. Use the Internet to find and list ten civic groups in your area that are open to you. What is the mission of each? Had you heard of any of them before? Contact one **organization** to ask about the work they do and their membership. Do you think they serve a vital function in your community?

EMILE DURKHEIM

On the Normality of Crime

from *The Rules of the Sociological Method*

H ow is it that **society** can produce both a Hitler and a Shakespeare? Emile Durkheim, the cofounder of the discipline of **sociology**, argues that the kind of deviation from the **norm** that leads to both **crime** and genius is necessary to society. In this excerpt from *The Rules of Sociological Method* (first published in 1895), Durkheim asserts that crime is "normal": like pain, it is unpleasant and to be avoided, but it also serves to remind us of our limits. As you read Durkheim's reasoning that society sets standards for what is and is not criminal behavior, consider how you think that might apply to twenty-first-century society.

* * *

IF THERE IS A FACT WHOSE PATHOLOGICAL NATURE APPEARS indisputable, it is crime. All criminologists agree on this score. Although they explain this pathology differently, they none the less unanimously acknowledge it. However, the problem needs to be treated less summarily.

* * * Crime is not only observed in most societies of a particular species, but in all societies of all types. There is not one in which criminality does not exist, although it changes in form and the actions which are termed criminal are not everywhere the same. Yet everywhere and always there have been men who have conducted themselves in such a way as to bring down punishment upon their heads. If at least, as societies pass from lower to higher types, the crime rate (the relationship between the annual crime figures and population figures) tended to fall, we might believe that, although still remaining a normal phenomenon, crime tended to lose that character of normality. Yet there is no single ground for believing such a regression to be real. Many facts would rather seem to point to the existence of a movement in the opposite direction. From the beginning of the century statistics provide us with a means of following the progression of criminality. It has everywhere increased, and in France the increase is of the order of 300 per cent. Thus there is no phenomenon which represents more incontrovertibly all the symptoms of normality, since it appears to be closely bound up with the conditions of all collective life. To make crime a social illness would be to concede that sickness is not something accidental, but on the contrary derives in certain cases from the fundamental constitution of the living creature. This would be to erase any distinction between the physiological and the pathological. It can certainly happen that crime itself has normal forms; this is what happens, for instance, when it reaches an excessively high level. There is no doubt that this excessiveness is pathological in nature. What is normal is simply that criminality exists, provided that for each social type it does not reach or go beyond a certain level which it is perhaps not impossible to fix in conformity with the previous rules.[1]

We are faced with a conclusion which is apparently somewhat paradoxical. Let us make no mistake: to classify crime among the phenomena of normal sociology is not merely to declare that it is an inevitable though regrettable phenomenon arising from the incorrigible wickedness of men; it is to assert that it is a factor in public health, an integrative element in any healthy society. At first sight this result is so surprising that it disconcerted even ourselves for a long time. However, once that first impression of surprise has been overcome it is not difficult to discover reasons to explain this normality and at the same time to confirm it.

In the first place, crime is normal because it is completely impossible for any society entirely free of it to exist.

Crime, as we have shown elsewhere, consists of an action which offends certain collective feelings which are especially strong and clear-cut. In any society, for actions regarded as criminal to cease, the feelings that they offend would need to be found in each individual consciousness without exception and in the degree of strength requisite to counteract the opposing feelings. Even supposing that this condition could effectively be fulfilled, crime would not thereby disappear; it would merely change in form, for the very cause which made the well-springs of criminality to dry up would immediately open up new ones.

Indeed, for the collective feelings, which the penal law of a people at a particular moment in its history protects, to penetrate individual consciousnesses that had hitherto remained closed to them, or to assume greater authority—whereas previously they had not possessed enough—they would have to acquire an intensity greater than they had had up to then. The community as a whole must feel them more keenly, for they cannot draw from any other source the additional force which enables them to bear down upon individuals who formerly were the most refractory. For murderers to disappear, the horror of bloodshed must increase in those strata of society from which murderers are recruited; but for this to happen the abhorrence must increase throughout society. Moreover, the very absence of crime would contribute directly to bringing about that result, for a sentiment appears much more respectable when it is always and uniformly respected. But we overlook the fact that these strong states of the common consciousness cannot be reinforced in this way without the weaker states, the violation of which previously gave rise to mere breaches of convention, being reinforced at the same time, for the weaker states are no more than the extension and attenuated form of the stronger ones. Thus, for example, theft and mere misappropriation of property offend the same altruistic sentiment, the respect for other people's possessions. However, this sentiment is offended less strongly by the latter action than the former. Moreover, since the average consciousness does not have sufficient intensity of feeling to feel strongly about the lesser of these two offences, the latter is the object of greater tolerance. This is why the misappropriator is merely censured, while the thief is punished. But if this sentiment grows stronger, to such a degree that it extinguishes in the consciousness the tendency to theft that men possess, they will become more sensitive to these minor offences, which up to then had had only a marginal effect upon them. They will react with greater intensity against these lesser faults, which will become the object of severer condemnation, so that, from the mere moral errors that they were, some will pass into the category of crimes. For example, dishonest contracts or those fulfilled dishonestly, which only incur public censure or civil redress, will become crimes. Imagine a community of saints in an exemplary and perfect monastery. In it crime as such will be unknown, but faults that appear venial to the ordinary person will arouse the same scandal as does normal crime in ordinary consciences. If therefore that community has the power to judge and punish, it will term such acts criminal and deal with them as such. It is for the same reason that the completely honourable man judges his slightest moral failings with a severity that the mass of people reserves for acts that are truly criminal. In former times acts of violence against the person were more frequent than they are today because respect for individual dignity was weaker. As it has increased, such crimes have become less frequent, but many acts which offended against that sentiment have been incorporated into the penal code, which did not previously include them.[2]

In order to exhaust all the logically possible hypotheses, it will perhaps be asked why this unanimity should not cover all collective sentiments without exception, and why even the weakest sentiments should not evoke sufficient power to forestall any dissentient voice. The moral conscience of society would be found in its entirety in every individual, endowed with sufficient force to prevent the commission of any act offending against it, whether purely conventional failings or crimes. But such universal and absolute uniformity is utterly impossible, for the immediate physical environment in which each one of us is placed, our hereditary antecedents, the social influences upon which we depend, vary from one individual to another and consequently cause a diversity of consciences. It is impossible for everyone to be alike in this matter, by virtue of the fact that we each have our own organic constitution and occupy different areas in space. This is why, even among lower peoples where individual originality is very little developed, such originality does however exist. Thus, since there cannot be a society in which individuals do not diverge to some extent from the collective type, it is also inevitable that among these deviations some assume a criminal character. What confers upon them this character is not the intrinsic importance of the acts but the importance which the common consciousness ascribes to them. Thus if the latter is stronger and possesses sufficient authority to make these divergences very weak in absolute terms, it will also be more sensitive and exacting. By reacting against the slightest deviations with an energy which it elsewhere employs against those what are more weighty, it endues them with the same gravity and will brand them as criminal.

Thus crime is necessary. It is linked to the basic conditions of social life, but on this very account is useful, for the conditions to which it is bound are themselves indispensable to the normal evolution of morality and law.

Indeed today we can no longer dispute the fact that not only do law and morality vary from one social type to another, but they even change within the same type if the conditions of collective existence are modified. Yet for these transformations to be made possible, the collective sentiments at the basis of morality should not prove unyielding to change, and consequently should be only moderately intense. If they were too strong, they would no longer be malleable. Any arrangement is indeed an obstacle to a new arrangement; this is even more the case the more deep-seated the original arrangement. The more strongly a structure is articulated, the more it resists modification; this is as true for functional as for anatomical patterns. If there were no crimes, this condition would not be fulfilled, for such a hypothesis presumes that collective sentiments would have attained a degree of intensity unparalleled in history. Nothing is good indefinitely and without limits. The authority which the moral consciousness enjoys must not be excessive, for otherwise no one would dare to attack it and it would petrify too easily into an immutable form. For it to evolve, individual originality must be allowed to manifest itself. But so that the originality of the idealist who dreams of transcending his era may display itself, that of the criminal, which falls short of the age, must also be possible. One does not go without the other.

Nor is this all. Beyond this indirect utility, crime itself may play a useful part in this evolution. Not only does it imply that the way to necessary changes remains open, but in certain cases it also directly prepares for these changes. Where crime exists, collective sentiments are not only in the state of plasticity necessary to assume a new form, but sometimes it even contributes to determining beforehand the shape they will take on. Indeed, how often is it only an anticipation of the morality to come, a progression towards what will be! According to Athenian law, Socrates was a criminal and his condemnation was entirely just. However, his crime—his independence of thought—was useful not only for humanity but for his country. It served to prepare a way for a new morality and a new faith, which the Athenians then needed because the traditions by which they had hitherto lived no longer corresponded to the conditions of their existence. Socrates's case is not an isloated one, for it recurs periodically in history. The freedom of thought that we at present enjoy could never have been asserted if the rules that forbade it had not been violated before they were solemnly abrogated. However, at the time the violation was a crime, since it was an offence against sentiments still keenly felt in the average consciousness. Yet this crime was useful since it was the prelude to changes which were daily becoming more necessary. Liberal philosophy has had as its precursors heretics of all kinds whom the secular arm rightly punished throught the Middle Ages and has continued to do so almost up to the present day.

From this viewpoint the fundamental facts of criminology appear to us in an entirely new light. Contrary to current ideas, the criminal no longer appears as an utterly unsociable creature, a sort of parasitic element, a foreign, unassimilable body introduced into the bosom of society.[3] He plays a normal role in social life. For its part, crime must no longer be conceived of as an evil which cannot be circumscribed closely enough. Far from there being cause for congratulation when it drops too noticeably below the normal level, this apparent progress assuredly coincides with and is linked to some social disturbance. Thus the number of crimes of assault never falls so low as it does in times of scarcity.[4] Consequently, at the same time, and as a reaction, the theory of punishment is revised, or rather should be revised. If in fact crime is a sickness, punishment is the cure for it and cannot be conceived of otherwise; thus all the discussion aroused revolves round knowing what punishment should be to fulfil its role as a remedy. But if crime is in no way pathological, the object of punishment cannot be to cure it and its true function must be sought elsewhere.

* * *

NOTES

1. From the fact that crime is a phenomenon of normal sociology it does not follow that the criminal is a person normally constituted from the biological and psychological viewpoints. The two questions are independent of each other. This independence will be better understood when we have shown later the difference which exists between psychical and sociological facts.
2. Calumny, insults, slander, deception, etc.
3. We have ourselves committed the error of speaking of the criminal in this way through not having applied our rule (cf. *Division du travail social*, pp.395, 396).
4. But, although crime is a fact of normal sociology, it does not follow that we should not abhor it. Pain has likewise nothing desirable about it: the individual detests it just as society detests crime, and yet it is a normal physiological function. Not only does it necessarily derive from the very constitution of every living creature, but it plays a useful and

irreplaceable role in life. Thus it would be a peculiar distortion to represent our thinking as an apologia for crime. We would not even have envisaged protesting against such an interpretation were we not aware of the strange accusations and misunderstandings to which one is exposed in undertaking to study moral facts objectively and to speak of them in language that is not commonly used.

STUDY QUESTIONS

1. Where does **crime** exist? Why?

2. According to Durkheim, what happens to crime as a **society**'s feelings toward weaker crimes or faults grow stronger?

3. Examine the part of this selection in which Durkheim argues that crime is useful. He uses the example of Socrates. What other examples can you think of that would support Durkheim's point that transgression of laws prefigures a change in society?

4. Durkheim's conclusion points to a practical application of his theory: it's our job to figure out what kinds of punishment will "cure" the sickness of crime. In small groups or as a class, discuss the following (or other) crimes: murder, burglary, and computer hacking. What are the punishments for these crimes? Do you think that the punishments can "cure" the crimes or the criminals? Why or why not?

WILLIAM J. CHAMBLISS

The Saints and the Roughnecks

kipping class, drinking like fish, pulling absurd pranks, and engaging in reckless and wild behavior—this is how William Chambliss describes some of the most "promising" students at a U.S. high school. For two years Chambliss followed two groups of students. The "Roughnecks" were always in trouble with the law and were seen as a drain on **society**, while the "Saints" behaved much worse but were seen as "good kids." Chambliss contends that the Saints used their **social class** to avoid public scrutiny. As you read this report pay attention to how the class differences between the two groups impacts which **crimes** they commit and how the **community** responds.

EIGHT PROMISING YOUNG MEN—CHILDREN OF GOOD, STABLE, white upper-middle-class families, active in school affairs, good pre-college students—were some of the most delinquent boys at Hanibal High School. While community residents knew that these boys occasionally sowed a few wild oats, they were totally unaware that sowing wild oats completely occupied the daily routine of these young men. The Saints were constantly occupied with truancy, drinking, wild driving, petty theft, and vandalism. Yet no one was officially arrested for any misdeed during the two years I observed them.

This record was particularly surprising in light of my observations during the same two years of another gang of Hanibal High School students, six lower-class white boys known as the Roughnecks. The Roughnecks were constantly in trouble with police and community even though their rate of delinquency was about equal

"The Saints and the Roughnecks" by William J. Chambliss from *Society*, Vol. 11, No. 1 (1973), pages 24–31. Copyright © 1973 Springer. With kind permission from Springer Science and Business Media.

with that of the Saints. What was the cause of this disparity? the result? The following consideration of the activities, social class, and community perceptions of both gangs may provide some answers.

THE SAINTS FROM MONDAY TO FRIDAY

The Saints' principal daily concern was with getting out of school as early as possible. The boys managed to get out of school with minimum danger that they would be accused of playing hookey through an elaborate procedure for obtaining "legitimate" release from class. The most common procedure was for one boy to obtain the release of another by fabricating a meeting of some committee, program, or recognized club. Charles might raise his hand in his 9:00 chemistry class and ask to be excused— a euphemism for going to the bathroom. Charles would go to Ed's math class and inform the teacher that Ed was needed for a 9:30 rehearsal of the drama club play. The math teacher would recognize Ed and Charles as "good students" involved in numerous school activities and would permit Ed to leave at 9:30. Charles would return to his class, and Ed would go to Tom's English class to obtain his release. Tom would engineer Charles's escape. The strategy would continue until as many of the Saints as possible were freed. After a stealthy trip to the car (which had been parked in a strategic spot), the boys were off for a day of fun.

Over the two years I observed the Saints, this pattern was repeated nearly every day. There were variations on the theme, but in one form or another, the boys used this procedure for getting out of class and then off the school grounds. Rarely did all eight of the Saints manage to leave school at the same time. The average number avoiding school on the days I observed them was five.

Having escaped from the concrete corridors the boys usually went either to a pool hall on the other (lower-class) side of town or to a café in the suburbs. Both places were out of the way of people the boys were likely to know (family or school officials), and both provided a source of entertainment. The pool hall entertainment was the generally rough atmosphere, the occasional hustler, the sometimes drunk proprietor and, of course, the game of pool. The café's entertainment was provided by the owner. The boys would "accidentally" knock a glass on the floor or spill cola on the counter—not all the time, but enough to be sporting. They would also bend spoons, put salt in sugar bowls and generally tease whoever was working in the café. The owner had opened the café recently and was dependent on the boys' business which was, in fact, substantial since between the horsing around and the teasing they bought food and drinks.

THE SAINTS ON WEEKENDS

On weekends the automobile was even more critical than during the week, for on weekends the Saints went to Big Town—a large city with a population of over a million 25 miles from Hanibal. Every Friday and Saturday night most of the Saints would meet between 8:00 and 8:30 and would go into Big Town. Big Town activities included drinking heavily in taverns or nightclubs, driving drunkenly through the streets, and committing acts of vandalism and playing pranks.

By midnight on Fridays and Saturdays the Saints were usually thoroughly high, and one or two of them were often so drunk they had to be carried to the cars. Then the boys drove around town, calling obscenities to women and girls; occasionally trying (unsuccessfully so far as I could tell) to pick girls up; and driving recklessly through red lights and at high speeds with their lights out. Occasionally they played "chicken." One boy would climb out the back window of the car and across the roof to the driver's side of the car while the car was moving at high speed (between 40 and 50 miles an hour); then the driver would move over and the boy who had just crawled across the car roof would take the driver's seat.

Searching for "fair game" for a prank was the boy's principal activity after they left the tavern. The boys would drive alongside a foot patrol-man and ask directions to some street. If the policeman leaned on the car in the course of answering the question, the driver would speed away, causing him to lose his balance. The Saints were careful to play this prank only in an area where they were not going to spend much time and where they could quickly disappear around a corner to avoid having their license plate number taken.

Construction sites and road repair areas were the special province of the Saints' mischief. A soon-to-be-repaired hole in the road inevitably invited the Saints to remove lanterns and wooden barricades and put them in the car, leaving the hole unprotected. The boys would find a safe vantage point and wait for an unsuspecting motorist to drive into the hole. Often, though not always, the boys would go up to the motorist and commiserate with him about the dreadful way the city protected its citizenry.

Leaving the scene of the open hole and the motorist, the boys would then go searching for an appropriate place to erect the stolen barricade. An "appropriate place" was often a spot on a highway near a curve in the road where the barricade would not be seen by an oncoming motorist. The boys would wait to watch an unsuspecting motorist attempt to stop and (usually) crash into the wooden barricade. With saintly bearing the boys might offer help and understanding.

A stolen lantern might well find its way onto the back of a police car or hang from a street lamp. Once a lantern served as a prop for a reenactment of the "midnight ride of Paul Revere" until the "play," which was taking place at 2:00 A.M. in the center of a main street of Big Town, was interrupted by a police car several blocks away. The boys ran, leaving the lanterns on the street, and managed to avoid being apprehended.

Abandoned houses, especially if they were located in out-of-the-way places, were fair game for destruction and spontaneous vandalism. The boys would break windows, remove furniture to the yard and tear it apart, urinate on the walls, and scrawl obscenities inside.

Through all the pranks, drinking, and reckless driving the boys managed miraculously to avoid being stopped by police. Only twice in two years was I aware that they had been stopped by a Big Town policeman. Once was for speeding (which they did every time they drove whether they were drunk or sober), and the driver managed to convince the policeman that it was simply an error. The second time they were stopped they had just left a nightclub and were walking through an alley. Aaron stopped to urinate and the boys began making obscene remarks. A foot patrolman came into the alley, lectured the boys and sent them home. Before the boys got to the car one began talking in a loud voice again. The policeman, who had followed them down the alley, arrested this boy for disturbing the peace and took him to the police station where the other Saints gathered. After paying a $5.00 fine, and with the assurance that there would be no permanent record of the arrest, the boy was released.

The boys had a spirit of frivolity and fun about their escapades. They did not view what they were engaged in as "delinquency," though it surely was by any reasonable definition of that word. They simply viewed themselves as having a little fun and who, they would ask, was really hurt by it? The answer had to be no one, although this fact remains one of the most difficult things to explain about the gang's behavior. Unlikely though it seems, in two years of drinking, driving, carousing, and vandalism no one was seriously injured as a result of the Saints' activities.

THE SAINTS IN SCHOOL

The Saints were highly successful in school. The average grade for the group was "B," with two of the boys having close to a straight "A" average. Almost all of the boys were popular and many of them held offices in the school. One of the boys was vice president of the student body one year. Six of the boys played on athletic teams.

At the end of their senior year, the student body selected ten seniors for special recognition as the "school wheels"; four of the ten were Saints. Teachers and school officials saw no problem with any of these boys and anticipated that they would all "make something of themselves."

How the boys managed to maintain this impression is surprising in view of their actual behavior in school. Their technique for covering truancy was so successful that teachers did not even realize that the boys were absent from school much of the time.

Occasionally, of course, the system would backfire and then the boy was on his own. A boy who was caught would be most contrite, would plead guilty and ask for mercy. He inevitably got the mercy he sought.

Cheating on examinations was rampant, even to the point of orally communicating answers to exams as well as looking at one another's papers. Since none of the group studied, and since they were primarily dependent on one another for help, it is surprising that grades were so high. Teachers contributed to the deception in their admitted inclination to give these boys (and presumably others like them) the benefit of the doubt. When asked how the boys did in school, and when pressed on specific examinations, teachers might admit that they were disappointed in John's performance, but would quickly add that they "knew that he was capable of doing better," so John was given a higher grade than he had actually earned. How often this happened is impossible to know. During the time that I observed the group, I never saw any of the boys take homework home. Teachers may have been "understanding" very regularly.

One exception to the gang's generally good performance was Jerry, who had a "C" average in his junior year, experienced disaster the next year, and failed to graduate. Jerry had always been a little more nonchalant than the others about the liberties he took in school. Rather than wait for someone to come get him from class, he would offer his own excuse and leave. Although he probably did not miss any more class than most of the others in the group, he did not take the requisite pains to cover his absences. Jerry was the only Saint whom I ever heard talk back to a teacher. Although teachers often called him a "cut up" or a "smart kid," they never referred to him as a trouble-maker or as a kid headed for trouble. It seems likely, then, that Jerry's failure his senior year and his mediocre performance his junior year were consequences of his not playing the game the proper way (possibly because he was disturbed by his parents' divorce). His teachers regarded him as "immature" and not quite ready to get out of high school.

THE POLICE AND THE SAINTS

The local police saw the Saints as good boys who were among the leaders of the youth in the community. Rarely, the boys might be stopped in town for speeding or for running a stop sign. When this happened the boys were always polite, contrite and pled for mercy. As in school, they received the mercy they asked for. None ever received a ticket or was taken into the precinct by the local police.

The situation in Big Town, where the boys engaged in most of their delinquency, was only slightly different. The police there did not know the boys at all, although occasionally the boys were stopped by a patrolman. Once they were caught taking a lantern from a construction site. Another time they were stopped for running a stop sign, and on several occasions they were stopped for speeding. Their behavior was as before: contrite, polite and penitent. The urban police, like the local police, accepted their demeanor as sincere. More important, the urban police were convinced that these were good boys just out for a lark.

THE ROUGHNECKS

Hanibal townspeople never perceived the Saints' high level of delinquency. The Saints were good boys who just went in for an occasional prank. After all, they were well dressed, well mannered and had nice cars. The Roughnecks were a different story. Although the two gangs of boys were the same age, and both groups engaged in an equal amount of wild-oat sowing, everyone agreed that the not-so-well-dressed, not-so-well-mannered, not-so-rich boys were heading for trouble. Townspeople would say, "You can see the gang members at the drugstore, night after night, leaning against the storefront (sometimes drunk) or slouching around inside buying cokes, reading magazines, and probably stealing old Mr. Wall blind. When they are outside and girls walk by, even respectable girls, these boys make suggestive remarks. Sometimes their remarks are downright lewd."

From the community's viewpoint, the real indication that these kids were in trouble was that they were constantly involved with the police. Some of them had been picked up for stealing, mostly small stuff, of course, "but still it's stealing small stuff that leads to big time crimes." "Too bad," people said. "Too bad that these boys couldn't behave like the other kids in town; stay out of trouble, be polite to adults, and look to their future."

The community's impression of the degrees to which this group of six boys (ranging in age from 16 to 19) engaged in delinquency was somewhat distorted. In some ways the gang was more delinquent than the community thought; in other ways they were less.

The fighting activities of the group were fairly readily and accurately perceived by almost everyone. At least once a month, the boys would get into some sort of fight, although most fights were scraps between members of the group or involved only one member of the group and some peripheral hanger-on. Only three times in the period of observation did the group fight together: once against a gang from across town, once against two blacks, and once against a group of boys from another school. For the first two fights the group went out "looking for trouble"—and they found it both times. The third fight followed a football game and began spontaneously with an argument on the football field between one of the Roughnecks and a member of the opposition's football team.

Jack has a particular propensity for fighting and was involved in most of the brawls. He was a prime mover of the escalation of arguments into fights.

More serious than fighting, had the community been aware of it, was theft. Although almost everyone was aware that the boys occasionally stole things, they did not realize the extent of the activity. Petty stealing was a frequent event for the Roughnecks. Sometimes they stole as a group and coordinated their efforts; other things they stole in pairs. Rarely did they steal alone.

The thefts ranged from very small things like paperback books, comics, and ballpoint pens to expensive items like watches. The nature of the thefts varied from time to time. The gang would go through a period of systematically lifting items from automobiles or school lockers. Types of thievery varied with the whim of the gang. Some forms of thievery were more profitable than others, but all thefts were for profit, not just thrills.

Roughnecks siphoned gasoline from cars as often as they had access to an automobile, which was not very often. Unlike the Saints, who owned their own cars, the Roughnecks would have to borrow their parents' cars, an event which occurred only eight or nine times a year. The boys claimed to have stolen cars for joy rides from time to time.

Ron committed the most serious of the group's offenses. With an unidentified associate the boy attempted to burglarize a gasoline station. Although this station had been robbed twice previously in the same month, Ron denied any involvement in either of the other thefts. When Ron and his accomplice approached the station, the owner was hiding in the bushes beside the station. He fired both barrels of a double-barreled shotgun at the boys. Ron was severely injured; the other boy ran away and was never caught. Though he remained in critical condition for several months, Ron finally recovered and served six months of the following year in reform school. Upon release from reform school, Ron was put back a grade in school, and began running around with a different gang of boys. The Roughnecks considered the new gang less delinquent than themselves, and during the following year Ron had no more trouble with the police.

The Roughnecks, then, engaged mainly in three types of delinquency: theft, drinking, and fighting. Although community members perceived that this gang of kids was delinquent, they mistakenly believed that their illegal activities were primarily drinking, fighting, and being a nuisance to passersby. Drinking was limited among the gang members, although it did occur, and theft was much more prevalent than anyone realized.

Drinking would doubtless have been more prevalent had the boys had ready access to liquor. Since they rarely had automobiles at their disposal, they could not travel very far, and the bars in town would not serve them. Most of the boys had little money, and this, too, inhibited their purchase of alcohol. Their major source of liquor was a local drunk who would buy them a fifth if they would give him enough extra to buy himself a pint of whiskey or a bottle of wine.

The community's perception of drinking as prevalent stemmed from the fact that it was the most obvious delinquency the boys engaged in. When one of the boys had been drinking, even a casual observer seeing him on the corner would suspect that he was high.

There was a high level of mutual distrust and dislike between the Roughnecks and the police. The boys felt very strongly that the police were unfair and corrupt. Some evidence existed that the boys were correct in their perception.

The main source of the boys' dislike for the police undoubtedly stemmed from the fact that the police would sporadically harass the group. From the standpoint of the boys, these acts of occasional enforcement of the law were whimsical and uncalled for. It made no sense to them, for example, that the police would come to the corner occasionally and threaten them with arrest for loitering when the night before the boys had been out siphoning gasoline from cars and the police had been nowhere in sight. To the boys, the police were stupid on the one hand, for not being where they should have been and catching the boys in a serious offense, and unfair on the other hand, for trumping up "loitering" charges against them.

From the viewpoint of the police, the situation was quite different. They knew, with all the confidence necessary to be a policeman, that these boys were engaged in criminal activities. They knew this partly from occasionally catching them, mostly from circumstantial evidence ("the boys were around when those tires were slashed"), and partly because the police shared the view of the community in general that this was a bad bunch of boys. The best the police could hope to do was to be sensitive to the fact that these boys were engaged in illegal acts and arrest them whenever there was some evidence that they had been involved. Whether or not the boys had in fact committed a particular act in a particular way was not especially important. The police had a broader view: their job was to stamp out these kids' crimes; the tactics were not as important as the end result.

Over the period that the group was under observation, each member was arrested at least once. Several of the boys were arrested a number of times and spent at least one night in jail. While most were never taken to court, two of the boys were sentenced to six months' incarceration in boys' schools.

THE ROUGHNECKS IN SCHOOL

The Roughnecks' behavior in school was not particularly disruptive. During school hours they did not all hang around together, but tended instead to spend most of their time with one or two other members of the gang who were their special buddies. Although every member of the gang attempted to avoid school as much as possible, they were not particularly successful and most of them attended school with surprising regularity. They considered school a burden—something to be gotten through with a minimum of conflict. If they were "bugged" by a particular teacher, it could lead to trouble. One of the boys, Al, once threatened to beat up a teacher and, according to the other boys, the teacher hid under a desk to escape him.

Teachers saw the boys the way the general community did, as heading for trouble, as being uninterested in making something of themselves. Some were also seen as being incapable of meeting the academic standards of the school. Most of the teachers expressed concern for this group of boys and were willing to pass them despite poor performance, in the belief that failing them would only aggravate the problem.

The group of boys had a grade point average just slightly above "C." No one in the group failed either grade, and no one had better than a "C" average. They were very consistent in their achievement or, at least, the teachers were consistent in their perception of the boys' achievement.

Two of the boys were good football players, Herb was acknowledged to be the best player in the school and Jack was almost as good. Both boys were criticized for their failure to abide by training rules, for refusing to come to practice as often as they should, and for not playing their best during practice. What they lacked in sportsmanship they made up for in skill, apparently, and played every game no matter how poorly they had performed in practice or how many practice sessions they had missed.

TWO QUESTIONS

Why did the community, the school, and the police react to the Saints as though they were good, upstanding, nondelinquent youths with bright futures but to the Roughnecks as though they were tough, young criminals who were headed for trouble? Why did the Roughnecks and the Saints in fact have quite different careers after high school—careers which, by and large, lived up to the expectations of the community?

The most obvious explanation for the differences in the community's and law enforcement agencies' reactions to the two gangs is that one group of boys was "more delinquent" than the other. Which group was more delinquent? The answer to this question will determine in part how we explain the differential responses to these groups by the members of the community and, particularly, by law enforcement and school officials.

In sheer number of illegal acts, the Saints were the more delinquent. They were truant from school for at least part of the day almost every day of the week. In addition, their drinking and vandalism occurred with surprising regularity. The Roughnecks, in contrast, engaged sporadically in delinquent episodes. While these episodes were frequent, they certainly did not occur on a daily or even a weekly basis.

The difference in frequency of offenses was probably caused by the Roughnecks' inability to obtain liquor and to manipulate legitimate excuses from school. Since the Roughnecks had less money than the Saints, and teachers carefully supervised their school activities, the Roughnecks' hearts may have been as black as the Saints', but their misdeeds were not nearly as frequent.

There are really no clear-cut criteria by which to measure qualitative differences in antisocial behavior. The most important dimension is generally referred to as the "seriousness" of the offenses.

If seriousness encompasses the relative economic costs of delinquent acts, then some assessment can be made. The Roughnecks probably stole an average of about $5.00 worth of goods a week. Some weeks the figure was considerably higher, but these times must be balanced against long periods when almost nothing was stolen.

The Saints were more continuously engaged in delinquency but their acts were not for the most part costly to property. Only their vandalism and occasional theft of gasoline would so qualify. Perhaps once or twice a month they would siphon a tankful of gas. The other costly items were street signs, construction lanterns, and the like. All of these acts combined probably did not quite average $5.00 a week, partly because much of the stolen equipment was abandoned and presumably could be recovered. The difference in cost of stolen property between the two groups was trivial, but the Roughnecks probably had a slightly more expensive set of activities than did the Saints.

Another meaning of seriousness is the potential threat of physical harm to members of the community and to the boys themselves. The Roughnecks were more prone to physical violence; they not only welcomed an opportunity to fight; they went seeking it. In addition, they fought among themselves frequently. Although the fighting never included deadly weapons, it was still a menace, however minor, to the physical safety of those involved.

The Saints never fought. They avoided physical conflict both inside and outside the group. At the same time, though, the Saints frequently endangered their own and other people's lives. They did so almost every time they drove a car, especially if they had been drinking. Sober, their driving was risky; under the influence of alcohol it was horrendous. In addition, the Saints endangered the lives of others with their pranks. Street excavations left unmarked were a very serious hazard.

Evaluating the relative seriousness of the two gangs' activities is difficult. The community reacted as though the behavior of the Roughnecks was a problem, and they reacted as though the behavior of the Saints was not. But the members of the community were ignorant of the array of delinquent acts that characterized the Saints' behavior. Although concerned citizens were unaware of much of the Roughnecks' behavior as well, they were much better informed about the Roughnecks' involvement in delinquency than they were about the Saints'.

VISIBILITY

Differential treatment of the two gangs resulted in part because one gang was infinitely more visible than the other. This differential visibility was a direct function of the economic standing of the families. The Saints had access to automobiles and were able to remove themselves from the sight of the community. In as routine a decision as to where to go to have a milkshake after school, the Saints stayed away from the mainstream of community life. Lacking transportation, the Roughnecks could not make it to the edge of town. The center of town was the only practical place for them to meet since their homes were scattered throughout the town and any non-central meeting place put an undue hardship on some members. Through necessity the Roughnecks congregated in a crowded area where everyone in the community passed frequently, including teachers and law enforcement officers. They could easily see the Roughnecks hanging around the drugstore.

The Roughnecks, of course, made themselves even more visible by making remarks to passersby and by occasionally getting into fights on the corner. Meanwhile, just as regularly, the Saints were either at the café on one edge of town or in the pool hall at the other edge of town. Without any particular realization that they were making themselves inconspicuous, the Saints were able to hide their time-wasting. Not only were they removed from the mainstream of traffic, but they were almost always inside a building.

On their escapades the Saints were also relatively invisible, since they left Hanibal and traveled to Big Town. Here, too, they were mobile, roaming the city, rarely going to the same area twice.

DEMEANOR

To the notion of visibility must be added the difference in the responses of group members to outside intervention with their activities. If one of the Saints was confronted with an accusing policeman, even if he felt he was truly innocent of a wrongdoing, his demeanor was apologetic and penitent. A Roughneck's attitude was almost the polar opposite. When confronted with a threatening adult authority, even one who tried to be pleasant, the Roughneck's hostility and disdain were clearly observable. Sometimes he might attempt to put up a veneer of respect, but it was thin and was not accepted as sincere by the authority.

School was no different from the community at large. The Saints could manipulate the system by feigning compliance with the school norms. The availability of cars at school meant that once free from the immediate sight of the teacher, the boys could disappear rapidly. And this escape was well enough planned that no administrator or teacher was nearby when the boys left. A Roughneck who wished to escape for a few hours was in a bind. If it were possible to get free from class, downtown was still a mile away, and even if he arrived there, he was still very visible. Truancy for the Roughnecks meant almost certain detection, while the Saints enjoyed almost complete immunity from sanctions.

BIAS

Community members were not aware of the transgressions of the Saints. Even if the Saints had been less discreet, their favorite delinquencies would have been perceived as less serious than those of the Roughnecks.

In the eyes of the police and school officials, a boy who drinks in an alley and stands intoxicated on the street corner is committing a more serious offense than is a boy who drinks to inebriation in a nightclub or a tavern and drives around afterwards in a car. Similarly, a boy who steals a wallet from a store will be viewed as having committed a more serious offense than a boy who steals a lantern from a construction site.

Perceptual bias also operates with respect to the demeanor of the boys in the two groups when they are confronted by adults. It is not simply that adults dislike the posture affected by boys of the Roughneck ilk; more important is the conviction that the posture adopted by the Roughnecks is an indication of their devotion and commitment to deviance as a way of life. The posture becomes a cue, just as the type of the offense is a cue, to the degree to which the known transgressions are indicators of the youths' potential for other problems.

Visibility, demeanor, and bias are surface variables which explain the day-to-day operations of the police. Why do these surface variables operate as they do? Why did the police choose to disregard the Saints' delinquencies while breathing down the backs of the Roughnecks?

The answer lies in the class structure of American society and the control of legal institutions by those at the top of the class structure. Obviously, no representative of the upper class drew up the operational chart for the police which led them to look in the ghettos and on street corners—which led them to see the demeanor of lower-class youth as troublesome and that of upper-middle-class youth as tolerable. Rather, the procedures simply developed from experience—experience with irate and influential upper-middle-class parents insisting that their son's vandalism was simply a prank and his drunkenness only a momentary "sowing of wild oats"—experience with cooperative or indifferent, powerless, lower-class parents who acquiesced to the law's definition of their son's behavior.

ADULT CAREERS OF THE SAINTS AND THE ROUGHNECKS

The community's confidence in the potential of the Saints and the Roughnecks apparently was justified. If anything, the community members underestimated the degree to which these youngsters would turn out "good" or "bad."

Seven of the eight members of the Saints went on to college immediately after high school. Five of the boys graduated from college in four years. The sixth one finished college after two years in the army, and the seventh spent four years in the air force before returning to college and receiving a B.A. degree. Of these seven college graduates, three went on for advanced degrees. One finished law school and is now active in state politics, one finished medical school and is practicing near Hanibal, and one boy is now working for a Ph.D. The other four college graduates entered submanagerial, managerial, or executive training positions with larger firms.

The only Saint who did not complete college was Jerry. Jerry had failed to graduate from high school with the other Saints. During his second senior year, after the other Saints had gone on to college, Jerry began to hang around with what several teachers described as a "rough crowd"—the gang that was heir apparent to the Roughnecks. At the end of his second senior year, when he did graduate from high school, Jerry took a job as a used-car salesman, got married, and quickly had a child. Although he made several abortive attempts to go to college by attending night school, when I last saw him (ten years after high school) Jerry was unemployed and had been living on unemployment for almost a year. His wife worked as a waitress.

Some of the Roughnecks have lived up to community expectations. A number of them were headed for trouble. A few were not.

Jack and Herb were the athletes among the Roughnecks and their athletic prowess paid off handsomely. Both boys received unsolicited athletic scholarships to college. After Herb received his scholarship (near the end of his senior year), he apparently did an about-face. His demeanor became very similar to that of the Saints. Although he remained a member in good standing of the Roughnecks, he stopped participating in most activities and did not hang on the corner as often.

Jack did not change. If anything, he became more prone to fighting. He even made excuses for accepting the scholarship. He told the other gang members that the school had guaranteed him a "C" average if he would come to play football—an idea that seems far-fetched, even in this day of highly competitive recruiting.

During the summer after graduation from high school, Jack attempted suicide by jumping from a tall building. The jump would certainly have killed most people trying it, but Jack survived. He entered college in the fall and played four years of football. He and Herb graduated in four years, and both are teaching and coaching in high schools. They are married and have stable families. If anything, Jack appears to have a more prestigious position in the community than does Herb, though both are well respected and secure in their positions.

Two of the boys never finished high school. Tommy left at the end of his junior year and went to another state. That summer he was arrested and placed on probation on a manslaughter charge. Three years later he was arrested for murder; he pleaded guilty to second-degree murder and is serving a 30-year sentence in the state penitentiary.

Al, the other boy who did not finish high school, also left the state in his senior year. He is serving a life sentence in a state penitentiary for first-degree murder.

Wes is a small-time gambler. He finished high school and "bummed around." After several years he made contact with a bookmaker who employed him as a runner. Later he acquired his own area and has been working it ever since. His position among the bookmakers is almost identical to the position he had in the gang; he is always around but no one is really aware of him. He makes no trouble and he does not get into any. Steady, reliable, capable of keeping his mouth closed, he plays the game by the rules, even though the game is an illegal one.

That leaves only Ron. Some of his former friends reported that they had heard he was "driving a truck up north," but no one could provide any concrete information.

REINFORCEMENT

The community responded to the Roughnecks as boys in trouble, and the boys agreed with that perception. Their pattern of deviancy was reinforced, and breaking away from it became increasingly unlikely. Once the boys acquired an image of themselves as deviants, they selected new friends who affirmed that self-image. As that self-conception became more firmly entrenched, they also became willing to try new and more extreme deviances. With their growing alienation came freer expression of disrespect and hostility for representatives of the legitimate society. This disrespect increased the community's negativism, perpetuating the entire process of commitment to deviance. Lack of a commitment to deviance works the same way. In either case, the process will perpetuate itself unless some event (like a scholarship to college or a sudden failure) external to the established relationship intervenes. For two of the Roughnecks (Herb and Jack), receiving college athletic scholarships created new relations and culminated in a break with the established pattern of deviance. In the case of one of the Saints (Jerry), his parents' divorce and his failing to graduate from high school changed some of his other relations. Being held back in school for a year and losing his place among the Saints had sufficient impact on Jerry to alter his self-image and virtually to assure that he would not go on to college as his peers did. Although the experiments of life can rarely be reversed, it seems likely in view of the behavior of the other boys who did not enjoy this special treatment by the school that Jerry, too, would have "become something" had he graduated as anticipated. For Herb and Jack outside intervention worked to their advantage; for Jerry it was his undoing.

Selective perception and labeling—finding, processing, and punishing some kinds of criminality and not others—means that visible, poor, non-mobile, outspoken, undiplomatic "tough" kids will be noticed, whether their actions are seriously delinquent or not. Other kids, who have established a reputation for being bright (even though underachieving), disciplined, and involved in respectable activities, who are mobile and monied, will be invisible when they deviate from sanctioned activities. They'll sow their wild oats—perhaps even wider and thicker than their lower-class cohorts—but they won't be noticed. When it's time to leave adolescence most will follow the expected path, settling into the ways of the middle class, remembering fondly the delinquent but unnoticed fling of their youth. The Roughnecks and others like them may turn around, too. It is more likely that their noticeable deviance will have been so reinforced by police and community that their lives will be effectively channeled into careers consistent with their adolescent background.

STUDY QUESTIONS

1. Who commits fewer delinquent acts: the Roughnecks or the Saints?

2. A self-fulfilling prophecy means something happens simply because someone said or believed that it would. How did teacher expectations of the Saints and of the Roughnecks affect how the teachers treated each group? Is this an example of a self-fulfilling prophecy?

3. Chambliss argues that those with more **power** in **society** are able to get away with deviant behaviors their less powerful counterparts cannot. Can you think of a **crime** or act of **deviance** that a more wealthy person can get away with that a poorer person would be punished or sanctioned for?

4. Watch Dalton Conley's discussion with Victor Rios about youth control theory (http://bit.ly/victorrios). What connections can you see between the ways institutions treat young African American males in Oakland, CA, and how the school administrators and the police treated the Roughnecks?

KARL MARX AND FRIEDRICH ENGELS

Bourgeois and Proletarians

From *Manifesto of the Communist Party*

Karl Marx and Friedrich Engels's *Manifesto of the Communist Party* is one of the most influential documents in history. First published in 1848, the manifesto describes the history of **class** struggle in **society**, from feudal serfs against their lords to the **proletariat**, or **working class**, against the **bourgeoisie**, or merchant class, of the mid-nineteenth century. Just as **capitalism** took over the means of production from feudalism, the authors argue, the proletariat will rise to retake the means of production from the bourgeoisie. As you read, consider whether you agree that the history of society *is* the history of class struggle.

THE HISTORY OF ALL HITHERTO EXISTING SOCIETY IS THE HIStory of class struggles.

Freeman and slave, patrician and plebeian, lord and serf, guild-master[1] and journeyman, in a word, oppressor and oppressed, stood in constant opposition to one another, carried on an uninterrupted, now hidden, now open fight, a fight that each time ended, either in a revolutionary re-constitution of society at large, or in the common ruin of the contending classes.

In the earlier epochs of history, we find almost everywhere a complicated arrangement of society into various orders, a manifold gradation of social rank. In ancient Rome we have patricians, knights, plebeians, slaves; in the Middle Ages, feudal lords,

---

[1] That is, a full member of a guild, a master within, not a head of a guild.

vassals, guild-masters, journey-men, apprentices, serfs; in almost all of these classes, again, subordinate gradations.

The modern bourgeois society that has sprouted from the ruins of feudal society has not done away with class antagonisms. It has but established new classes, new conditions of oppression, new forms of struggle in place of the old ones.

Our epoch, the epoch of the bourgeoisie,[2] possesses, however, this distinctive feature: it has simplified the class antagonisms: Society as a whole is more and more splitting up into two great hostile camps, into two great classes directly facing each other: Bourgeoisie and Proletariat.

From the serfs of the Middle Ages sprang the chartered burghers of the earliest towns. From these burgesses the first elements of the bourgeoisie were developed.

The discovery of America, the rounding of the Cape,[3] opened up fresh ground for the rising bourgeoisie. The East-Indian and Chinese markets, the colonisation of America, trade with the colonies, the increase in the means of exchange and in commodities generally, gave to commerce, to navigation, to industry, an impulse never before known, and thereby, to the revolutionary element in the tottering feudal society, a rapid development.

The feudal system of industry, under which industrial production was monopolised by closed guilds, now no longer sufficed for the growing wants of the new markets. The manufacturing system took its place. The guild-masters were pushed on one side by the manufacturing middle class; division of labour between the different corporate guilds vanished in the face of division of labour in each single workshop.

Meantime the markets kept ever growing, the demand ever rising. Even manufacture no longer sufficed. Thereupon, steam and machinery revolutionised industrial production. The place of manufacture was taken by the giant, Modern Industry, the place of the industrial middle class, by industrial millionaires, the leaders of whole industrial armies, the modern bourgeois.

Modern industry has established the world-market, for which the discovery of America paved the way. This market has given an immense development to commerce, to navigation, to communication by land. This development has, in its turn, reacted on the extension of industry; and in proportion as industry, commerce, navigation, railways extended, in the same proportion the bourgeoisie developed, increased its capital, and pushed into the background every class handed down from the Middle Ages.

We see, therefore, how the modern bourgeoisie is itself the product of a long course of development, of a series of revolutions in the modes of production and of exchange.

Each step in the development of the bourgeoisie was accompanied by a corresponding political advance of that class. An oppressed class under the sway of the

---

[2] Specifically, capitalists, or owners of factories and other means of production. *Proletariat*: here, wage laborers.

[3] That is, the cape of Good Hope, which provided an alternative trade route to the East.

feudal nobility, an armed and self-governing association in the mediaeval commune; here independent urban republic (as in Italy and Germany), there taxable "third estate" of the monarchy (as in France), afterwards, in the period of manufacture proper, serving either the semi-feudal or the absolute monarchy as a counterpoise against the nobility, and, in fact, corner-stone of the great monarchies in general, the bourgeoisie has at last, since the establishment of Modern Industry and of the world-market, conquered for itself, in the modern representative State, exclusive political sway. The executive of the modern State is but a committee for managing the common affairs of the whole bourgeoisie.

The bourgeoisie, historically, has played a most revolutionary part.

The bourgeoisie, wherever it has got the upper hand, has put an end to all feudal, patriarchal, idyllic relations. It has pitilessly torn asunder the motley feudal ties that bound man to his "natural superiors," and has left remaining no other nexus between man and man than naked self-interest, than callous "cash payment." It has drowned the most heavenly ecstasies of religious fervour, of chivalrous enthusiasm, of philistine sentimentalism, in the icy water of egotistical calculation. It has resolved personal worth into exchange value, and in place of the numberless indefeasible chartered freedoms, has set up that single, unconscionable freedom—Free Trade. In one word, for exploitation, veiled by religious and political illusions, it has substituted naked, shameless, direct, brutal exploitation.

The bourgeoisie has stripped of its halo every occupation hitherto honoured and looked up to with reverent awe. It has converted the physician, the lawyer, the priest, the poet, the man of science, into its paid wage-labourers.

The bourgeoisie has torn away from the family its sentimental veil, and has reduced the family relation to a mere money relation.

The bourgeoisie has disclosed how it came to pass that the brutal display of vigour in the Middle Ages, which Reactionists so much admire, found its fitting complement in the most slothful indolence. It has been the first to show what man's activity can bring about. It has accomplished wonders far surpassing Egyptian pyramids, Roman aqueducts, and Gothic cathedrals; it has conducted expeditions that put in the shade all former Exoduses of nations and crusades.

The bourgeoisie cannot exist without constantly revolutionising the instruments of production, and thereby the relations of production, and with them the whole relations of society. Conservation of the old modes of production in unaltered form, was, on the contrary, the first condition of existence for all earlier industrial classes. Constant revolutionising of production, uninterrupted disturbance of all social conditions, everlasting uncertainty and agitation distinguish the bourgeois epoch from all earlier ones. All fixed, fast-frozen relations, with their train of ancient and venerable prejudices and opinions, are swept away, all new-formed ones become antiquated before they can ossify. All that is solid melts into air, all that is holy is profaned, and man is at last compelled to face with sober senses, his real conditions of life, and his relations with his kind.

The need of a constantly expanding market for its products chases the bourgeoisie over the whole surface of the globe. It must nestle everywhere, settle everywhere, establish connexions everywhere.

The bourgeoisie has through its exploitation of the world-market given a cosmopolitan character to production and consumption in every country. To the great chagrin of Reactionists, it has drawn from under the feet of industry the national ground on which it stood. All old-established national industries have been destroyed or are daily being destroyed. They are dislodged by new industries, whose introduction becomes a life and death question for all civilised nations, by industries that no longer work up indigenous raw material, but raw material drawn from the remotest zones; industries whose products are consumed, not only at home, but in every quarter of the globe. In place of the old wants, satisfied by the productions of the country, we find new wants, requiring for their satisfaction the products of distant lands and climes. In place of the old local and national seclusion and self-sufficiency, we have intercourse in every direction, universal inter-dependence of nations. And as in material, so also in intellectual production. The intellectual creations of individual nations become common property. National one-sidedness and narrow-mindedness become more and more impossible, and from the numerous national and local literatures, there arises a world literature.

The bourgeoisie, by the rapid improvement of all instruments of production, by the immensely facilitated means of communication, draws all, even the most barbarian, nations into civilisation. The cheap prices of its commodities are the heavy artillery with which it batters down all Chinese walls, with which it forces the barbarians' intensely obstinate hatred of foreigners to capitulate. It compels all nations, on pain of extinction, to adopt the bourgeois mode of production; it compels them to introduce what it calls civilisation into their midst, *i.e.*, to become bourgeois themselves. In one word, it creates a world after its own image.

The bourgeoisie has subjected the country to the rule of the towns. It has created enormous cities, has greatly increased the urban population as compared with the rural, and has thus rescued a considerable part of the population from the idiocy of rural life. Just as it has made the country dependent on the towns, so it has made barbarian and semi-barbarian countries dependent on the civilised ones, nations of peasants on nations of bourgeois, the East on the West.

The bourgeoisie keeps more and more doing away with the scattered state of the population, of the means of production, and of property. It has agglomerated population, centralised means of production, and has concentrated property in a few hands. The necessary consequence of this was political centralisation. Independent, or but loosely connected provinces, with separate interests, laws, governments and systems of taxation, became lumped together into one nation, with one government, one code of laws, one national class-interest, one frontier and one customs-tariff.

The bourgeoisie, during its rule of scarce one hundred years, has created more massive and more colossal productive forces than have all preceding generations together. Subjection of Nature's forces to man, machinery, application of chemistry to industry and agriculture, steam-navigation, railways, electric telegraphs, clearing of whole continents for cultivation, canalisation of rivers, whole populations conjured out of the ground—what earlier century had even a presentiment that such productive forces slumbered in the lap of social labour?

We see then: the means of production and of exchange, on whose foundation the bourgeoisie built itself up, were generated in feudal society. At a certain stage in the development of these means of production and of exchange, the conditions under which feudal society produced and exchanged, the feudal organisation of agriculture and manufacturing industry, in one word, the feudal relations of property became no longer compatible with the already developed productive forces; they became so many fetters. They had to be burst asunder; they were burst asunder.

Into their place stepped free competition, accompanied by a social and political constitution adapted to it, and by the economical and political sway of the bourgeois class.

A similar movement is going on before our own eyes. Modern bourgeois society with its relations of production, of exchange and of property, a society that has conjured up such gigantic means of production and of exchange, is like the sorcerer, who is no longer able to control the powers of the nether world whom he has called up by his spells. For many a decade past the history of industry and commerce is but the history of the revolt of modern productive forces against modern conditions of production, against the property relations that are the conditions for the existence of the bourgeoisie and of its rule. It is enough to mention the commercial crises that by their periodical return put on its trial, each time more threateningly, the existence of the entire bourgeois society. In these crises a great part not only of the existing products, but also of the previously created productive forces, are periodically destroyed. In these crises there breaks out an epidemic that, in all earlier epochs, would have seemed an absurdity—the epidemic of over-production. Society suddenly finds itself put back into a state of momentary barbarism; it appears as if a famine, a universal war of devastation had cut off the supply of every means of subsistence; industry and commerce seem to be destroyed; and why? Because there is too much civilisation, too much means of subsistence, too much industry, too much commerce. The productive forces at the disposal of society no longer tend to further the development of the conditions of bourgeois property; on the contrary, they have become too powerful for these conditions, by which they are fettered, and so soon as they overcome these fetters, they bring disorder into the whole of bourgeois society, endanger the existence of bourgeois property. The conditions of bourgeois society are too narrow to comprise the wealth created by them. And how does the bourgeoisie get over these crises? On the one hand by enforced destruction of a mass of productive forces; on the other, by the conquest of new markets, and by the more thorough exploitation of the old ones. That is to say, by paving the way for more extensive and more destructive crises, and by diminishing the means whereby crises are prevented.

The weapons with which the bourgeoisie felled feudalism to the ground are now turned against the bourgeoisie itself.

But not only has the bourgeoisie forged the weapons that bring death to itself; it has also called into existence the men who are to wield those weapons—the modern working class—the proletarians.

In proportion as the bourgeoisie, *i.e.*, capital, is developed, in the same proportion is the proletariat, the modern working class, developed—a class of labourers, who live only so long as they find work, and who find work only so long as their labour increases capital. These labourers, who must sell themselves piece-meal, are a commodity, like every other article of commerce, and are consequently exposed to all the vicissitudes of competition, to all the fluctuations of the market.

Owing to the extensive use of machinery and to division of labour, the work of the proletarians has lost all individual character, and consequently, all charm for the workman. He becomes an appendage of the machine, and it is only the most simple, most monotonous, and most easily acquired knack, that is required of him. Hence, the cost of production of a workman is restricted, almost entirely, to the means of subsistence that he requires for his maintenance, and for the propagation of his race. But the price of a commodity, and therefore also of labour, is equal to its cost of production. In proportion, therefore, as the repulsiveness of the work increases, the wage decreases. Nay more, in proportion as the use of machinery and division of labour increases, in the same proportion the burden of toil also increases, whether by prolongation of the working hours, by increase of the work exacted in a given time or by increased speed of the machinery, etc.

Modern industry has converted the little workshop of the patriarchal master into the great factory of the industrial capitalist. Masses of labourers, crowded into the factory, are organised like soldiers. As privates of the industrial army they are placed under the command of a perfect hierarchy of officers and sergeants. Not only are they slaves of the bourgeois class, and of the bourgeois State; they are daily and hourly enslaved by the machine, by the over-looker, and, above all, by the individual bourgeois manufacturer himself. The more openly this despotism proclaims gain to be its end and aim, the more petty, the more hateful and the more embittering it is.

The less the skill and exertion of strength implied in manual labour, in other words, the more modern industry becomes developed, the more is the labour of men superseded by that of women. Differences of age and sex have no longer any distinctive social validity for the working class. All are instruments of labour, more or less expensive to use, according to their age and sex.

No sooner is the exploitation of the labourer by the manufacturer, so far, at an end, that he receives his wages in cash, than he is set upon by the other portions of the bourgeoisie, the landlord, the shopkeeper, the pawnbroker, etc.

The lower strata of the middle class—the small tradespeople, shopkeepers, and retired tradesmen generally, the handicraftsmen and peasants—all these sink gradually into the proletariat, partly because their diminutive capital does not suffice for the scale on which Modern Industry is carried on, and is swamped in the competition with the large capitalists, partly because their specialised skill is rendered worthless by new methods of production. Thus the proletariat is recruited from all classes of the population.

The proletariat goes through various stages of development. With its birth begins its struggle with the bourgeoisie. At first the contest is carried on by individual labourers, then by the workpeople of a factory, then by the operatives of one trade, in one locality, against the individual bourgeois who directly exploits them. They direct their attacks not against the bourgeois conditions of production, but against the instruments of production themselves; they destroy imported wares that compete with their labour, they smash to pieces machinery, they set factories ablaze, they seek to restore by force the vanished status of the workman of the Middle Ages.

At this stage the labourers still form an incoherent mass scattered over the whole country, and broken up by their mutual competition. If anywhere they unite to form more compact bodies, this is not yet the consequence of their own active union, but of the union of the bourgeoisie, which class, in order to attain its own political ends, is compelled to set the whole proletariat in motion, and is moreover yet, for a time, able to do so. At this stage, therefore, the proletarians do not fight their enemies, but the enemies of their enemies, the remnants of absolute monarchy, the landowners, the non-industrial bourgeois, the petty bourgeoisie. Thus the whole historical movement is concentrated in the hands of the bourgeoisie; every victory so obtained is a victory for the bourgeoisie.

But with the development of industry the proletariat not only increases in number; it becomes concentrated in greater masses, its strength grows, and it feels that strength more. The various interests and conditions of life within the ranks of the proletariat are more and more equalised, in proportion as machinery obliterates all distinctions of labour, and nearly everywhere reduces wages to the same low level. The growing competition among the bourgeois, and the resulting commercial crises, make the wages of the workers ever more fluctuating. The unceasing improvement of machinery, ever more rapidly developing, makes their livelihood more and more precarious; the collisions between individual workmen and individual bourgeois take more and more the character of collisions between two classes. Thereupon the workers begin to form combinations (Trade Unions) against the bourgeois; they club together in order to keep up the rate of wages; they found permanent associations in order to make provision beforehand for these occasional revolts. Here and there the contest breaks out into riots.

Now and then the workers are victorious, but only for a time. The real fruit of their battles lies, not in the immediate result, but in the ever-expanding union of the workers. This union is helped on by the improved means of communication that are created by modern industry and that place the workers of different localities in contact with one another. It was just this contact that was needed to centralise the numerous local struggles, all of the same character, into one national struggle between classes. But every class struggle is a political struggle. And that union, to attain which the burghers of the Middle Ages, with their miserable highways, required centuries, the modern proletarians, thanks to railways, achieve in a few years.

This organisation of the proletarians into a class, and consequently into a political party, is continually being upset again by the competition between the workers themselves. But it ever rises up again, stronger, firmer, mightier. It compels legislative recognition of particular interests of the workers, by taking advantage of the divisions among the bourgeoisie itself. Thus the ten-hours' bill[4] in England was carried.

Altogether collisions between the classes of the old society further, in many ways, the course of development of the proletariat. The bourgeoisie finds itself involved in a constant battle. At first with the aristocracy, later on, with those portions of the bourgeoisie itself, whose interests have become antagonistic to the progress of industry; at all times, with the bourgeoisie of foreign countries. In all these battles it sees itself compelled to appeal to the proletariat, to ask for its help, and thus, to drag it into the political arena. The bourgeoisie itself, therefore, supplies the proletariat with its own elements of political and general education, in other words, it furnishes the proletariat with weapons for fighting the bourgeoisie.

Further, as we have already seen, entire sections of the ruling classes are, by the advance of industry, precipitated into the proletariat, or are at least threatened in their conditions of existence. These also supply the proletariat with fresh elements of enlightenment and progress.

Finally, in times when the class struggle nears the decisive hour, the process of dissolution going on within the ruling class, in fact within the whole range of society, assumes such a violent, glaring character, that a small section of the ruling class cuts itself adrift, and joins the revolutionary class, the class that holds the future in its hands. Just as, therefore, at an earlier period, a section of the nobility went over to the bourgeoisie, so now a portion of the bourgeoisie goes over to the proletariat, and in particular, a portion of the bourgeois ideologists, who have raised themselves to the level of comprehending theoretically the historical movement as a whole.

Of all the classes that stand face to face with the bourgeoisie today, the proletariat alone is a really revolutionary class. The other classes decay and finally disappear in the face of Modern Industry; the proletariat is its special and essential product.

The lower middle class, the small manufacturer, the shopkeeper, the artisan, the peasant, all these fight against the bourgeoisie, to save from extinction their existence as fractions of the middle class. They are therefore not revolutionary, but conserva-

---

[4] Passed in 1847, the bill restricted the number of hours women and children could work in factories to ten hours a day, fifty-eight hours per week.

tive. Nay more, they are reactionary, for they try to roll back the wheel of history. If by chance they are revolutionary, they are so only in view of their impending transfer into the proletariat, they thus defend not their present, but their future interests, they desert their own standpoint to place themselves at that of the proletariat.

The "dangerous class," the social scum, that passively rotting mass thrown off by the lowest layers of old society, may, here and there, be swept into the movement by a proletarian revolution; its conditions of life, however, prepare it far more for the part of a bribed tool of reactionary intrigue.

In the conditions of the proletariat, those of old society at large are already virtually swamped. The proletarian is without property; his relation to his wife and children has no longer anything in common with the bourgeois family-relations; modern industrial labour, modern subjection to capital, the same in England as in France, in America as in Germany, has stripped him of every trace of national character. Law, morality, religion, are to him so many bourgeois prejudices, behind which lurk in ambush just as many bourgeois interests.

All the preceding classes that got the upper hand, sought to fortify their already acquired status by subjecting society at large to their conditions of appropriation. The proletarians cannot become masters of the productive forces of society, except by abolishing their own previous mode of appropriation, and thereby also every other previous mode of appropriation. They have nothing of their own to secure and to fortify; their mission is to destroy all previous securities for, and insurances of, individual property.

All previous historical movements were movements of minorities, or in the interests of minorities. The proletarian movement is the self-conscious, independent movement of the immense majority, in the interests of the immense majority. The proletariat, the lowest stratum of our present society, cannot stir, cannot raise itself up, without the whole superincumbent strata of official society being sprung into the air.

Though not in substance, yet in form, the struggle of the proletariat with the bourgeoisie is at first a national struggle. The proletariat of each country must, of course, first of all settle matters with its own bourgeoisie.

In depicting the most general phases of the development of the proletariat, we traced the more or less veiled civil war, raging within existing society, up to the point where that war breaks out into open revolution, and where the violent overthrow of the bourgeoisie lays the foundation for the sway of the proletariat.

Hitherto, every form of society has been based, as we have already seen, on the antagonism of oppressing and oppressed classes. But in order to oppress a class, certain conditions must be assured to it under which it can, at least, continue its slavish existence. The serf, in the period of serfdom, raised himself to membership in the commune, just as the petty bourgeois, under the yoke of feudal absolutism, managed to develop into a bourgeois. The modern labourer, on the contrary, instead of rising with the progress of industry, sinks deeper and deeper below the conditions of existence of his own class. He becomes a pauper, and pauperism develops more rapidly than population and wealth. And here it becomes evident, that the bourgeoisie is unfit any longer to be the ruling class in society, and to impose its conditions of existence upon society as an over-riding law. It is unfit to rule because it is incompetent to assure an existence to its slave within his slavery, because it cannot help letting him sink into such a state, that it has to feed him, instead of being fed by him. Society can no longer live under this bourgeoisie, in other words, its existence is no longer compatible with society.

The essential condition for the existence, and for the sway of the bourgeois class, is the formation and augmentation of capital; the condition for capital is wage-labour. Wage-labour rests exclusively on competition between the labourers. The advance of industry, whose involuntary promoter is the bourgeoisie, replaces the isolation of the labourers, due to competition, by their revolutionary combination, due to association. The development of Modern Industry, therefore, cuts from under its feet the very foundation on which the bourgeoisie produces and appropriates products. What the bourgeoisie, therefore, produces, above all, is its own grave-diggers. Its fall and the victory of the proletariat are equally inevitable.

STUDY QUESTIONS

1. How did the **bourgeoisie** gain power? Describe the previous system.

2. How is the bourgeoisie contributing to its own demise according to the *Manifesto*? How does competition among wage laborers slow the progress of the **proletarian** rise?

3. Considered within the context of the *Manifesto of the Communist Party,* what should the rise in electronic communication do for workers? Do you think worldwide electronic communication has improved the lot of workers? Why or why not?

4. In most places, the Communist system has not succeeded (in, for example, East Germany and the Soviet Union). Researching **communism** if necessary, discuss some reasons for its failure. Are "Communists" really practicing communism? Are there places where the proletariat rules?

GREGORY MANTSIOS

Class in America—2009

W e hold these truths to be self-evident, that all men are created equal, that they are endowed by their Creator with certain unalienable Rights, that among these are Life, Liberty, and the pursuit of Happiness." So reads a famous portion of the United States' Declaration of Independence. In theory, if you work hard you can succeed. But Gregory Mantsios points out that the American Dream is complicated by our distinct **social classes**; he identifies four myths about class in contemporary America. Before reading this article, think about how fair you perceive American life to be; when you're finished, reconsider the question. Has Mantsios confirmed or challenged your perceptions?

PEOPLE IN THE UNITED STATES DON'T LIKE TO TALK ABOUT CLASS. Or so it would seem. We don't speak about class privileges, or class oppression, or the class nature of society. These terms are not part of our everyday vocabulary, and in most circles they are associated with the language of the rhetorical fringe. Unlike people in most other parts of the world, we shrink from using words that classify along economic lines or that point to class distinctions: phrases like "working class," "upper class," and "ruling class" are rarely uttered by Americans.

For the most part, avoidance of class-laden vocabulary crosses class boundaries. There are few among the poor who speak of themselves as lower class; instead, they refer to their race, ethnic group, or geographic location. Workers are more likely to

"Class in America—2009," by Gregory Mantsios in *Race, Class, and Gender in the United States: An Integrated Study* (8th Edition), Paula S. Rothenberg, editor, Worth Publishers: 2010. Used by permission of the author.

identify with their employer, industry, or occupational group than with other workers, or with the working class.[1]

Neither are those at the other end of the economic spectrum likely to use the word "class." In her study of thirty-eight wealthy and socially prominent women, Susan Ostrander asked participants if they considered themselves members of the upper class. One participant responded, "I hate to use the word 'class.' We are responsible, fortunate people, old families, the people who have something."

Another said, "I hate [the term] upper class. It is so non-upper class to use it. I just call it 'all of us,' those who are wellborn."[2]

It is not that Americans, rich or poor, aren't keenly aware of class differences— those quoted above obviously are; it is that class is not in the domain of public discourse. Class is not discussed or debated in public because class identity has been stripped from popular culture. The institutions that shape mass culture and define the parameters of public debate have avoided class issues. In politics, in primary and secondary education, and in the mass media, formulating issues in terms of class is unacceptable, perhaps even un-American.

There are, however, two notable exceptions to this phenomenon. First, it is acceptable in the United States to talk about "the middle class." Interestingly enough, such references appear to be acceptable precisely because they mute class differences. References to the middle class by politicians, for example, are designed to encompass and attract the broadest possible constituency. Not only do references to the middle class gloss over differences, but these references also avoid any suggestion of conflict or injustice.

This leads us to the second exception to the class-avoidance phenomenon. We are, on occasion, presented with glimpses of the upper class and the lower class (the language used is "the wealthy" and "the poor"). In the media, these presentations are designed to satisfy some real or imagined voyeuristic need of "the ordinary person." As curiosities, the ground-level view of street life and the inside look at the rich and the famous serve as unique models, one to avoid and one to aspire to. In either case, the two models are presented without causal relation to each other: one is not rich because the other is poor.

Similarly, when social commentators or liberal politicians draw attention to the plight of the poor, they do so in a manner that obscures the class structure and denies any sense of exploitation. Wealth and poverty are viewed as one of several natural and inevitable states of being: differences are only differences. One may even say differences are the American way, a reflection of American social diversity.

We are left with one of two possibilities: either talking about class and recognizing class distinctions are not relevant to U.S. society, or we mistakenly hold a set of beliefs that obscure the reality of class differences and their impact on people's lives.

Let us look at four common, albeit contradictory, beliefs about the United States.

Myth 1: The United States is fundamentally a classless society. Class distinctions are largely irrelevant today, and whatever differences do exist in economic standing, they are—for the most part—insignificant. Rich or poor, we are all equal in the eyes of the law, and such basic needs as health care and education are provided to all regardless of economic standing.

Myth 2: We are, essentially, a middle-class nation. Despite some variations in economic status, most Americans have achieved relative affluence in what is widely recognized as a consumer society.

Myth 3: We are all getting richer. The American public as a whole is steadily moving up the economic ladder, and each generation propels itself to greater economic well-being. Despite some fluctuations, the U.S. position in the global economy has brought previously unknown prosperity to most, if not all, Americans.

Myth 4: Everyone has an equal chance to succeed. Success in the United States requires no more than hard work, sacrifice, and perseverance: "In America, anyone can become a millionaire; it's just a matter of being in the right place at the right time."

In trying to assess the legitimacy of these beliefs, we want to ask several important questions. Are there significant class differences among Americans? If these differences do exist, are they getting bigger or smaller, and do these differences have a significant impact on the way we live? Finally, does everyone in the United States really have an equal opportunity to succeed?

THE ECONOMIC SPECTRUM

Let's begin by looking at difference. An examination of available data reveals that variations in economic well-being are, in fact, immense. Consider the following:

- The wealthiest 1 percent of the American population holds 34 percent of the total national wealth. That is, they own over one-third of all the consumer durables (such as houses, cars, and stereos) and financial assets (such as stocks, bonds, property, and savings accounts). The richest 20 percent of Americans hold nearly 85 percent of the total household wealth in the country.[3]

- Approximately 338,761 Americans, or approximately eight-tenths of 1 percent of the adult population, earn more than $1 million *annually*.[4] There are nearly 400 billionaires in the U.S today, more than three dozen of them worth more than $10 billion each. It would take the typical (median) American (earning $49,568 and spending absolutely nothing at all) a total of 20,174 years (or approximately 298 lifetimes) to earn just $1 billion.

Affluence and prosperity are clearly alive and well in certain segments of the U.S. population. However, this abundance is in contrast to the poverty and despair that is also prevalent in the United States. At the other end of the spectrum:

- Approximately 13 percent of the American population—that is, nearly one of every eight people in this country—live below the official poverty line (calculated in 2007 at $10,590 for an individual and $21,203 for a family of four).[5] An estimated 3.5 million people—of whom nearly 1.4 million are children—experience homelessness in any given year.[6]

The contrast between rich and poor is sharp, and with nearly one-third of the American population living at one extreme or the other, it is difficult to argue that we live in a classless society. Big-payoff reality shows, celebrity salaries, and multimillion dollar lotteries notwithstanding, evidence suggests that the level of inequality in the United States is getting higher. Census data show the gap between the rich and the poor to be the widest since the government began collecting information in 1947[7] and that this gap is continuing to grow. In one year alone, from 2003 to 2004, the average after-tax income of the top 1 percent increased by 20 percent to $145,500 per year. This is the largest one-year increase going to the top 1 percent in fifteen years. On average the income of the bottom 80 percent increased only 2.7 percent.[8]

Nor is such a gap between rich and poor representative of the rest of the industrialized world. In fact, the United States has by far the most unequal distribution of household income.[9] The income gap between rich and poor in the United States (measured as the percentage of total income held by the wealthiest 10 percent of the population as compared to the poorest 10 percent) is approximately 5.4 to 1, the highest ratio in the industrialized world.[10]

Reality 1: There are enormous differences in the economic standing of American citizens. A sizable proportion of the U.S. population occupies opposite ends of the economic spectrum. In the middle range of the economic spectrum:

- Sixty percent of the American population holds less than 4 percent of the nation's wealth.[11]
- While the real income of the top 1 percent of U.S. families more than doubled (111 percent) between 1979 and 2003, the income of the middle fifth of the population grew only slightly (9 percent over that same 24-year period and its share of income (15 percent of the total compared to 48 percent of the total for the wealthiest fifth) actually declined during this period.[12]
- Regressive changes in governmental tax policies and the weakening of labor unions over the last quarter century have led to a significant rise in the level of inequality between the rich and the middle class. Between 1979 and 2005, the gap in household income between the top fifth and middle fifth of the population rose

by almost 40 percent.[13] From 1962 to 2004, the wealth held by most Americans (80 percent of the total population) increased from $40,000 to $82,000 (not adjusted for inflation). During that same period, the average wealth of the top 1 percent increased from $5.6 million to $14.8 million.[14] One prominent economist described economic growth in the United States as a "spectator sport for the majority of American families."[15] Economic decline, on the other hand, is much more "inclusive," with layoffs impacting hardest on middle- and lower-income families—those with fewer resources to fall back on.

The level of inequality is sometimes difficult to comprehend fully by looking at dollar figures and percentages. To help his students visualize the distribution of income, the well-known economist Paul Samuelson asked them to picture an income pyramid made of children's blocks, with each layer of blocks representing $1,000. If we were to construct Samuelson's pyramid today, the peak of the pyramid would be much higher than the Eiffel Tower, yet almost all of us would be within six feet of the ground.[16] In other words, the distribution of income is heavily skewed; a small minority of families take the lion's share of national income, and the remaining income is distributed among the vast majority of middle-income and low-income families. Keep in mind that Samuelson's pyramid represents the distribution of income, not wealth. The distribution of wealth is skewed even further.

Reality 2: The middle class in the United States holds a very small share of the nation's wealth and that share is declining steadily. The gap between rich and poor and between rich and the middle class is larger than it has ever been.

AMERICAN LIFE-STYLES

At last count, nearly 37 million Americans across the nation lived in unrelenting poverty.[17] Yet, as political scientist Michael Harrington once commented, "America has the best dressed poverty the world has ever known."[18] Clothing disguises much of the poverty in the United States, and this may explain, in part, its middle-class image. With increased mass marketing of "designer" clothing and with shifts in the nation's economy from blue-collar (and often better-paying) manufacturing jobs to white-collar and pink-collar jobs in the service sector, it is becoming increasingly difficult to distinguish class differences based on appearance.[19] The dress-down environment prevalent in the high-tech industry (what one author refers to as the "no-collars movement") has reduced superficial distinctions even further.[20]

Beneath the surface, there is another reality. Let's look at some "typical" and not-so-typical life-styles.

American Profile

Name:	Harold S. Browning
Father:	manufacturer, industrialist
Mother:	prominent social figure in the community
Principal child-rearer:	governess
Primary education:	an exclusive private school on Manhattan's Upper East Side
	Note: a small, well-respected primary school where teachers and administrators have a reputation for nurturing student creativity and for providing the finest educational preparation
	Ambition: "to become President"
Supplemental tutoring:	tutors in French and mathematics
Summer camp:	sleep-away camp in northern Connecticut
	Note: camp provides instruction in the creative arts, athletics, and the natural sciences
Secondary education:	a prestigious preparatory school in Westchester County
	Note: classmates included the sons of ambassadors, doctors, attorneys, television personalities, and well-known business leaders
	Supplemental education: private SAT tutor
	After-school activities: private riding lessons
	Ambition: "to take over my father's business"
	High-school graduation gift: BMW
Family activities:	theater, recitals, museums, summer vacations in Europe, occasional winter trips to the Caribbean
	Note: as members of and donors to the local art museum, the Brownings and their children attend private receptions and exhibit openings at the invitation of the museum director
Higher education:	an Ivy League liberal arts college in Massachusetts
	Major: economics and political science
	After-class activities: debating club, college newspaper, swim team
	Ambition: "to become a leader in business"
First full-time job (age 23):	assistant manager of operations, Browning Tool and Die, Inc. (family enterprise)

Subsequent employment:	*3 years*—executive assistant to the president, Browning Tool and Die *Responsibilities included:* purchasing (materials and equipment), personnel, and distribution networks *4 years*—advertising manager, Lackheed Manufacturing (home appliances) *3 years*—director of marketing and sales, Comerex, Inc. (business machines)
Present employment (age 38):	executive vice president, SmithBond and Co. (digital instruments) *Typical daily activities:* review financial reports and computer printouts, dictate memoranda, lunch with clients, initiate conference calls, meet with assistants, plan business trips, meet with associates *Transportation to and from work:* chauffeured company limousine *Annual salary:* $324,000 *Ambition:* "to become chief executive officer of the firm, or one like it, within the next five to ten years"
Present residence:	eighteenth-floor condominium on Manhattan's Upper West Side, eleven rooms, including five spacious bedrooms and terrace overlooking river *Interior:* professionally decorated and accented with elegant furnishings, valuable antiques, and expensive artwork *Note:* building management provides doorman and elevator attendant; family employs au pair for children and maid for other domestic chores
Second residence:	farm in northwestern Connecticut, used for weekend retreats and for horse breeding (investment/hobby) *Note:* to maintain the farm and cater to the family when they are there, the Brownings employ a part-time maid, groundskeeper, and horse breeder

Harold Browning was born into a world of nurses, maids, and governesses. His world today is one of airplanes and limousines, five-star restaurants, and luxurious living accommodations. The life and life-style of Harold Browning is in sharp contrast to that of Bob Farrell.

American Profile

Name:	Bob Farrell
Father:	machinist
Mother:	retail clerk
Principal child-rearer:	mother and sitter
Primary education:	a medium-size public school in Queens, New York, characterized by large class size, outmoded physical facilities, and an educational philosophy emphasizing basic skills and student discipline
	Ambition: "to become President"
Supplemental tutoring:	none
Summer camp:	YMCA day camp
	Note: emphasis on team sports, arts and crafts
Secondary education:	large regional high school in Queens
	Note: classmates included the sons and daughters of carpenters, postal clerks, teachers, nurses, shopkeepers, mechanics, bus drivers, police officers, salespersons
	Supplemental education: SAT prep course offered by national chain
	After-school activities: basketball and handball in school park
	Ambition: "to make it through college"
	High-school graduation gift: $500 savings bond
Family activities:	family gatherings around television set, softball, an occasional trip to the movie theater, summer Sundays at the public beach
Higher education:	a two-year community college with a technical orientation
	Major: electrical technology
	After-school activities: employed as a part-time bagger in local supermarket
	Ambition: "to become an electrical engineer"

First full-time job (age 19):	service-station attendant
	Note: continued to take college classes in the evening
Subsequent employment:	mail clerk at large insurance firm; manager trainee, large retail chain
Present employment (age 38):	assistant sales manager, building supply firm
	Typical daily activities: demonstrate products, write up product orders, handle customer complaints, check inventory
	Transportation to and from work: city subway
Annual salary:	$45,261
	Ambition: "to open up my own business"
	Additional income: $6,100 in commissions from evening and weekend work as salesman in local men's clothing store
Present residence:	the Farrells own their own home in a working class neighborhood in Queens, New York.

Bob Farrell and Harold Browning live very differently: the life-style of one is privileged; that of the other is not so privileged. The differences are class differences, and these differences have a profound impact on the way they live. They are differences between playing a game of handball in the park and taking riding lessons at a private stable; watching a movie on television and going to the theater; and taking the subway to work and being driven in a limousine. More important, the difference in class determines where they live, who their friends are, how well they are educated, what they do for a living, and what they come to expect from life.

Yet, as dissimilar as their life-styles are, Harold Browning and Bob Farrell have some things in common; they live in the same city, they work long hours, and they are highly motivated. More important, they are both white males.

Let's look at someone else who works long and hard and is highly motivated. This person, however, is black and female.

American Profile	
Name:	Cheryl Mitchell
Father:	janitor
Mother:	waitress
Principal child-rearer:	grandmother
Primary education:	large public school in Ocean Hill-Brownsville, Brooklyn, New York

	Note: rote teaching of basic skills and emphasis on conveying the importance of good attendance, good manners, and good work habits; school patrolled by security guards
	Ambition: "to be a teacher"
Supplemental tutoring:	none
Summer camp:	none
Secondary education:	large public school in Ocean Hill-Brownsville
	Note: classmates included sons and daughters of hairdressers, groundskeepers, painters, dressmakers, dishwashers, domestics
	Supplemental education: none
	After-school activities: domestic chores, part-time employment as babysitter and housekeeper
	Ambition: "to be a social worker"
	High-school graduation gift: corsage
Family activities:	church-sponsored socials
Higher education:	one semester of local community college
	Note: dropped out of school for financial reasons
First full-time job (age 17):	counter clerk, local bakery
Subsequent employment:	file clerk with temporary-service agency, supermarket checker
Present employment (age 38):	nurse's aide at a municipal hospital
	Typical daily activities: make up hospital beds, clean out bedpans, weigh patients and assist them to the bathroom, take temperature readings, pass out and collect food trays, feed patients who need help, bathe patients, and change dressings
	Annual salary: $16,850
	Ambition: "to get out of the ghetto"
Present residence:	three-room apartment in the South Bronx, needs painting, has poor ventilation, is in a high-crime area
	Note: Cheryl Mitchell lives with her four-year-old son and her elderly mother

When we look at the lives of Cheryl Mitchell, Bob Farrell, and Harold Browning, we see life-styles that are very different. We are not looking, however, at economic extremes. Cheryl Mitchell's income as a nurse's aide puts her above the government's official poverty line.[21] Below her on the income pyramid are 37 million poverty-stricken Americans. Far from being poor, Bob Farrell has an annual income as an assistant sales manager that puts him well above the median income level—that is, more than 50 percent of the U.S. population earns less money than Bob Farrell.[22] And while Harold Browning's income puts him in a high-income bracket, he stands only a fraction of the way up Samuelson's income pyramid. Well above him are the 338,761 individuals whose annual salary exceeds $1 million. Yet Harold Browning spends more money on his horses than Cheryl Mitchell earns in a year.

Reality 3: Even ignoring the extreme poles of the economic spectrum, we find enormous class differences in the life-styles among the haves, the have-nots, and the have-littles.

Class affects more than life-style and material well-being. It has a significant impact on our physical and mental well-being as well.

Researchers have found an inverse relationship between social class and health. Lower-class standing is correlated to higher rates of infant mortality, eye and ear disease, arthritis, physical disability, diabetes, nutritional deficiency, respiratory disease, mental illness, and heart disease.[23] In all areas of health, poor people do not share the same life chances as those in the social class above them. Furthermore, lower-class standing is correlated with a lower quality of treatment for illness and disease. The results of poor health and poor treatment are borne out in the life expectancy rates within each class. Researchers have found that the higher your class standing, the higher your life expectancy. Conversely, they have also found that within each age group, the lower one's class standing, the higher the death rate; in some age groups, the figures are as much as two and three times as high.[24]

Reality 4: From cradle to grave, class standing has a significant impact on our chances for survival.

The lower one's class standing, the more difficult it is to secure appropriate housing, the more time is spent on the routine tasks of everyday life, the greater is the percentage of income that goes to pay for food and other basic necessities, and the greater is the likelihood of crime victimization.[25] Class can accurately predict chances for both survival and success.

CLASS AND EDUCATIONAL ATTAINMENT

School performance (grades and test scores) and educational attainment (level of schooling completed) also correlate strongly with economic class. Furthermore, despite some efforts to make testing fairer and schooling more accessible, current data suggest that the level of inequity is staying the same or getting worse.

In his study for the Carnegie Council on Children in 1978, Richard De Lone examined the test scores of over half a million students who took the College Board exams (SATs). His findings were consistent with earlier studies that showed a relationship between class and scores on standardized tests; his conclusion: "the higher the student's social status, the higher the probability that he or she will get higher grades."[26] Today, more than thirty years after the release of the Carnegie report, College Board surveys reveal data that are no different: test scores still correlate strongly with family income.

Average Combined Scores by Income (400 to 1600 scale)[27]

Family Income	Median Score
More than $100,000	1113
$80,000 to $100,000	1057
$70,000 to $80,000	1032
$60,000 to $70,000	1020
$50,000 to $60,000	1009
$40,000 to $50,000	994
$30,000 to $40,000	966
$20,000 to $30,000	936
$10,000 to $20,000	910
less than $10,000	886

These figures are based on the test results of 1,465,744 SAT takers in 2006.

In another study conducted thirty years ago, researcher William Sewell showed a positive correlation between class and overall educational achievement. In comparing the top quartile (25 percent) of his sample to the bottom quartile, he found that students from upper-class families were twice as likely to obtain training beyond high school and four times as likely to attain a postgraduate degree. Sewell concluded: "Socioeconomic background . . . operates independently of academic ability at every stage in the process of educational attainment."[28]

Today, the pattern persists. There are, however, two significant changes. On the one hand, the odds of getting into college have improved for the bottom quartile of the population, although they still remain relatively low compared to the top. On the other hand, the chances of completing a college degree have deteriorated markedly for the bottom quartile. Researchers estimate the chances of completing a four-year college degree (by age 24) to be nineteen times as great for the top 25 percent of the population as it is for the bottom 25 percent.[29]

Reality 5: Class standing has a significant impact on chances for educational achievement.

Class standing, and consequently life chances, are largely determined at birth. Although examples of individuals who have gone from rags to riches abound in the mass media, statistics on class mobility show these leaps to be extremely rare. In fact, dramatic advances in class standing are relatively infrequent. One study showed that fewer than one in five men surpass the economic status of their fathers.[30] For those whose annual income is in six figures, economic success is due in large part to the wealth and privileges bestowed on them at birth. Over 66 percent of the consumer units with incomes of $100,000 or more have inherited assets. Of these units, over 86 percent reported that inheritances constituted a substantial portion of their total assets.[31]

Economist Harold Wachtel likens inheritance to a series of Monopoly games in which the winner of the first game refuses to relinquish his or her cash and commercial property for the second game. "After all," argues the winner, "I accumulated my wealth and income by my own wits." With such an arrangement, it is not difficult to predict the outcome of subsequent games.[32]

Reality 6: All Americans do not have an equal opportunity to succeed. Inheritance laws ensure a greater likelihood of success for the offspring of the wealthy.

SPHERES OF POWER AND OPPRESSION

When we look at society and try to determine what it is that keeps most people down—what holds them back from realizing their potential as healthy, creative productive individuals—we find institutional forces that are largely beyond individual control. Class domination is one of these forces. People do not choose to be poor or working class; instead, they are limited and confined by the opportunities afforded or denied them by a social and economic system. The class structure in the United States is a function of its economic system: capitalism, a system that is based on private rather than public ownership and control of commercial enterprises. Under capitalism, these enterprises are governed by the need to produce a profit for the owners, rather than to fulfill societal needs. Class divisions arise from the differences between those who own and control corporate enterprise and those who do not.

Racial and gender domination are other forces that hold people down. Although there are significant differences in the way capitalism, racism, and sexism affect our lives, there are also a multitude of parallels. And although class, race, and gender act independently of each other, they are at the same time very much interrelated.

On the one hand, issues of race and gender cut across class lines. Women experience the effects of sexism whether they are well-paid professionals or poorly paid clerks. As women, they are not only subjected to catcalls and stereotyping, but face discrimination and are denied opportunities and privileges that men have. Similarly, a wealthy black man faces racial oppression, is subjected to racial slurs, and is denied opportunities because of his color. Regardless of their class standing, women and members of minority races are constantly dealing with institutional forces that are holding them down precisely because of their gender, the color of their skin, or both.

On the other hand, the experiences of women and minorities are differentiated along class lines. Although they are in subordinate positions vis-à-vis white men, the particular issues that confront women and people of color may be quite different depending on their position in the class structure.

Power is incremental, and class privileges can accrue to individual women and to individual members of a racial minority. While power is incremental, oppression is cumulative, and those who are poor, black, and female are often subject to all of the forces of class, race, and gender discrimination simultaneously. This cumulative situation is what is meant by the double and triple jeopardy of women and minorities.

Furthermore, oppression in one sphere is related to the likelihood of oppression in another. If you are black and female, for example, you are much more likely to be poor or working class than you would be as a white male. Census figures show that the incidence of poverty varies greatly by race and gender.

Chances of Being Poor in America[33]

White male/female	White female head*	Hispanic male/female	Hispanic female head*	Black male/female	Black female head*
1 in 12	1 in 5	1 in 5	1 in 3	1 in 4	1 in 3

*Persons in families with female householder, no husband present.

In other words, being female and being nonwhite are attributes in our society that increase the chances of poverty and of lower-class standing.

Reality 7: Racism and sexism significantly compound the effects of class in society.

None of this makes for a very pretty picture of our country. Despite what we like to think about ourselves as a nation, the truth is that opportunity for success and life itself are highly circumscribed by our race, our gender, and the class we are born into. As individuals, we feel hurt and anger when someone is treating us unfairly; yet as a society we tolerate unconscionable injustice. A more just society will require a radical redistribution of wealth and power. We can start by reversing the current trends that further polarize us as a people and adapt policies and practices that narrow the gaps in income, wealth, and privilege.

NOTES

1. See Jay MacLead, *Ain't No Makin' It: Aspirations and Attainment in a Lower-Income Neighborhood* (Boulder, CO: Westview Press, 1995); Benjamin DeMott, *The Imperial*

Middle (New York: Morrow, 1990); Ira Katznelson, *City Trenches: Urban Politics and Patterning of Class in the United States* (New York: Pantheon Books, 1981); Charles W. Tucker, "A Comparative Analysis of Subjective Social Class: 1945–1963," *Social Forces*, no. 46, June 1968, pp. 508–514; Robert Nisbet, "The Decline and Fall of Social Class," *Pacific Sociological Review*, vol. 2, Spring 1959, pp. 11–17; and Oscar Glantz, "Class Consciousness and Political Solidarity," *American Sociological Review*, vol. 23, August 1958, pp. 375–382.

2. Susan Ostander, "Upper-Class Women: Class Consciousness as Conduct and Meaning," in G. William Domhoff, *Power Structure Research* (Beverly Hills, CA: Sage Publications, 1980), pp. 78–79. Also see Stephen Birmingham, *America's Secret Aristocracy* (Boston: Little Brown, 1987).

3. Lawrence Mishel, Jared Bernstein, and Sylvia Allegretto, *State of Working America: 2006/2007* (Ithaca, NY: Cornell University Press, 2007), pp. 251, 253.

4. The number of individuals filing tax returns showing a gross adjusted income of $1 million or more in 2006 was 355,204 (Tax Stats at a Glance, Internal Revenue Service, U.S. Treasury Department, available at http://www.irs.gov/taxstats/article/0,,id=102886,00 .html).

5. Carmen DeNavas-Walt, Bernadette D. Proctor, and Jessica C. Smith, U.S. Census Bureau, Current Population Reports, P60–235, *Income, Poverty, and Health Insurance Coverage in the United States: 2007* (Washington, DC: U.S. Government Printing Office, 2008), pp. 12–19, available at http://pubdb3.census.gov/macro/032008/pov/new01_100_01.htm.

6. National Coalition for the Homeless, "How Many People Experience Homelessness?" NCH Fact Sheet #2 (June 2008), available at http://www.nationalhomeless.org/publica tions/facts/How_Many.html. Also see National Coalition for the Homeless, "How Many People Experience Homelessness?" NCH Fact Sheet #2 (June 2006), citing a 2004 National Law Center on Homelessness and Poverty study, available at http://www.national homeless.org/publications/facts/How_Many.pdf; U.S. Conference of Mayors, *Hunger and Homelessness Survey, 2008: A Survey Report on Homelessness and Hunger in American Cities* (Washington, DC: U.S. Conference of Mayors, 2008), pp. 13–23; Martha Burt, *What Will it Take to End Homelessness?* (Washington, DC: Urban Institute, September 2001); Martha Burt, "Chronic Homelessness: Emergence of a Public Policy," *Fordham Urban Law Journal*, 30, no. 3 (2003), pp. 1267–1279; and Kim Hopper, *Reckoning with Homelessness* (Ithaca, NY: Cornell University Press, 2002).

7. Mishel et al., op. cit., p. 253.

8. Arloc Sherman and Aviva Aron-Dine, "New CBO Data Show Income Inequality Continues to Widen" (Washington, DC: Center on Budget and Policy Priorities, January 2007), p. 3.

9. Based on a comparison of 19 industrialized states: Mishel et al., op. cit., pp. 344–349.

10. Mishel et al., op. cit., p. 345.

11. Derived from Mishel et al., p. 255, Table 5.3.

12. Mishel et al., op. cit., p. 64.

13. *Ibid.*, p. 59.

14. *Ibid.*, p. 255.

15. Alan Blinder, quoted by Paul Krugman, in "Disparity and Despair," *U.S. News and World Report*, March 23, 1992, p. 54.

16. Paul Samuelson, *Economics*, 10th ed. (New York: McGraw-Hill, 1976), p. 84.

17. DeNavas-Walt et al., op. cit., p. 12.

18. Michael Harrington, *The Other America* (New York: Macmillan, 1962), pp. 12–13.

19. Stuart Ewen and Elizabeth Ewen, *Channels of Desire: Mass Images and the Shaping of American Consciousness* (New York: McGraw-Hill, 1982).

20. Andrew Ross, *No-Collar: The Humane Work Place and Its Hidden Costs* (New York: Basic Books, 2002).

21. Based on a poverty threshold for a three-person household in 2007 of $16,650. DeNavas-Walt et al., op. cit., p. 1.

22. The median income in 2007 was $45,113 for men working full time, year round; $35,102 for women; and $50,233 for households. DeNavas-Walt et al., op. cit, p. 6.

23. U. S. Government Accountability Office, *Poverty in America: Economic Research Shows Adverse Impacts on Health Status and Other Social Conditions* (Washington, DC: U.S. Government Accountability Office, 2007), pp. 9–16. Also see E. Pamuk, D. Makuc, K. Heck, C. Reuben, and K. Lochner, *Socioeconomic Status and Health Chartbook, Health, United States, 1998* (Hyattsville, MD: National Center for Health Statistics, *1998*), pp. 145–159; Vincente Navarro, "Class, Race, and Health Care in the United States," in Bersh Berberoglu, *Critical Perspectives in Sociology*, 2nd ed. (Dubuque, IA: Kendall/Hunt, 1993), pp. 148–156; Melvin Krasner, *Poverty and Health in New York City* (New York: United Hospital Fund of New York, 1989); U.S. Department of Health and Human Services, *Health Status of Minorities and Low Income Groups, 1985*; and Dan Hughes, Kay Johnson, Sara Rosenbaum, Elizabeth Butler, and Janet Simons, *The Health of America's Children* (The Children's Defense Fund, 1988).

24. E. Pamuk et al., op. cit.; Kenneth Neubeck and Davita Glassberg, *Sociology: A Critical Approach* (New York: McGraw-Hill, 1996), pp. 436–438; Aaron Antonovsky, "Social Class, Life Expectancy, and Overall Mortality," in *The Impact of Social Class* (New York: Thomas Crowell, 1972), pp. 467–491. See also Harriet Duleep, "Measuring the Effect of Income on Adult Mortality Using Longitudinal Administrative Record Data," *Journal of Human Resources*, vol. 21, no. 2, Spring 1986. See also Paul Farmer, *Pathologies of Power: Health, Human Rights, and the New War on the Poor* (Berkeley: University of California Press, 2005).

25. E. Pamuk et al., op. cit., fig. 20; Dennis W. Roncek, "Dangerous Places: Crime and Residential Environment." *Social Forces*, vol. 60, no. 1, September 1981, pp. 74–96. Also see Steven D. Levitt, "The Changing Relationship between Income and Crime Victimization," *Economic Policy Review*, 5, No. 3, September 1999.

26. Richard De Lone, *Small Futures* (New York: Harcourt Brace Jovanovich, 1978), pp. 14–19.

27. Derived from Viji Sathy, Sandra Barbuti, and Krista Mattern, "The New SAT and Trends in Test Performance," *College Board*, 2006, pp. 18–20.

28. William H. Sewell, "Inequality of Opportunity for Higher Education," *American Sociological Review*, vol. 36, no. 5, 1971, pp. 793–809.

29. The Mortenson Report on Public Policy Analysis of Opportunity for Postsecondary Education, "Postsecondary Education Opportunity" (Iowa City, IA; September 1993, no. 16).

30. De Lone, op. cit., pp. 14–19. Also see Daniel McMurrer, Mark Condon, and Isabel Sawhill, "Intergenerational Mobility in the United States" (Washington, DC: Urban Institute, 1997), available at http://www.Urbaninstitute.org/url.cfm?ID=406796; and Bhashkar Mazumder, "Earnings Mobility in the US: A New Look at Intergenerational Inequality" (March 21, 2001), FRB Chicago Working Paper No. 2001–18, available at SSRN: http://ssrn.com/abstract=295559, or DOI: 10.2139/ssm.295559.

31. Howard Tuchman, *Economics of the Rich* (New York: Random House, 1973), p. 15. Also see Greg Duncan, Ariel Kalil, Susan Mayer, Robin Tepper, and Monique Payne. "The Apple

Does not Fall Far from the Tree," in Samuel Bowles, Herbert Gintis, and Melissa Groves, *Unequal Chances: Family Background and Economic Success* (Princeton, NJ: Princeton University Press, 2008), pp. 23–79; Bhashkar Mazumder, "The Apple Falls Even Closer to the Tree than We Thought," in Bowles et. al., pp. 80–99. For more information on inheritance, see Sam Bowles and Herbert Gintis, "The Inheritance of Inequality," *The Journal of Economic Perspectives*, 16, no. 3 (Summer 2002), pp. 2–30, and Tom Hertz, *Understanding Mobility in America*, Center for American Progress, available at http://www.american progress.org/kf/hertz_mobility_analysis.pdf.

32. Howard Wachtel, *Labor and the Economy* (Orlando, FL: Academic Press, 1984), pp. 161–162.

33. Derived from U.S. Census Bureau, *Current Population Survey*, Tables POV01 and POV2, available at http://pubdb3.census.gov/macro/032008/pov/toc.htm.

FURTHER READING

Baird, Robert M., and Stuart E. Rosenbaum, eds. *Bigotry, Prejudice, and Hatred.* Buffalo, NY: Prometheus Press, 1992.

Bonilla-Silva, Eduardo. *Racism without Racists: Colorblind Racism and the Persistence of Racial Inequality in the U.S.* New York: Rowman & Littlefield, 2003.

——. *White Supremacy and Racism in the Post Civil Rights Era.* Boulder CO: Rienner, 2001.

Brandt, Eric, ed. *Dangerous Liaisons: Blacks, Gays and the Struggle for Equality.* New York: New Press, 1999.

Brown, Michael K., et al. *Whitewashing Race in America: The Myth of a Colorblind Society.* Berkeley: University of California Press, 2005.

Cose, Ellis. *The Rage of a Privileged Class.* New York: Collins, 1994.

DeMott, Benjamin. *The Trouble with Friendship: Why Americans Can't Think Straight about Race.* New York: Atlantic Monthly Press, 1995.

Dusky, Lorraine. *Still Unequal: The Shameful Truth about Women and Justice in America.* New York: Crown Books, 1996.

Dyer, Richard. *White.* London and New York: Routledge, 1997.

Faludi, Susan. *Backlash: The Undeclared War against American Women.* New York: Crown Publishers, 1991.

Feagin. Joe R. *Racist America: Roots, Realities, and Future Reparations.* New York: Routledge, 2000.

Harris, Leonard. *Racism.* New York: Humanities Books, 1999.

Kadi, Joanne. *Thinking Class: Sketches from a Cultural Worker.* Boston: South End Press, 1996.

Katznelson, Ira. *When Affirmative Action Was White: An Untold History of Racial Inequality in 20th C. America*, New York: W.W. Norton, 2005.

Kimmel, Michael. *The Gendered Society.* New York: Oxford University Press, 2000.

Lipsitz, George. *The Possessive Investment in Whiteness.* Philadelphia, PA: Temple University Press, 1998.

Perry, Barbara. *In the Name of Hate: Understanding Hate Crimes.* New York and London: Routledge, 2001.

Pharr, Suzanne. *Homophobia as a Weapon of Sexism.* Inverness, CA: Chardon Press, 1988.

Pincus, F. L., and H. J. Erlich. *Race and Ethnic Conflict: Contending Views on Prejudice, Discrimination and Ethnoviolence.* Boulder, CO: Westview, 1994.

Rhode, Deborah L. *Speaking of Sex: The Denial of Gender Inequality.* Cambridge, MA, and London, England: Harvard University Press, 1997.

Ronai, Carol R., et al. *Everyday Sexism in the Third Millenium,* New York and London: Routledge, 1997.

Shipler, David K. *A Country of Strangers: Blacks and Whites in America.* New York: Knopf, 1997.

Wellman, David T. *Portraits of White Racism.* Cambridge: Cambridge University Press, 1977.

Williams, Lena. *It's the Little Things: the Everyday Interactions That Get Under the Skin of Blacks and Whites.* New York: Harcourt, 2000.

STUDY QUESTIONS

1. What evidence does Mantsios present in support of his argument that **wealth inequality** is a problem in the United States?

2. What key differences do you think explain why Harold S. Browning and Bob Farrell have had such different trajectories? How do their aspirations and **work** ethics compare? Their achievements and salaries? What might their lives tell us about the idea of **meritocracy** in the United States?

3. Based on the known effect of **family income** on SAT scores, do you think standardized testing should be used as a basis of admission for institutions of higher learning? What might be a fairer, but still feasible, measure of a student's capacity to succeed at a given college or university?

4. Today, an overwhelming majority of Americans report that they are **middle class**. Based on your reading of this article, what do you think defines the middle class? Why might people be less likely to refer to themselves as **working class** or **upper class** than in the past?

THOMAS SHAPIRO

The Cost of Being Black and the Advantage of Being White

from *The Hidden Cost of Being African American: How Wealth Perpetuates Inequality*

W hat does it cost to be black in America? Put another way, what financial advantages do whites receive just for being white in America? Thomas Shapiro takes up both of these questions, providing extensive evidence showing large differences in the **wealth** and net worth of white Americans compared to their black counterparts. As you read make note of each of the social forces that can explain the wide (and growing) racial gaps in America.

WEALTH AND INEQUALITY

What portion of the racial wealth gap results from merit-based differences like education, jobs, and earnings, and what portion springs from nonmerit-based sources, like inheritance, institutional discrimination, and discriminatory public policy? This question is crucial not because we can hope to explain all causes of the racial wealth gap but rather because it allows us to identify some significant sources of the gap. A commonsense explanation of why some people have more wealth than others is that

The Hidden Cost of Being African American: How Wealth Perpetuates Inequality by Thomas Shapiro (2004). 7040 words from Chapter Two "The Cost of Being Black and the Advantage of Being White," pp. 42–59, 213–215. Copyright © 2003 by Thomas M. Shapiro. By permission of Oxford University Press, Inc.

wealth is accumulated primarily through high salaries, wise and timely investments, and prudent spending. Many contend that the racial wealth gap principally results from income inequality. That is, people with similar incomes will have similar wealth, regardless of race. Do differences in income explain nearly all the racial differences in wealth? If so, then policies need to continue focusing primarily on the workplace to further narrow job and earnings inequality. If not, however, then public policy must address dynamics outside the labor market as well as those within.

The remarkable growth of wealth resulting from the sustained economic prosperity after World War II changed forever its role in American society. Until the baby boomers started coming of age, family wealth was the prerogative of a tiny minority of upper-crust American families. In the baby boom years, between 1946 and 1964, a significant number of middle-class families accumulated substantial amounts of wealth for the first time. Middle-class families now are passing along about $9 trillion to their adult children. How they use this unprecedented wealth transfer is an important part of the increasing inequality and racial inequality stories.

When we discuss a family's *net worth*, we mean all assets minus all debts and specifically include home equity. Net worth, then, is like a family's total asset balance sheet and indicates all of its financial resources. The median (or typical; half of all families have more and half have less) and mean (average) net worth of families in 1999 was $40,000 and $179,800, respectively. *Net financial assets*, on the other hand, are restricted to liquid assets (those immediately available), specifically excluding home equity and cars. Net financial assets indicate those resources immediately available to families, and net worth gives a better idea of those resources that might be available to the next generation. Median and mean net financial assets in 1999 stood at $15,000 and $134,700. Which is a better sense of what the "average" American family possesses: $15,000 or $134,700? In the case of the latter, adding a billionaire's wealth raises the statistical average substantially. It does not affect the median.

The significant difference between net worth and net financial assets is the inclusion or exclusion of home equity. Because net worth indicates wealth that may be bequeathed at death to the next generation and net financial assets indicate resources available today, I will present both throughout.

The remarkable post–World War II growth in wealth saw average net worth increase nearly $60,000 per household between 1962 and 1995. Of course, this figure is misleading, because the growth in wealth did not occur evenly for all families. Net worth increased from $31,000 to $39,000 for typical families during this period. The huge difference here between the mean and median figures demonstrates again the lopsided nature of wealth accumulation. Meanwhile, net financial assets for typical families remained unchanged between 1962 and 1995, although the average figures, again, show a hefty increase from $92,000 to $135,000. Keeping the important top-heavy caveat in mind, it does mean that larger shares of wealth created by the tremendous postwar prosperity in America spread out into more families than at any time in our past. The difference between net worth and net financial assets also indicates that for average Americans housing wealth continues to be the largest reservoir of assets. In fact, for families in the middle three-fifths of America's net worth distribution, ranging from $1,650 to $153,000, equity in their principal residence represents 60 percent of their wealth.

While overall wealth has been increasing at this staggering rate, wealth inequality has been increasing since 1980. By 1998 it had reached its worse level since 1929. The richest 1 percent of families controls 38 percent of total household wealth, and the top 20 percent controls 84 percent. Financial wealth is even more lopsided: The richest 1 percent owns 47 percent of the value of stocks, bonds, real estate, businesses, and other financial instruments, and one-fifth of America's families controls 93 percent. In contrast, the top 20 percent receives about 42 percent of all income.

The financial wealth of the bottom two-fifths of the population actually falls into negative numbers; that is, family debts overshadow financial assets. Nearly three in ten households have zero or negative financial wealth. These figures illustrate the extreme concentration of wealth, and when we view American families' economic health through this wealth lens we see that it is more fragile than acknowledged previously. Economic inequality increased markedly as the boom of the 1990s fizzled. The wealth of those in the top 10 percent of incomes surged much more than the wealth of those in any other group. The net worth of families in the top 10 percent jumped 69 percent from 1998 to 2001.

These numbers present a staggering portrait of inequality in America, but, as aggregate statistics, they cannot show us what wealth means in people's lives. I will turn to one of the wealthiest families we interviewed to put financial assets into the concrete and human context of real families and to glimpse the organizing role that assets play in family life.

THE DOUCETTE FAMILY STORY

In 1982, Jen and Sam Doucette bought a home on a quiet residential street in the Mar Vista section of West Los Angeles—bordered by Santa Monica to the north and Culver City to the east—from a friend who had moved away and was looking for someone to take over his mortgage. They had just married, and both held well-paying jobs they liked. Like the others in their immediate neighborhood, their home was a small, one-story, stucco tract home built right after World War II, probably for workers from the nearby Hughes and Douglas defense plants. They were the first on their block to add a second story, which not only doubled and modernized their living space but also began an upscaling of this neighborhood from working class to upper middle class. Their street is considerably west and south of what most call Mar Vista, but according to local real estate agents I spoke to, Mar Vista is becoming more a state of mind and status than a precise geographic area.

The Doucettes' part of Mar Vista is a section of Los Angeles that is increasing in value rapidly because it is only one mile to the ocean and because of its location on the affluent west side. Many homeowners have, like the Doucettes, recently expanded vertically to bring them more in tune with upper-middle-class urban lifestyles. The activity and newness of the construction brighten the neighborhood and give it a different air from the areas that surround it. Their block clearly has the sorts of amenities and new city services—like freshly painted crosswalks and curbs, neatly trimmed trees, buried electric lines—that herald up-and-coming neighborhoods. It sends out an air of rising property values.

In terms of financial wealth, the Doucettes are the wealthiest family we interviewed. Their net worth (including their house) of $1 million places them among the richest 1 percent of Americans. Sam is a corporate executive and makes more than $200,000 a year. Jen used to work at one of the motion picture studios but has been a homemaker since Blaine, their 5-year-old, was born. They possess an assortment of mutual funds, IRAs, 401(k)s, CDs, and pension plans that total about $450,000. Sam and Jen have access to over $700,000 in net financial assets tomorrow to take advantage of an opportunity, meet a crisis, or plan for their future.

In addition to their various savings plans, they bought another house in their neighborhood two years ago and fixed it up to rent as an investment property, and they feel very confident that it will rise in value with their neighborhood. They were able to put down about half of the purchase price for this investment property in cash. Several years ago on a vacation to Lake Arrowhead, they fell in love with the area and decided to buy a second home. Jen recalls,

> Homes could be had for a very reasonable price. I don't think we ever dreamed in a million years that we would have a vacation home this early in our lives. It fell into our lives, basically. We almost immediately decided that we wanted to buy up there.

They found a three-bedroom, two-bath vacation home and bought it for $140,000, using $65,000 as a down payment. Both of their additional properties have appreciated considerably, adding another $100,000 or so in property to their wealth portfolio. At the time of our interview, their house was worth about $160,000 more than it had cost them, including the improvements.

This is a very prosperous family, and evidence of this prosperity came through throughout the interview. Like most Americans, though, Jen and Sam do not believe it is appropriate to disclose financial details. Jen was so guarded about family finances that I had to ask for details more than once. When asked to rank her family's wealth as compared to other American families, Jen guessed about the 80th percentile, though in fact they are about the 99th percentile. At the other end of the spectrum, we talked to families with zero or even negative assets who ranked themselves at 50 on this scale. It seems that the commonly held perception that all think of themselves as middle class is accurate. The Doucettes responded to questions about wealth with discomfort, even though they had been clearly informed beforehand that I would ask them. Interestingly, we rarely got this attitude from families with few assets, who had perhaps more embarrassing and less "successful" stories to tell.

Despite their initial reticence, the Doucettes told us that they treat their wealth as a special kind of money different from income. According to Jen, wealth "is definitely long term. We act as if it's not even there." She is expressing her sense of economic security grounded in wealth.

Like many wealthy city residents, the Doucettes live in a community that they like but feel trapped in a school jurisdiction in which they have no confidence. Mar Vista may be a state of mind, as the local real estate agents like to say, but it unambiguously falls within the boundaries of the Los Angeles Unified School District, notorious for weak schools, drug problems, and violence. Blaine is attending a Montessori preschool. I ask Jen what will happen when he is ready for kindergarten and decisions must be made. Jen is clear and adamant: "Our neighborhood school is not an option." Instead, they are looking into a couple of charter and magnet schools, and they plan to petition neighboring Culver City for admission since this city's schools have a very good reputation. These are backup plans because Pacifica Oaks, "the private school that we applied to, is our first choice." It is one of the most expensive private schools in Los Angeles; the cost of kindergarten for Blaine would start at $12,000.

The capacity of wealth is powerful in the Doucette family. It allowed them to buy a house in a desirable location and a vacation home that gets them out of Los Angeles in the hot and smoggy summer months and into Southern California's mountains and lakes. They can use their wealth to acquire the kind of educational environment and experience they think best for Blaine. At the end of the interview, I ask Jen if she has a sense of economic security: "Very much, yes." I then ask her to tell me a few things she is able to do because of her sense of security. "Take trips, buy additional property, make certain investments," Jen says. "We definitely have freedom to do things." The Doucettes are a delightful family and seem quite happy. We have no way of knowing how important money is to their happiness, but for this family wealth is important for homeownership, community, a vacation home, and shaping the life of their child.

THE RACIAL WEALTH GAP

Surprisingly, household surveys did not begin collecting detailed information about wealth until the mid-1980s, when a couple of surveys began including questions about family assets. This information provides the basis for analyzing the racial wealth gap. The charts below look at data from 1999. (See Figures 1 and 2.) The typical black household earns 59 cents for every dollar earned by the typical white household. This income comparison closely matches other national data and is the most widely used

FIGURE 1. Family Income and Family Wealth

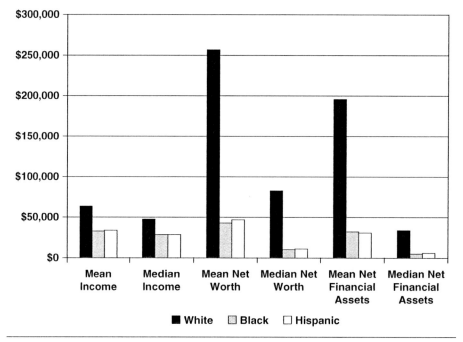

Source: PSID, 1999

FIGURE 2. Family Income and Family Wealth: Minority Cents-to-Dollar Values

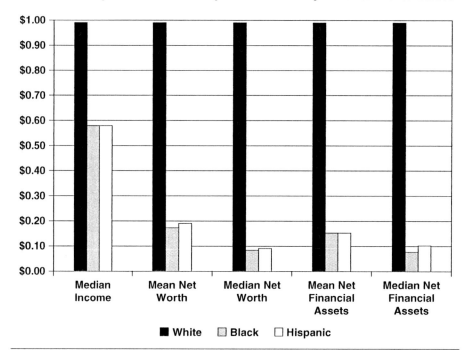

Source: PSID, 1999

indicator of current racial and ethnic material inequality. However, changing the lens of analysis to wealth dramatically shifts the perspective. The net worth of typical white families is $81,000 compared to $8,000 for black families. This *baseline racial wealth gap*, then, shows that black families possess only 10 cents for every dollar of wealth held by white families. The issue is no longer how to think about closing the gap from 59 cents on the dollar to a figure approaching parity but how to think about going from 10 cents on the dollar to parity. In dollars, the baseline racial wealth gap is robust: The typical white family's wealth is $73,450 more than the typical black family's. Even though both white and black families increased their net worth between 1988 and 1999, the black-white gap actually grew by $16,000 (in 1999 dollars).

The figures for net financial assets do not improve the picture. The typical black family possesses $3,000 in net financial assets compared to $53,500 for the typical white family. These figures represent wealth accumulation for both whites and blacks between 1988 and 1999, indicating that the typical white and black families had progressed financially. These figures also show a whopping $20,000 increase in the net financial asset gap. While families were doing better, inequality increased.

THE CONNECTION BETWEEN INCOME AND WEALTH

Why does this huge racial wealth gap persist, and why is it getting worse? One alternative explanation that minimizes the significance of race argues that wealth is a product of income and savings: that is, as incomes rise, people save and invest more, which leads to greater wealth accumulation. This classical economic view attributes the racial wealth gap primarily to income differences between whites and blacks. The explanation points to narrowing the income gap as the principal remedy for the racial wealth gap. In order to test this perspective, it is critically important to address whether the wealth of blacks is quite similar to that of whites with comparable incomes. In fact, while the evidence supports the importance of high salaries to wealth accumulation, the evidence also suggests that income is only part of a larger picture.

Table 1 shows that white households in every income quintile have significantly higher median wealth than similar-earning black households. In the lowest quintile, net worth for typical white households is $17,066, while black households in the same quintile possess only $2,400. Among highest-earning households, white median net worth is $133,607, while net worth for black households in the highest income group registers $43,806. The median net financial assets data is just as revealing: At the middle quintile, for example, typical net financial assets for white households are $6,800, which is markedly higher than for black households, $800.[1]

TABLE 1. Wealth by Income and Race

	White		Black	
	Net Worth	Net Financial Assets	Net Worth	Net Financial Assets
Highest fifth median	$133,607	$40,465	$43,806	$7,448
Second highest fifth median	$65,998	$13,362	$29,851	$2,699
Middle fifth median	$50,350	$6,800	$14,902	$800
Second lowest fifth median	$39,908	$3,599	$6,879	$249
Lowest fifth median	$17,066	$7,400	$2,400	$100

Source: PSID, 1999

It is important to observe that controlling for income in this manner does lessen significantly the white-to-black wealth ratios. The baseline median white-to-black net worth gap is a dime to a dollar overall but narrows when comparing white and black households in similar income quintiles. The gap, as expressed in black-to-white dollar ratios, stays about the same for people at the lower end but narrows to 30 cents on the dollar, 45 cents, and 33 cents, respectively, for people in the $25,000–$39,000, $39,001–$60,000, and highest earning ranges. In brief, as shown by this comparative procedure, controlling for income indeed narrows the gap, but a significantly large gap persists. This factual record does not support hypothetical propositions that whites and blacks at similar income levels possess similar wealth.[2]

No matter how much or how little you make, then, wealth is dramatically higher for white households. The evidence shows that higher incomes lead to high wealth accumulation, but the same evidence does not support the contention that the racial wealth gap derives principally from white-black income differences. This alternative explanation of the racial wealth gap lacks evidence. Lest my rejection of the income explanation sound too dismissive, let me be clear: The racial wealth gap does decline as incomes rise. At the same time, even when incomes are equal and high, a cavernous gap remains.

But aren't things improving for younger people? We might expect to find a more sizable racial wealth gap among older people than among younger people because of progress in other areas of racial inequality. As younger generations begin and go through life with more equal opportunities than previous generations, the wealth gap should narrow. And yet there is a consistent pattern. Further, the racial wealth gap is not simply a matter of starting at different places and then maintaining this constant gap; the gap widens as people advance through the life course. For whites and blacks who were 20–29 years old in 1984, the gap increased $23,926 by 1994. As white and black families progress through the life course, the different opportunities afforded by increasingly disparate financial resources continue to compound racial inequality and make it worse.

Earlier in this chapter we detailed the extraordinary magnitudes of wealth inequality between whites and blacks that remain even when they are matched on key characteristics such as income. The research findings support my contention that a single source or even a few sources cannot account for the racial wealth gap. Rather, its roots run more deeply in contemporary American life. A more informed and comprehensive analysis therefore needs to (1) identify which factors are most important in creating the wealth gulf; (2) explore how much of the racial wealth gap can be explained by a combination of key factors; and (3) assess the contribution of merit and nonmerit factors in creating the racial wealth gulf.

We now can use a statistical method called multiple regression to examine the relationship between wealth and the variables we think predict wealth, such as income, age, marital status, family size, region, job, and education. It allows us to see how changes in the various variables affect wealth. For example, multiple regression can give us a good understanding of how much wealth increases for each additional year of education completed net of changes in the other factors. The first step in regression analysis is to identify a set of variables that are expected to have an impact on wealth. Income? Education? Jobs? Age? Family? What combination of factors? I want to emphasize that this sort of analysis best identifies key factors and the contributions they make for the variance in wealth. Later, I will use our family interviews to assess the importance of head-start assets in launching a family's well-being.

The results in Table 2 show that in this survey income, inheritance, and having one full-time (highly paid) family worker are the most significant predictors of differences in net worth, followed by home ownership. When one has a college degree, the number of children in one's family, marital status, female-headed family, and full-time employment are less important. Income is the most important factor in net financial assets variation, followed by inheritance and one full-time family worker. Table 2 also allows us to observe the contribution each variable makes to wealth accumulation.

Income is the most important variable determining net worth. Each additional dollar of annual income generates $3.26 in net worth; thus the net worth difference between a family with a $30,000 income and a family with $60,000 in earnings is nearly $100,000. This wealth disparity is built upon years of income difference. Owning a home returns about $56,000, which is another indication of how important home equity is for building wealth. For net financial assets, each additional income dollar generates $2.95, and middle-class occupation nets $31,000 in comparison to working-class jobs.[3]

The results just presented include all families, and thus they do not tell us about racial differences. Now we can investigate whether, for example, a college education rewards blacks as well as it does whites. Table 3 opposite presents separate analyses for blacks and whites. Income translates, for example, into more wealth for whites than for blacks. Everything else being equal, blacks accrue only $1.98 in wealth for

TABLE 2. What Accounts for Wealth Differences?

	Net Worth	Net Financial Assets
White	32,509.00	24,503.00
Age	1,011.00	586.00
Age Squared	38.04	33.80
Live in South	−3,121.00	−4,782.00
Education in Years	5,695.00	3,693.00
Bachelor's Degree	54,398.00+	41,933.00
Middle-Class Occupation	26,108.00	31,748.00
Number of Children	−15,161.00+	−10,840.00
Widowed	−73,541.00	−73,333.00+
Married	12,353.00	45.86
Female-Headed w/ Children	62,509.00	43,993.00
Experienced Unemployment	7,902.00	5,575.00
Employed Full-Time	−68,163.00*	−55,476.00*
Retired	39,746.00	28,457.00
Own Home	56,238.00*	15,899.00
Income $	3.26***	2.95***
Inheritance $	0.13**	0.10**
CONSTANT	−229,954.00*	−171,773.00+
N	6367	6583
R Squared	0.174	0.139
Adjusted R Squared	0.171	0.137
Total Model Significance	0.00	0.00

+ < = .10; * < = .05; ** < = .01; *** < = .001

each additional dollar earned, in comparison to $3.25 for whites, so that, net of all other factors, the average black family earning $60,000 possesses $76,000 less wealth than the average white family with the same earnings. The most dramatic difference is the wealth effect of homeownership, which is worth about $60,000 more for whites than blacks. This evidence bolsters my core argument that the way homes are bought and sold, where they are located, and how the market values them provides a contemporary foundation for racial inequality.

These findings using 1999 data vividly show the continuing importance of race in the wealth accumulation process. We noted that demographic, achievement, and inheritance factors actually explain a small portion of the racial wealth gap. Examining wealth accumulation in 1999 in this way provides an excellent snapshot for the United States at one point in time and thus provides valuable insight into racial inequality. We can track families over time and examine their wealth accumulation and ask questions beyond the capabilities of cross-sectional data.[4] What distinguishes wealth-gaining families from families whose wealth does not change or from families whose wealth declines?[5] ... Income, inheritance, and retirement during this period

TABLE 3. What Accounts for Wealth Differences among Blacks and Whites?

	Net Worth		Net Financial Assets	
	WHITE	**BLACK**	**WHITE**	**BLACK**
Age	3040	–157	2041	–101.576
Age Squared	26	8	28	2.479
Live in South	–2908	–1741	–9376	–2162.824
Education in Years	14170	1530	9484–	235.308
Bachelor's Degree	35654	5974	28176	15516.457
Middle-Class Occupation	36356	24682	42808	27125.477+
Number of Children	–30210+	2564	–25713+	6122.664
Widowed	–78336	–4211	–85342	–4756.381
Married	22051	–12846	4329	–17886.824
Female-Headed w/ Children	61031	–1648	41959	–9432.589
Experienced Unemployment	–17216	16699	–14752	1188.436
Employed Full-Time	–81635+	–22750	–67562	–19695.876
Retired	55255	6120	37753	3476.659
Own Home	86658*	27324*	39427	1467.46
Income $	3.250***	1.974***	2.951***	1.938***
Inheritance $	0.118*	0.141	0.093*	0.05208
CONSTANT	–382,178.00*	–50,836.00	–277,028.50+	23670.359
N	3981	1859	4074	1963
R Squared	0.169	0.064	0.137	0.049
Adjusted R Squared	0.166	0.056	0.134	0.041
Total Model Significance	***	***	***	***

+ < = .10; * < = .05; ** < = .01; *** < = .001

Source: PSID, 1999

distinguish wealth-gaining families from those who did not gain much wealth. All the factors explain about 15 percent of the change in wealth between 1989 and 1999.

Change in family income is the most important factor in wealth changes. Each additional dollar in family income generates over $3.22 in net worth. Surprisingly, family educational status changing from no college graduates to college degrees is not important in distinguishing wealth-gainers from others. Becoming a homeowner during this period is not significant, in my view; homes do not rise in value very much in short time spans. However, homeownership will magnify differences over longer time periods. Finally, every dollar inherited between 1989 and 1999 created 60 cents in net worth.

* * * One can note for each racial group how different factors are significant in distinguishing wealth-gainers from others. Change in family income, again, is the most important factor, but income once more translates into more wealth for whites than for blacks. Blacks accrue only $2.00 in net worth wealth for each additional dollar earned, in comparison to $3.22 for whites. Receiving an inheritance in this period is an important characteristic distinguishing white wealth-gainers, adding 59 cents in

net worth for every dollar inherited.[6] Significantly, inheritance does not distinguish wealth-building among black families, perhaps because inheritance is so much more infrequent in black families and, when they do inherit, the amounts are small. I will pursue this key finding about the relative importance of inheritance in white and black families further in the next chapter.

To make our finding even more graphic we can look at what would happen if whites received the same returns as blacks on all factors. We know already, for instance, that whites receive $3.25 in additional wealth for each new dollar of income and that for blacks one additional income dollar generates only $1.98 in wealth. The idea here is to demonstrate the wealth effect of using blacks' wealth return for income instead of whites', and so on for every factor under analysis. We already know that a typical white family's mean net worth is $247,730, but what happens when we swap white functions for black ones? This method yields an easy way of projecting the cost of being African American. Swapping functions in this way lowers a family's net worth to $111,556. Thus the cost of being black amounts to $136,174. In net financial assets, the cost of being African American amounts to $94,426. These numbers present our best attempt to put a dollar figure on penalties African Americans pay.

In my view, it is equally important to explore the relationship between the hidden cost of being African American and the advantage of being white. This involves some tough reckoning. Do advantages in some areas translate into disadvantages for others? Is whites' well-being related to blacks' hardship? The white advantage in housing markets, as we have suggested already and will explore in detail later, seems to result in fewer homeownership opportunities and less built up in home equity for blacks. Advantages in education opportunity also come at the expense of disadvantaging others. In other areas, whites' advantage may not translate directly into blacks' disadvantage; instead, it may limit opportunities for minorities.

The idea of calculating white advantage is a good deal more threatening. The reason for this incongruity is that our national discourse typically frames racial discussions around why black Americans are not as successful as others are. Depending upon viewpoints, framing our national discussion on racial inequality this way puts the onus for black disadvantage on overt racism or on blacks themselves for not doing better. Both perspectives tend to see African Americans as victims. In my view, part of the power of dominant groups (in this case, whites) is their seeming invisibility and the fact that their status is often taken for granted, as if they are not active actors, agents, or benefactors in an unequal relationship. I believe we must begin to discuss white advantage and its direct impact on blacks. In the context of the next two chapters, which examine inheritance and middle-class achievements, I develop more fully the relationship between white advantage and black disadvantage.

For now, however, the focus remains on placing an objective dollar figure on white advantage. Class enters the picture once again because the figures tell us about the average white family. In reality, many do not benefit at all while the dollar advantage to others far exceeds the average. The figures for the cost of being black are also—

obversely—the dollar figures for white advantage: The hidden net worth advantage of being white also amounts to $136,173; similarly, the net financial assets advantage for being white is $94,426.

The Doucette family, described earlier in this chapter, gave us a glimpse at what wealth means to a very prosperous family. But what of families more firmly situated in the middle class and more like an "average" American family? In fact, the more typical case, as people's stories showed us repeatedly, is that addition or subtraction of a relatively small amount of assets can lead to radically changed lives. Take, for example, the Andrews family, a professional, middle-class family living in St. Louis.

THE ANDREWS FAMILY

Judith Andrews is the kind of person who anchors a community—energetic, bright, and involved. She was 7 years old when her family moved from the public housing projects into their own home and became the first African American family on the block. Her father was a musician, and her mother was a seamstress. She was educated in the Catholic schools of Cleveland before becoming the first in her family to go to college. Using a combination of scholarships, working, and school loans, she earned her bachelor's degree at Cleveland State and then a master's degree in public affairs from Occidental College. After college, she moved to St. Louis for additional training in public affairs and started working as a planner at an agency focusing on housing for low- and moderate-income families.

Judith Andrews loves to tell the story of how she found and bought her home in 1982. Through her work in urban planning, she found a condemned house in the "dicey" but potentially up-and-coming Vandeventer neighborhood of north St. Louis. Just out of college, single, and with little in the way of savings, she took a calculated risk, bought a dilapidated house for $1,500, and completely rehabbed it from pipes in the ground to roof tiles. Fixing the roof was more expensive than the purchase price. Since first buying the house, she has put $30,000 into making the once-condemned property a comfortable home. In 1990, a few years after she bought her home, the average selling price for a single-family residence in this area was $32,000. In 2000 Vandeventer is 97 percent African American, 29 percent of the housing units are vacant, abandoned, or boarded up, and the poverty rate is high. When I ask why she chose her neighborhood, she says, "I kind of liked the urban pioneer spirit that St. Louis seemed to exhibit at that time." Judith particularly enjoys the liveliness of the nearby Central West End neighborhood, with its restaurants, shops, activity, and integrated feel.

In 1994 Judith married Steve, who works as a paralegal. The Andrewses' block fits sociologist Mary Patillo-McCoy's description of black middle-class neighborhoods in her book *Black Picket Fences*. More poverty, worse schools, higher crime, and fewer services than middle-class white neighborhoods characterize them. This results from the geography of residential segregation that typically situates black middle-class neighborhoods between poor black communities and whites. The Andrewses share space and public services with poor blacks, and thus the problems associated with poor black urban neighborhoods, while they serve as a buffer between the largely white, upscale West End they identify with and those same problems.

The street Judith lives on is a block north of a major thoroughfare that many consider the northern perimeter of the Central West End. As with the Doucettes defining themselves as a part of Mar Vista, it is important for Judith to identify as a Central West Ender, which supplies a middle-class persona that Vandeventer cannot. Her block is like many others in sections of St. Louis that are all black. Judith's home is a three-story brick house in good shape set back about 15 feet from the street with trimmed grass and plants in front. Trees provide much-needed shade on this block and some separation between houses that otherwise are close together. The houses on either side look like hers and add to the spruced-up, middle-class feel of her block, but across the street, and indeed interspersed every three or four houses, buildings are boarded up and broken windows and tall weeds designate obviously vacant homes. Turner Park, located near Judith's house, is a perfect example of the mixed economic condition of the Vandeventer neighborhood: At one corner there is a playground that could be the cornerstone of the surrounding blocks; at the other corner there is an unmaintained baseball diamond whose teams have long since moved from the neighborhood.

Judith enjoys seeing herself as a pioneer, but she also talks about needing to play frontier sheriff when drug activity increases and she must intensify her neighborhood commitments. She discusses her constant quest to "turn houses over to families who would make an investment in the neighborhood." She fears that many of the homes could be "wiped out overnight."

> Just wiped out. Like one year, the man across the street died. The man next door to him died. The man next door to me died. And two doors down across the street, the lady died. And they were all like in their eighties. . . . And those houses were all vacant. I mean, that's a scary thought. One day, they're occupied and fully functional; and then you wake up and they're vacant.

Judith calls this the "scourge" of her community, which she and others regularly combat with constant vigilance and by marketing the area to prospective homeowners and small businesses.

Judith and Steven are successful in their professional careers, earning more than $80,000 between them. This urban-pioneer story is not just a tale about boldness and risk rewarded. It also is an asset success story. They live and find part of their urban identity in the "lively" Central West End. They probably could not afford to live within the traditional borders of the Central West End, where homes are far more expensive, but they are helping to stretch its boundary. The wealth accumulated in their home also means they do not have to shoulder the burden of poor urban public schools. Judith's 17-year-old son goes to an all-black parochial high school with excellent educational standards. Their young daughter will go to day care full-time until she reaches school age, when she too will go to private school, if she does not get into the city magnet school for gifted children. Their healthy incomes cannot pay the private school and day care bills, which total $18,000 annually. Judith and Steven have taken out a home equity loan to provide for their children's needs and other family expenses.

The house is worth about $70,000 in the current Vandeventer real estate market. We will analyze this in more detail in later chapters, but the real estate mantra of *location, location, location* clearly is evident here. Everything about this house—its architecture, its size, its condition, the way it feels—suggests that if we moved it to a more affluent community its value would rise significantly. Its Vandeventer location puts a racialized ceiling on its value because middle-class white families will not choose to move to this neighborhood. With the pool of potential buyers limited to blacks who can afford the Andrews house, the law of supply and demand values homes in black communities at considerably lower prices. Even though their home provides the Andrews about $40,000 in equity, if it were in a white middle-class community, the value of the house would be higher and their home equity would be much larger. This is one of the ways being black disadvantages even successful, hard-working, playing-by-the-rules, middle-class blacks. Several later chapters will pick up this theme and break down these dynamics in detail.

END NOTES

1. I switch the data in this table to SIPP because in my estimation this dataset is more appropriate for detailed breakdowns, especially if one wants to include useful information on Hispanics. The lowest income quintile includes the elderly; thus the wealth figures for this quintile appear larger than one might otherwise expect.

2. Yet another way to test this, almost to the point of absurdity, compares wealth controlling for white and black income distributions. Calibrating the white-to-black income distributions means, for example, comparing the 25th percentile of the white wealth data to the 45th in the black distribution, the 50th white to the black 70th, and the white 75th to the black 88th.

   These results show, for example, that at the 25th percentile (white), median white NW is $7,671, but the black NW now adjusts upward to $3,548. At the 50th white percentile, white NW is $52,944, compared to $30,000 for equivalent earning blacks. At the 75th percentile, white wealth stands at $141,491 versus $72,761 for blacks.

   At the 50th percentile, then, the original uncontrolled gap weighs in at $46,817 with a ratio of .12. Controlling for income reduces this gap to $22,944. The black-white wealth ratio closes as well to .57.

3. These tables are unweighted PSID data. Social scientists disagree about whether regressions like these should be weighted and/or logged. We examined every combination

possible. We present the unweighted data because it allows us to preserve as many cases as possible. In addition, results from the weighted data are not much different from the unweighted, although more factors become significant. Using the logged data does not allow us to discuss the dollar contribution of each factor to wealth accumulation.

4. PSID has collected information on family assets since 1984, asking questions that are more comprehensive about family assets and liability issues every five years, and thus we can examine changes in family wealth over a 15-year period, 1984–99. For technical reasons, we use the most recent 10-year period, 1989–99. The 1984 survey reported too many families who did not answer some critical wealth questions for us to use the 1984 survey with confidence.

5. Of course, this longitudinal window is another way to examine racial differences and see if the most significant factors—income, middle-class occupations, and inheritance—remain the same. We can examine whether the wealth gap between equally achieving families narrows, stays the same, or increases over time. Do the disadvantages and advantages wealth confers accumulate, magnify, and sediment into racial stratification? We compute changes in wealth accumulation by subtracting a family's 1989 wealth from their reported wealth in 1999. We regressed the same set of independent variables identified in our previous regression on the 10-year change in family wealth. Now we convert these factors to changes because we want to know, for example, how change in family income between 1989 and 1999 affects a family's wealth.

6. In a different regression model, not shown here, receiving an inheritance between 1989 and 1999 added $131,000 net worth for white families.

STUDY QUESTIONS

1. How has African American net worth changed since the mid-1980s? How does this compare to the change in net worth for whites during the same time period?

2. Why does **wealth** inequality matter so much? That is, why is having wealth so advantageous?

3. Think about your community. Where is the lower income part of town? What are the social disadvantages to living in this area? Your answer should include a discussion of disadvantages in **education**, health, safety, property values, and any other social factor you can think of.

4. What can be done about economic racial inequality? Brainstorm a few possible solutions, pick one, and explain why you think this solution has the best likelihood of success.

JOE FEAGIN

Contemporary Racial Attitudes and Racial Oppression in Everyday Practice

from Racist America: Roots, Current Realities, and Future Reparations

s **racism** even a big deal anymore? I mean, look how much progress we've made. Won't this all resolve itself soon?" These are common student reactions when racism is brought up in class. Social research is clear, though: **race** still advantages some and disadvantages others. Yet the "is this still even an issue" perspective is common. How can a world with inequality be perceived as equal? Why, when someone says they've been **discriminated** against, do many people say, "You're seeing something that's not there," or, "You're too sensitive"? In this essay the author explains how the way we conceptualize race affects how we perceive it in **society**.

CONTEMPORARY RACIAL ATTITUDES AND IMAGES

Denying Discrimination and Racism: The White Public

Denying the Reality of Discrimination Soon after the 1960s civil rights movement declined in intensity, most whites were moving toward the view that racial

"Contemporary Racial Attitudes & Images," by Joe R. Feagin from *Racist America: Roots, Current Realities, and Future Reparations.* Reprinted by permission of Routledge, Taylor & Francis Group LLC.

discrimination is no longer an important problem for the nation. In a 1976 survey, for example, most (71 percent) whites agreed that "blacks and other minorities no longer face unfair employment conditions. In fact they are favored in many training and job programs." A meager 12 percent of whites agreed with the statement that "discrimination affects all black people. The only way to handle it is for blacks to organize together and demand rights for all."[1] In a 1980 survey respondents were asked, "How much discrimination do you feel there is against blacks and other minorities in any area of life that limits their chances to get ahead?"[2] Just over half of blacks replied "a lot," compared to only a quarter of whites. In these surveys only a minority of whites viewed discrimination as a major hurdle.

In more recent surveys, black and white Americans still differ dramatically in how they view discrimination. A 1990 NORC survey question asked why blacks have worse jobs, income, and housing than whites. Choosing among alternative explanations, two-thirds of black respondents said that it was "mainly due to discrimination," compared to only 35 percent of whites.[3] Similarly, in a mid-1990s Pennsylvania survey researchers found that eight in ten black respondents thought inequality in jobs, housing, and income stemmed mostly from discrimination, while the majority of whites viewed this inequality as resulting from blacks' lack of motivation. Respondents were asked whether the quality of life for black Americans had gotten better in the last decade. Nearly six in ten whites said it had gotten better, compared to less than a third of black respondents.[4] Recent national polls have shown the same pattern. A 1997 ABC/*Washington Post* poll found that only 17 percent of the white respondents felt there was a lot of racial discrimination, compared to nearly half the blacks polled. In addition, several other surveys have found that on questions dealing with specific institutional areas such as housing, education, and jobs less than a majority of whites believe that blacks currently face discrimination.[5]

Several recent surveys have found that many whites think blacks are as well off as or are better off than whites in regard to education, health care, and jobs. For example, a Massachusetts survey found a majority of the white respondents saying that African Americans, Asian Americans, and Latino Americans now have *equality* in life chances with whites.[6] However, government statistical data indicate that such views are very much in error. Perhaps because of erroneous or misleading media reports, most whites do not understand just how much worse off blacks actually are than whites in most areas of political and economic life.[7]

"I Am Not a Racist": Denying Individual Racism Clearly, a majority of whites do not see the United States as a nation that has a problem of serious and widespread racial discrimination. Apparently, most whites also do not view themselves as significantly racist in thought or action, often asserting "I am not a racist." In recent years many whites have also made such statements as "my family never owned slaves" or "my family did not segregate lunch counters." Many will say to black Americans something like, "Slavery happened hundreds of years ago—get over it." They do not know, or pretend they do not, that official slavery ended less than 140 years or so prior to their statements. In addition, whites making such assertions usually do not admit that they and their families have benefited greatly from slavery, segregation, and present-day discrimination.

Many whites seem to mix negative views of black Americans with images of white innocence, thereby giving specific expression to elements of a broader racial ideology. Take this example of a white college student's reply to a question about her first experience with black Americans, in this case children: "I switched from a private school which had no blacks to a public school, and I was thrown in the middle of a bunch of apes, no I'm just kidding. . . . And I don't know, my parents have always instilled in me that blacks aren't equal, because we are from [the Deep South]." In her interview she continues in this vein, making several negative comments about African Americans. Then at the end of her interview, she adds, "I don't consider myself racist. I, when I think of the word racist, I think of KKK, people in white robes burning black people on crosses and stuff, or I think of the Skinheads or some exaggerated form of racism."[8] We see here the imaging of the white self in positive terms.

It seems that most whites can assert that they are "not racist" because they see racism as something that *other* whites do. That is, they know other whites who are much more racist in thought or action than they are, and thus they see themselves as already beyond that racism. Jerome Culp has said, "To many white people, not being racist means having less racial animosity than their parents (something almost all can at least claim); having less racial animosity than someone they know (something all can claim); or not belonging to a white supremacist group. . . . For many white people, unless they believe overwhelmingly in the inferiority of black people, they are not collaborators with racism and are not racist."[9] As we saw in white views of athletes and actors on "The Cosby Show,"* many whites hold some more or less positive images of selected black men or women. However, these usually superficial positive views reduce the ability of whites to see their own culpability in personal and institutional racism. Indeed, many a white person has a false consciousness that occurs when a white "believes he or she is identifying with a person of color, but in fact is doing so only in a slight, superficial way."[10] It is possible to hold that black Americans can be good entertainers, musicians, or sports figures, yet also believe that most are inferior to whites in character, morality, or intelligence.

Historical changes in racism have also been misperceived by whites. When the legal segregation era came to an end with the passage of civil rights laws in the 1960s, most whites apparently concluded that serious racism was being rapidly extinguished. Today, most whites, like the young woman interviewed above, seem to view what

---

* American television sitcom (1984–92) that featured an upper-middle-class African American family.

racism remains as a matter of isolated Klan-type bigotry and not as a system of racism cutting across U.S. institutions. As a result, they do not see their own racism. Moreover, the level at which racist attitudes are held can vary in degree of consciousness. Psychologist Patricia Devine has suggested that whites who reject overtly prejudiced views can still hold less consciously prejudiced thoughts that stem from prior socialization. For many whites this attitudinal racism is a persisting bad habit that keeps coming up in everyday thought and behavior. One reason for this is the fact that human beings are characterized by automatic information processing, which involves the unintentional activation of previously socialized attitudes such as racist stereotypes and prejudices.[11] Racist attitudes can thus be conscious, half-conscious, or even subconscious.

White Views on Government Action against Discrimination

If antiblack discrimination is no longer regarded as a serious problem, then it is not surprising that most whites see less need, or no need, for strong antidiscrimination efforts by governments. From this perspective blacks pressing for continuing or enhanced antidiscrimination programs, such as aggressive affirmative action, are seen as making illegitimate demands. David Wellman has suggested that "the concrete problem facing white people is how to come to grips with the demands made by blacks while at the same time *avoiding* the possibility of institutional change and reorganization that might affect them."[12]

Symbolic and Laissez-Faire Racism Some researchers have described a contemporary white perspective called *symbolic racism.* Whites often combine the notion of declining or eradicated blatant racism with the idea that blacks are making illegitimate demands for societal changes. As these researchers see the current situation, a majority of whites have shifted away from old-fashioned racist ideas and have accepted modest desegregation while strongly resisting aggressive government action for large-scale desegregation. This symbolic racism is grounded in white resistance to substantial changes in the status quo. Central to white concerns is a fear whites have of losing status and power because of black attempts to bring change. Deeply-lying antiblack views—especially views of blacks violating traditional American work values—are still present, but white resentment of pressures for substantial change is central to the current racist ideology.[13] This symbolic racism perspective has been criticized by some scholars as playing down old-fashioned racism, when the latter still exists among whites and is directly connected to negative views of programs to eradicate discrimination.

Lawrence Bobo, James Kluegel, and Ryan Smith have suggested a more historical approach. Since the 1950s, and shaped by structural changes in the society, they say white attitudes have shifted from an accent on strict segregation and overt bigotry to "laissez-faire racism," by which they mean whites' continuing stereotyping of blacks and blaming of blacks for their problems. Roughly in line with, but probably lagging somewhat, the elite responses [I have] described, most ordinary whites have given up a commitment to compulsory racial segregation. Yet, also in line with the elite, they still strive to maintain white privilege and position. Survey data since the 1960s indicate a substantial discrepancy between white views on the *principle* of desegregation versus white views on the *implementation* of desegregation by government. While surveys in the mid-1960s indicated that nearly two-thirds of whites accepted integrated schooling in principle, just 38 percent accepted a role for government in pressing for more integration. By the mid-1980s white support for the principle of school integration had grown to 93 percent, while endorsement of government intervention had declined to 26 percent.[14] The survey data indicate similar discrepancies in white views of job and housing integration. Acceptance of the principle of racial integration does not mean that whites wish to see government intervene aggressively, or to personally have more contact with blacks. Whites maintain a positive sense of self and their claims to greater privileges and resources while fending off what whites see as illegitimate black demands for a fair share of those resources.

Views on Affirmative Action Affirmative action is a major example of a remedial program to deal with racial discrimination. Yet most whites, including most white leaders, have been opposed to *aggressive* affirmative action since at least the 1970s. In one 1977 survey of mostly white and male local and national leaders in business, farming, unions, the media, and academia, *most* were overwhelmingly opposed to affirmative-action quotas for black Americans in school admissions and jobs. Only 10 to 22 percent of the several leadership groups favored strong remedial quotas.[15] In addition, the overwhelming majority of these elites thought that equality of opportunity, not equality of results, was the best way to eradicate disparities. The white public seems to share this view. Earlier we noted mid-1970s surveys suggesting that the white majority views blacks as no longer facing serious job discrimination and expresses opposition to an expanded effort for civil rights.

Recent data show the same pattern: more than half of whites do not believe that government or private agencies should be making aggressive remedial efforts on behalf of black Americans or other Americans of color. In an ABC News/*Washington Post* survey only a quarter of whites thought minorities should receive some preferences in jobs and college admissions.[16] And a late-1990s Gallup poll found that 70 percent of Republicans, a heavily white group, felt the federal government should not make special efforts to help Americans of color, because they should help themselves.[17] A majority of whites took the same position in a late-1990s survey in Massachusetts.[18] Most national surveys have shown the same pattern of white opposition to strong programs with special preferences or quotas as a means of aggressively remedying past discrimination. (Milder remedial programs may sometimes be acceptable.) Indeed, today many whites believe that they are likely to be the victims of governmental policies helping black Americans. One recent Pennsylvania survey asked a question as to how likely it would be that a white worker might lose a job or a promotion to a less qualified black worker. Most black respondents (57 percent) thought this was unlikely, while most whites (80 percent) thought it was likely.[19] National polls using such a question have gotten similar responses: The majority of whites seem convinced that antiwhite discrimination is now commonplace.

White elites have periodically expended substantial effort to shape the public's views of remedial programs. Elite perspectives on antidiscrimination programs and related public policies generally shifted in a more conservative direction in the two decades after the 1960s. Moreover, researcher Robert Entman has examined trends in mass media reports of the controversy over affirmative action that recurred periodically in the 1980s and 1990s. He found significant peaking in media attention to affirmative action during the years 1987, 1991, and 1995—years that preceded presidential elections. This pattern suggests elite manipulation of the affirmative action issue for political purposes. The media elites and their white-collar employees tended to present the issue of affirmative action in white-framed ways or in terms of national controversy, using such phrases as the "tide of white anger" or the "growing white backlash." Entman concludes that "journalists, it seems, built their frame on claims by elite sources with an interest in promoting the impression of white arousal, filtered through the conflict norm that shapes story construction."[20] The media attention accelerated concerns about affirmative action in the white public.

Related to opposition to strong affirmative action programs is the old individualistic ethic, especially the blame-the-victim version. Recall the historical importance of the individualistic (work) ethic from our previous discussion of racist ideology. Today, as in the past, many whites comment about the problems of blacks with such statements as, "Why can't they be like us?" The notion here is that if "they" will work harder and improve their personal and family values, then the normal assimilation processes will enable them to have greater socioeconomic mobility. One recent survey asked whether respondents agreed with this statement: "The Irish, Italians, and many other groups overcame prejudice and worked their way up, African-Americans and other minorities should do the same without any special help from the government." Most whites (69 percent) agreed.[21] Most seem to perceive the black experience in terms of an individualistic mobility model. Black Americans, from this viewpoint, are little different from white immigrant groups, such as the southern and eastern European immigrants of the early 1900s. Like those immigrants, who are seen as having encountered discrimination, black Americans should be able to work themselves up the social ladder. If they do not make it, it is mostly their own fault.

Imaging the White Self

As we [have seen], the racist ideas and attitudes of white Americans encompass *much more* than their antiblack views. Among these racist attitudes are positive views of white superiority and merit. Generally, the broad white-racist ideology sees white history as meritorious. Indeed, in the United States, group merit and individual merit are judged by standards created by the white majority, [as in] the images of white superiority and virtue in many Hollywood films. From the first years of moviemaking to the present, when racial matters have been portrayed, whites as a group have almost always been portrayed as morally superior, intellectually superior, or otherwise meritorious. In these movies—including more recent television movies—there may be a few white individuals who are racist bigots, but the society as a whole is not portrayed as racist. Some white person is typically a central hero, even in movies mostly about black Americans (for example, *Glory**).

Among elites and in the general public, whites have developed numerous sincere fictions that reproduce aspects of the broad racist ideology at an everyday level. Such fictions may describe whites as "not racist" and as "good people" even as the same whites take part in racist actions or express racist ideas. This moral privileging of whiteness may be conscious or it can be half-conscious or unconscious. Ruth Frankenberg found evidence of this unconsciousness in her research on white women: whiteness, she noted, is "difficult for white people to name. . . . Those who are securely housed within its borders usually do not examine it."[22] The sense of whiteness is often hidden deeply in individual psyches and practices. Being white, one might say, means rarely or never having to think about it. Whiteness is the national norm, and thus the white majority's views, practices, and culture are generally seen as normal.

Examining commentaries on racial inequality written by white students, Joyce King found that most were "unaware of how their own subjective identities reflect an uncritical identification with the existing social order." Only one student out of fifty-seven linked persisting racial inequality to the larger system of racial oppression.[23] Thus, while whites get many substantial advantages from systemic racism, they do pay a subtle and hidden price. This may include a lack of conscious awareness about certain critical aspects of social reality. Many have an uncritical mind that accepts the existing racial order with little questioning.

Perhaps most amazing is that a majority of whites today do not see the centuries of slavery and segregation as bringing whites substantial socioeconomic benefit. One survey found that nearly two-thirds of white respondents did *not* think that whites as a group had benefited from past and present discrimination against black Americans. Nor did they think whites should take significant action to remedy continuing discrimination.[24] Moreover, as we have seen, many whites have asserted their innocence with a torrent of comments such as "my family never owned slaves." This white guiltlessness is professed at all class levels, even by presidential candidates. Clearly, much

---

* American war film (1989) about the first all–African American U.S. Army unit, starring Matthew Broderick as the white captain Robert Gould Shaw.

work has gone into reframing the American history of racial oppression so that white Americans can appear blameless for the brutality and carnage they and their ancestors created.

* * *

RACIAL OPPRESSION IN EVERYDAY PRACTICE

Everyday Racism: Subtle, Covert, and Blatant The character of discrimination varies. Whites may actively persecute blacks, or they may engage in an array of avoidance behaviors. Discrimination can be self-consciously motivated, or it can be half-conscious or unconscious and deeply imbedded in an actor's core beliefs. At the level of everyday interaction with black Americans, most whites can create racial tensions and barriers even without conscious awareness they are doing so. Examples of this include when white men lock their car doors as a black man walks by on the street or when white women step out or pull their purses close to them when a black man comes into an elevator they are on. Stereotyped images of black men as criminals probably motivate this and similar types of defensive action. Such practices represent, according to Philomena Essed, the "integration of racism into everyday situations."[25] Systemic racism is thus a system of oppression made up of many thousands of everyday acts of mistreatment of black Americans by white Americans, incidents that range from the subtle and hard to observe to the blatant and easy to notice. These acts of mistreatment can be nonverbal or verbal, nonviolent or violent. Moreover, many racist actions that crash in on everyday life are, from the victim's viewpoint, unpredictable and sporadic. Such actions are commonplace, recurring, and cumulative in their negative impact. They are, as one retired black American in her eighties put it, "little murders" that happen every day.[26]

In a specific setting, such as an employment setting, a white person in authority may select another white person over an equally or better qualified black person because of a preconceived notion that whites are more competent or because of discomfort with people perceived as somehow different. This latter type of subtle discrimination includes, in John Calmore's words, "the unconscious failure to extend to a minority the same recognition of humanity, and hence the same sympathy and care, given as a matter of course to one's own group." The selectivity results "often unconsciously—from our tendency to sympathize most readily with those who seem most like ourselves."[27] Yet oppression is not less serious because it is more subtle.

The racist system is made even more complex by its reinforcement in many other aspects of the everyday behavior of white Americans. When whites make racist comments to other whites, or when they think or say racist things when watching television by themselves or with their families, they also reinforce and maintain the white-racist system, even though no blacks are present. Racism is systemic because it infiltrates most aspects of life.

Who Does the Discriminating? Antiblack discrimination comes from all levels and categories of white Americans. Most whites are involved in some way in creating, reinforcing, or maintaining, the racist reality of U.S. society. Depending on the situation and the opportunity to discriminate, very large numbers of whites can and do discriminate. Judging from the housing audit studies cited below, perhaps half of all whites are inclined to discriminate in some fashion, whether subtly or blatantly, in situations where they have housing to rent or sell to black individuals or families. It may well be that whites discriminate at similarly high levels in other major institutional arenas.

There are actively antiracist whites scattered across the nation. They consistently and regularly speak out against white racism, even to the point of risking personal injury, friendships, and jobs. However, in regard to racist practice, most whites seem to fall into three other categories of action. One large group of whites regularly engage in overtly racist behavior; some of these whites are greatly consumed by their racist hatreds, as can be seen in lynchings and hate crimes. A second, much larger, group of whites discriminate against blacks in a variety of ways, as the occasion arises, but they frequently discriminate in less overt or more subtle ways and may often not be consciously aware of their discrimination. A third group of whites are consistently bystanders, engaging in less direct discrimination but knowingly providing support for those who do. Whites in the latter two groups often reject the type of blatant discrimination in which some in the first group engage, and may speak out against it, even as they themselves are engaging in more subtle or covert types of discrimination. Most whites in these three groups routinely think in white-oriented terms when choosing mates, neighborhoods, schools, and business partners. The racist system is thereby reinforced in daily interactions among whites. A sense of white superiority, however dim, seems to be part of the consciousness of most whites, including those who are relatively liberal on racial matters.

Interestingly, when issues of racism are discussed in the mass media, it is often working-class whites, the Archie Bunkers of television fame, who get tagged as the serious racists by the news and other media programs. Blue-collar violence against black Americans often does get significant news attention. Yet elite and middle-class whites are less frequently the focus of attention in media discussions of racial problems, and media discussions of discrimination that do involve a few middle class or elite discriminators usually avoid making connections to broader issues of systemic racism. Indeed, most elite and middle class whites vigorously deny that they are racist.

The portrait of discriminatory practice that emerges from research is quite different. Judging from hundreds of interviews that I and my colleagues have conducted with black and white Americans over the last decade, as well as from numerous other field studies of discrimination in housing, employment, and public accommodations, the majority of whites who do the serious discriminating are those with some power to bring harm, such as white employers, managers, teachers, social workers, real estate agents, lenders, landlords and apartment managers, and police officers.[28] Middle-income and upper-income men and women are heavily implicated in racial oppression, though it is likely that in most major institutional areas, such as corporate promotions and urban policing, white men account for the lion's share of discriminatory actions. Generally speaking, these middle-income and upper-income whites are the ones in a position to most significantly affect black lives. Certainly, whites with less social or economic power also discriminate against black Americans in all income categories. Blue-collar employees frequently harass black workers in the workplace, and blue-collar bigots may yell racist epithets or hurl beer cans at a black man, woman, or child on the street. And working-class whites do seem to predominate as perpetrators in violent attacks on blacks in public places.

Given the right circumstances, most whites in all income groups have the ability to put black Americans "in their place," to frustrate or sabotage their lives for racist reasons. However, the patterns of discrimination vary. Many in the employer class, for instance, may be most interested in the exploitation of black workers, whose lowest-paid members constitute a reserve army of workers. In contrast, those in the white working and middle classes may be more concerned about housing or educational competition with black Americans, and they appear to be the most likely to discriminate in these latter areas.

Facing Lifetimes of Racial Discrimination

Whether subtle, covert, or blatant, racist practices are commonplace and recurring in a great variety of settings, ranging from public accommodations to educational facilities, business arenas, workplaces, and neighborhoods. How frequent is the discrimination faced by black Americans? What forms does this discrimination take? We do not yet have full answers to these questions, but recent surveys are helpful.

Researchers Nancy Krieger and Stephen Sidney gave some 2,000 black respondents a list of seven settings, such as the workplace, where one can face discrimination. Seventy percent of the female and 84 percent of the male respondents reported encountering discrimination in at least one area. The majority reported discrimination in at least three settings.[29] Similarly, a survey in the Detroit area asked black respondents about facing discrimination in six situations. Thirty-two percent reported discrimination recently in at least one of the situations, and four in ten reported facing at least one form of discrimination frequently. In addition, a recent Gallup survey inquired of black respondents if they had experienced discrimination in five areas (work, dining out, shopping, with police, in public transportation) during the last month. Just under half reported discrimination in one or more of these areas, including 70 percent of black men under the age of 35.[30] Many black Americans frequently face racist barriers in an array of societal arenas.

Even these substantial data are likely to be serious underestimates of the frequency of racist obstacles. Short survey questions do not explore the great range of discrimination faced by black Americans in everyday life. Indeed, survey research on the black experience with discrimination is relatively recent and remarkably limited. Survey questions are usually brief and customarily deal with only a few of the many types of racial mistreatment in the society. Indeed, a few survey researchers have suggested that more detailed questioning would reveal a more substantial portrait of discrimination.[31]

There are other reasons why the existing survey data do not adequately describe the reality of everyday racism. Most black and white Americans are taught as children to focus on individual reasons for personal barriers or failures. Most are taught that blaming others, however legitimate that may seem, is generally not appropriate. The reasoning behind such socialization seems to be that a system-blame orientation makes a person seem weak to those she or he respects. Some black Americans who suffer from discrimination may thus feel that talking too much about racist barriers suggests that they as individuals are not capable of dealing with these difficulties. However, this reluctance to report to survey researchers some of the discrimination they experience does not mean that the discrimination is not harmful in the respondent's life.

In addition, the terminology used in most surveys leads to underestimates. The term "discrimination" itself is used by some black Americans only for very serious abuse by whites. Lesser forms of mistreatment, because they are so commonplace, may not be characterized as discrimination. For example, a young black college professor recently explained to me that he does not ordinarily think of certain everyday examples of differential treatment—such as white cashiers not putting money in his hand because they do not want to touch a black person—as "racial discrimination." It is the more serious incidents of racism that he would recall if asked a question by a pollster about having encountered racial discrimination recently. Racial obstacles are so much a part of black lives that they generally become a part of the societal woodwork. This "everydayness" of racist barriers means that for many black Americans a survey researcher's brief question about discrimination will bring quickly to mind primarily the more serious incidents that stay at the front of the mind—and sometimes not the many intrusions of more subtle racism that occur in one's life. A failure to recall some incidents with whites when questioned briefly does not mean these encounters are of little consequence. In order to survive in a racist society, black Americans cannot attend consciously to all the racist incidents that intrude on their lives. The personal and family cost of too-close attention to much discrimination is too great.

To my knowledge, there is no research on the frequency of the incidents and events of discrimination faced by individual black Americans over their lifetimes. In a few exploratory interviews with black respondents, I have asked a question about frequency and gotten large estimates in response. For example, I asked a retired printer from New York City how often he has faced discrimination over the course of his life. After some careful reflection, this man estimated that he confronts at least 250 significant incidents of discrimination from whites each year, if he only includes the incidents that he consciously notices and records. Blatant and subtle mistreatment by white clerks in stores and restaurants are examples he had in mind. Judging from my own field studies using in-depth interviews with black Americans, this man's experience seems representative. Over the course of a lifetime, a typical black man or woman likely faces *thousands* of instances of blatant, covert, or subtle discrimination at the hands of whites. Today, this omnipresent and routinized discrimination remains a key mechanism in the social reproduction of systemic racism.

Racial Discrimination in Public Places

The Ecology of Oppression Racial oppression has a distinctive spatial dimension, and its character can vary as a black person travels from the private home site to more public spaces. In one study that interviewed a large number of middle-class black Americans, a professor at a major university noted the stress that comes from dealing with whites in public places:

> If I'm in those areas that are fairly protected, within gatherings of my own group, other African Americans, or if I'm in the university where my status as a professor mediates against the way I might be perceived, mediates against the hostile perception, then it's fairly comfortable.... When I divide my life into encounters with the outside world, and of course that's ninety percent of my life, it's fairly consistently unpleasant at those sites where there's nothing that mediates between my race and what I have to do. For example, if I'm in a grocery store, if I'm in my car, which is a 1970 Chevrolet, a real old ugly car, all those things—being in a grocery store in casual clothes, or being in the car—sort of advertises something that doesn't have anything to do with my status as far as people I run into are concerned.[32]

The increase in unpleasant encounters that comes as this professor moves from her home into public arenas such as stores is attributed to the absence of mediating factors such as whites knowing that she is a professor. Much antiblack discrimination occurs outside social contexts where there are family or friends or symbols of status that may reduce the likelihood of discrimination. On the way to work or school there can be unpleasant contacts with white police officers, white clerks who will not touch your hand, white teenagers at a traffic light, or white customers in stores who are rude. These racist practices are not limited to one setting but rather take place across many public arenas.

Discrimination in Public Places Psychological researchers have staged situations of possible discrimination in public places, and have discovered that white bystanders will often not respond to a black person's call for help in a staged emergency situation. In contrast, whites are much more likely to respond to calls for help from a white person.[33] One study found that when a black woman drops a bag of groceries in a public setting, a white person is less likely to help her than to help a white woman who has the same mishap.[34] The racial identity of the person needing help strongly affects white responses. Overt dislike of black people is one likely reason. One analyst has suggested yet another possible reason for the white reactions: The more whites see of black people suffering, such as in the media, the more they come to see that condition as normal, and the less sympathy they have for blacks in difficulty.[35]

In a recent Gallup survey asking black respondents about discrimination in various settings in the preceding month, retail shopping was the area in which the largest percentage (30 percent) of the sample reported racial mistreatment. Indeed, 45 percent of the young men in this sample reported such discrimination. Twenty-one percent of the sample (and 32 percent of young men) also reported discrimination when dining out. Discrimination in dining includes very poor service that seems racially motivated and often being seated in an undesirable place, such as at the back of the restaurant near the kitchen. Discrimination in retail stores encompasses the extra surveillance often faced by black shoppers and other discrimination by white sales clerks. In this survey, moreover, those black respondents with higher incomes reported encountering more discrimination than those with lower incomes.[36] Leanita McClain, a prize-winning black columnist for the *Chicago Tribune*, once suggested an important difference between contemporary racist practices and the old segregationist practices: "The old racism wouldn't let blacks into some stores; the new racism assumes that any black person, no matter how well dressed, in a store is probably there to steal, not to buy." Undoubtedly drawing on her own experience, she added that the old racism "didn't have to address black people; the new racism is left speechless when a black, approached condescendingly, has an eloquent comeback."[37]

Black customers face discrimination in the buying process. One major Chicago study examined more than 180 buyer-salesperson negotiations at ninety car dealerships. Black and white testers, with similar economic characteristics and bargaining scripts, posed as car buyers. White male testers got much better prices from the salespeople than did white women or black men and women. Compared to the markup given to white men, black men paid twice the markup and black women paid more than three times the markup. The average dealer profit in the final offers to each category of tester was as follows: white men, $362; white women, $504; black men, $783; and black women, $1237. In another study the researchers used thirty-eight testers who bargained for some 400 cars at 242 dealers. Again, black testers were quoted much higher prices than white men, though this time black men were quoted the highest prices.[38] In some cases racist language was used by salespeople, but the researchers concluded that the more serious problem was stereotyping about how much black customers will pay. The cost of this commonplace discrimination is high. Given that black customers pay two to three times the markup offered to white men—if this holds across the nation—then black customers "annually would pay $150 million more for new cars than do white males."[39]

Discrimination has also been found in professional services. Recently, one group of researchers used actors to portray black and white patients with certain coronary disease symptoms. A total of 720 physicians were asked to look at these recorded interviews and other patient data, to assess the probability of coronary artery disease, and to suggest treatment. The researchers found differences in proposed treatment: blacks, and especially black women, were less likely to be recommended for cardiac catheterization, compared to whites with the same dress, occupations, and medical histories.[40] Another recent study reported in the *New England Journal of Medicine* found that black patients with lung cancer were less likely to receive the best surgical treatment than white patients.[41] The reasons for these patterns of differential medical treatment along racial lines are yet to be delineated, but they may include not only traditional racial stereotypes but also specific stereotypes shared by some white medical practitioners, such as the notion that black patients who get special or expensive treatments are not as likely as whites to take proper care of themselves after treatment. The explanation for differences in surgery may also include the reluctance on the part of some black patients to trust the recommendations of white physicians. More research remains to be done, but there is no reason to expect that the racism of the larger society does not extend into the medical professions.

NOTES

1. James R. Kluegel and Eliot R. Smith, *Beliefs about Inequality* (New York: Aldine de Gruyter, 1986), pp. 186–87.
2. Ibid., p. 190.
3. General Social Survey, National Opinion Research Center, Chicago, Illinois, 1990.
4. Matthew P. Smith, "Bridging the Gulf Between Blacks & Whites," *Pittsburgh Post-Gazette*, April 7, 1996, A1.
5. Robert J. Blendon et al., "The Public and the President's Commission on Race," *The Public Perspective*, February, 1998, 66.
6. Scot Lehigh, "Conflicting views of Massachusetts; Poll Shows a Sharp Racial Divide over the State of Equality," *Boston Globe*, June 14, 1998, B1.
7. See Joe R. Feagin and Clairece B. Feagin, *Racial and Ethnic Relations*, 6th ed. (Upper Saddle River, NJ: Prentice-Hall, 1999), pp. 254–62.
8. Feagin and Vera, *White Racism*, pp. 160–61.
9. Jerome M. Culp, Jr., "Water Buffalo and Diversity: Naming Names and Reclaiming the Racial Discourse," *Connecticut Law Review* 26 (Fall 1993): 209.
10. Richard Delgado, *The Coming Race War?* (New York: New York University Press, 1996), p. 12.
11. Patricia G. Devine, "Stereotypes and Prejudice: Their Automatic and Controlled Components," *Journal of Personality and Social Psychology* 56 (1989): 15–16. I draw on the summary of Devine's work in Feldman, *Social Psychology*, p. 97.

12. David Wellman, *Portraits of White Racism* (Cambridge: Cambridge University Press, 1977), p. 42.

13. David O. Sears, "Symbolic Racism," in *Eliminating Racism*, eds. Phyllis A. Katz and Dalmas A. Taylor (New York: Plenum, 1988), pp. 55–58; and Lawrence Bobo, "Group Conflict, Prejudice, and the Paradox of Contemporary Racial Attitudes," in *Eliminating Racism*, eds. Katz and Taylor, pp. 99–101; and Michael Hughes, "Symbolic Racism, Old-Fashioned Racism, and Whites' Opposition to Affirmative Action," in *Racial Attitudes in the 1990s: Continuity and Change*, eds. Steven A. Tuch and Jack K. Martin (Westport, CT: Praeger, 1997), p. 73–74.

14. Lawrence Bobo, James R. Kluegel, and Ryan A. Smith, "Laissez-Faire Racism: The Crystallization of a Kinder, Gentler, Antiblack Ideology," in *Racial Attitudes in the 1990s: Continuity and Change*, eds. Steven A. Tuch and Jack K. Martin (Westport, CT: Praeger, 1997), pp. 25, 39. They draw on the survey data in Schuman, Steeh, and Bobo, *Racial Attitudes in America: Trends and Interpretations*.

15. Sidney Verba and Gary R. Orren, *Equality in America: The View from the Top* (Cambridge, MA: Harvard University Press, 1985), p. 63.

16. Everett C. Ladd, "Rethinking the Sixties." *The American Enterprise*, May/June 1995, 102.

17. Blendon et al., "The Public and the President's Commission on Race," p. 66.

18. Lehigh, "Conflicting views of Massachusetts; Poll Shows a Sharp Racial Divide over the State of Equality," B1.

19. Smith, "Bridging the Gulf Between Blacks & Whites," p. A1.

20. Robert M. Entman, "Manufacturing Discord: Media in the Affirmative Action Debate," *Press/Politics* 2 (1997): 36.

21. Blendon et al., "The Public and the President's Commission on Race," p. 66.

22. Ruth Frankenberg, *White Women, Race Matters* (Minneapolis: University of Minnesota Press, 1993), pp 228–29.

23. Joyce E. King, "Dysconscious Racism: Ideology, Identity, and the Miseducation of Teachers," *Journal of Negro Education* 60 (1991): 138.

24. Survey results cited in Blendon et al., "The Public and the President's Commission on Race," p. 66.

25. Essed, *Understanding Everyday Racism*, p. 50.

26. Joe R. Feagin and Melvin P. Sikes, *Living With Racism: The Black Middle-Class Experience* (Boston: Beacon Press, 1994), p. 54.

27. John O. Calmore, "To Make Wrong Right: The Necessary and Proper Aspirations of Fair Housing," in *The State of Black America 1989* (New York: National Urban League, 1989), p. 89.

28. See Feagin and Sikes, *Living With Racism*; Joe R. Feagin, Hernan Vera, and Nikitah Imani, *The Agony of Education: Black Students at White Colleges and Universities* (New York: Routledge, 1996); and Yanick St. Jean and Joe R. Feagin, *Double Burden: Black Women and Everyday Racism* (New York: M. E. Sharpe, 1998).

29. Nancy Krieger and Stephen Sidney, "Racial Discrimination and Blood Pressure," *American Journal of Public Health* 86 (1996): 1370–78.

30. Tyrone Forman, David R. Williams, and James S. Jackson, "Race, Place, and Discrimination," in *Perspectives on Social Problems*, ed. Carol Brooks Gardner (Stamford, CT: JAI Press, 1997), pp. 231–61; Gallup Organization, *Black/White Relations in the United States* (Princeton, NJ: Gallup Organization, 1997), pp. 29–30, 108–10.

31. Lee Sigelman and Susan Welch, *Black Americans' Views of Racial Inequality: The Dream Deferred* (Cambridge: Cambridge University Press, 1991), p. 59.

32. Feagin and Sikes, *Living With Racism*, pp. 20–21.

33. John F. Dovidio, "The Subtlety of Racism," *Training and Development*, April 1993, 51–55.

34. Faye Crosby et al., "Recent Unobtrusive Studies of Black and White Discrimination and Prejudice: A Literature Review," *Psychological Bulletin* 87 (1980): 546.

35. Delgado, *The Coming Race War?*, p. 17.

36. Gallup, *Black/White Relations in the United States*, pp. 29–30, 108–10.

37. Leanita McClain, "The Insidious New Racism," in *A Foot in Each World*, ed. Clarence Page (Evanston, IL: Northwestern University Press, 1986), pp. 20–21.

38. Ian Ayres, "Fair Driving: Gender and Race Discrimination in Retail Car Negotiations," *Harvard Law Review* 104 (February 1991): 820, 829–30.

39. Ibid., p. 824.

40. Kevin A. Schulman et al., "The Effect of Race and Sex on Physicians' Recommendations for Cardiac Catherization," *New England Journal of Medicine* (February 25, 1999): 618–26; Peter B. Bach et al., "Racial Differences in the Treatment of Early-Stage Lung Cancer," *New England Journal of Medicine* (October 14, 1999): 1198–1205.

41. Benjamin B. Ringer, *"We the People" and Others* (New York: Tavistock, 1983), p. 327.

STUDY QUESTIONS

1. The author writes: "Being white, one might say, means rarely or never having to think about it." What does the author mean? Why do people of color have to think about their racial/ethnic identity?

2. Research shows that whites and non-whites disagree about how pervasive **racism** is and what causes it. What accounts for this difference in perspective? What does this conflict tell us about how our social statuses affect our perception of the world?

3. The author writes: "Psychologist Patricia Devine has suggested that whites who reject overtly prejudiced views can still hold less consciously prejudiced thoughts that stem from prior socialization." What do you think? Is it possible that you have **prejudices** or **biases** that are inconsistent with your self-image?

4. Feagin argues that many whites value and support the principles of equality, but do not support the policies needed to put these principles into action. How do such views allow whites to hold a positive sense of self while simultaneously supporting continued racial inequality?

MARY C. WATERS

Optional Ethnicities:
For Whites Only?

What are you?" asks a person you've just met at a party. How would you respond to this question? Would you describe your ethnic background? Would you say American? Would you be offended and walk away? In this article Mary Waters suggests that inside your answer we can learn a great deal about your ethnic **identity**, how much it influences your day-to-day life, and how people of your ethnic identity are treated by **society** at large.

ETHNIC IDENTITY FOR WHITES IN THE 1990S

WHAT DOES IT MEAN TO TALK ABOUT ETHNICITY AS AN OPTION for an individual? To argue that an individual has some degree of choice in their ethnic identity flies in the face of the common sense notion of ethnicity many of us believe in—that one's ethnic identity is a fixed characteristic, reflective of blood ties and given at birth. However, social scientists who study ethnicity have long concluded that while ethnicity is based in a *belief* in a common ancestry, ethnicity is primarily a *social* phenomenon, not a biological one (Alba 1985, 1990; Barth 1969; Weber [1921] 1968, p. 389). The belief that members of an ethnic group have that they share a common ancestry may not be a fact. There is a great deal of change in ethnic identities across generations through intermarriage, changing allegiances, and changing social categories. There is also a much larger amount of change in the identities of individuals over their life than is commonly believed. While most people are aware of the phenomena known as "passing"—people raised as one race who change at some point and claim a different race as their identity, there are similar life course changes in ethnicity that happen all the time and are not given the same degree of attention as "racial passing."

White Americans of European ancestry can be described as having a great deal of choice in terms of their ethnic identities. The two major types of options White Americans can exercise are (1) the option of whether to claim any specific ancestry, or to just be "White" or American, [Lieberson (1985) called these people "unhyphenated Whites"] and (2) the choice of which of their European ancestries to choose to include in their description of their own identities. In both cases, the option of choosing how to present yourself on surveys and in everyday social interactions exists for Whites because of social changes and societal conditions that have created a great deal of social mobility, immigrant assimilation, and political and economic power for Whites in the United States. Specifically, the option of being able to not claim any ethnic identity exists for Whites of European background in the United States because they are the majority group—in terms of holding political and social power, as well as being a numerical majority. The option of choosing among different ethnicities in their family backgrounds exists because the degree of discrimination and social distance attached to specific European backgrounds has diminished over time.

The Ethnic Miracle

When European immigration to the United States was sharply curtailed in the late 1920s, a process was set in motion whereby the European ethnic groups already in the United States were for all intents and purposes cut off from any new arrivals. As a result, the composition of the ethnic groups began to age generationally. The proportion of each ethnic group made up of immigrants or the first generation began to gradually decline, and the proportion made up of the children, grandchildren, and eventually great-grandchildren began to increase. Consequently, by 1990 most European-origin ethnic groups in the United States were composed of a very small number of immigrants, and a very large proportion of people whose link to their ethnic origins in Europe was increasingly remote.

This generational change was accompanied by unprecedented social and economic changes. The very success of the assimilation process these groups experienced makes it difficult to imagine how much the question of the immigrants' eventual assimilation was an open one at the turn of the century. At the peak of immigration from southern and central Europe there was widespread discrimination and hostility against the newcomers by established Americans. Italians, Poles, Greeks, and Jews were called derogatory names, attacked by nativist mobs, and derided in the press. Intermarriage across ethnic lines was very uncommon—castelike in the words of some sociologists (Pagnini and Morgan 1990). The immigrants and their children were residentially segregated, occupationally specialized, and generally poor.

After several generations in the United States, the situation has changed a great deal. The success and social mobility of the grandchildren and great-grandchildren of that massive wave of immigrants from Europe has been called "The Ethnic Miracle" (Greeley 1976). These Whites have moved away from the inner-city ethnic ghettos to White middle-class suburban homes. They are doctors, lawyers, entertainers, academics, governors, and Supreme Court justices. But contrary to what some social science theorists and some politicians predicted or hoped for, these middle-class Americans have not completely given up ethnic identity. Instead, they have maintained some connection with their immigrant ancestors' identities—becoming Irish American doctors, Italian American Supreme Court justices, and Greek American presidential candidates. In the tradition of cultural pluralism, successful middle-class Americans in the late twentieth century maintain some degree of identity with their ethnic backgrounds. They have remained "hyphenated Americans." So while social mobility and declining discrimination have created the option of not identifying with any European ancestry, most White Americans continue to report some ethnic background.

With the growth in intermarriage among people of European ethnic origins, increasingly these people are of mixed ethnic ancestry. This gives them the option of which ethnicity to identify with. The U.S. census has asked a question on ethnic ancestry in the 1980 and 1990 censuses. In 1980, 52 percent of the American public responded with a single ethnic ancestry, 31 percent gave multiple ethnic origins (up to three were coded, but some individuals wrote in more than three), and only 6 percent said they were American only, while the remaining 11 percent gave no response. In 1990 about 90 percent of the population gave some response to the ancestry question, with only 5 percent giving American as a response and only 1.4 percent reporting an uncodeable response such as "don't know" (McKenney and Cresce 1992; U.S. Bureau of the Census 1992b).

Several researchers have examined the pattern of responses of people to the census ancestry question. These analyses have shown a pattern of flux and inconsistency in ethnic ancestry reporting. For instance, Lieberson and Waters (1986; 1988, p. 93) have found that parents simplify children's ancestries when reporting them to the census. For instance, among the offspring in situations where one parent reports a specific single White ethnic origin and the other parent reports a different single White origin, about 40 percent of the children are not described as the logical combination of the parents ancestries. For example, only about 60 percent of the children of English-German marriages are labeled as English-German or German-English. About 15 percent of the children of these parents are simplified to just English, and another 15 percent are reported as just German. The remainder of the children are either not given an ancestry or are described as American (Lieberson and Waters 1986, 1993).

In addition to these intergenerational changes, researchers have found changes in reporting ancestry that occur at the time of marriage or upon leaving home. At the ages of eighteen to twenty-two, when many young Americans leave home for the first time, the number of people reporting a single as opposed to a multiple ancestry goes up. Thus while parents simplify children's ancestries when they leave home, children themselves tend to report less complexity in their ancestries when they leave their parents' homes and begin reporting their ancestries themselves (Lieberson and Waters 1986, 1988; Waters 1990).

These individual changes are reflected in variability over time in the aggregate numbers of groups determined by the census and surveys. Farley (1991) compared the consistency of the overall counts of different ancestry groups in the 1979 Current Population Survey, the 1980 census, and the 1986 National Content Test (a pretest for the 1990 census). He found much less consistency in the numbers for northern European ancestry groups whose immigration peaks were early in the nineteenth century—the English, Dutch, Germans, and other northern European groups. In other words each of these different surveys and the census yielded a different estimate of the number of people having this ancestry. The 1990 census also showed a great deal of flux and inconsistency in some ancestry groups. The number of people reporting English as an ancestry went down considerably from 1980, while the number reporting German ancestry went up. The number of Cajuns grew dramatically. This has led officials at the Census Bureau to assume that the examples used in the instructions strongly influence the responses people give. (Cajun was one of the examples of an ancestry given in 1990 but not in 1980, and German was the first example given. English was an example in the 1980 instructions, but not in 1990.)

All of these studies point to the socially variable nature of ethnic identity—and the lack of equivalence between ethnic ancestry and identity. If merely adding a category to the instructions to the question increases the number of people claiming that ancestry, what does that mean about the level of importance of that identity for people answering the census? Clearly identity and ancestry for Whites in the United States, who increasingly are from mixed backgrounds, involves some change and choice.

Symbolic Ethnicities for White Americans

What do these ethnic identities mean to people and why do they cling to them rather than just abandoning the tie and calling themselves American? My own field research with suburban Whites in California and Pennsylvania found that later-generation descendants of European origin maintain what are called "symbolic ethnicities." Symbolic ethnicity is a term coined by Herbert Gans (1979) to refer to ethnicity that is individualistic in nature and without real social cost for the individual. These symbolic identifications are essentially leisure time activities, rooted in nuclear family traditions and reinforced by the voluntary enjoyable aspects of being ethnic (Waters 1990). Richard Alba (1990) also found later-generation Whites in Albany, New York, who chose to keep a tie with an ethnic identity because of the enjoyable and voluntary aspects to those identities, along with the feelings of specialness they entailed. An example of symbolic ethnicity is individuals who identify as Irish, for example, on occasions such as Saint Patrick's Day, on family holidays, or for vacations. They do not usually belong to Irish American organizations, live in Irish neighborhoods, work in Irish jobs, or marry other Irish people. The symbolic meaning of being Irish American can be constructed by individuals from mass media images, family traditions, or other intermittent social activities. In other words, for later-generation White ethnics, ethnicity is not something that influences their lives unless they want it to. In the world of work and school and neighborhood, individuals do not have to admit to being ethnic unless they choose to. And for an increasing number of European-origin individuals whose parents and grandparents have intermarried, the ethnicity they claim is largely a matter of personal choice as they sort through all of the possible combinations of groups in their genealogies.

Individuals can choose those aspects of being Italian, for instance, that appeal to them, and discard those that do not. Or a person whose father is Italian, and mother part Polish and part French, might choose among the three ethnicities and present herself as a Polish American. For instance, a nineteen-year-old college student, interviewed in California in 1986, told me he would have answered Irish on the 1980 census form that asked about ethnic ancestry. These are his reasons:

Q: Why would you have answered that?

A: Well my Dad's name is Kerrigan and my mom's name is O'Leary, and I do have some German in me, but if you figure it out, I am about 75% Irish, so I usually say I am Irish.

Q: You usually don't say German when people ask?

A: No, no, I never say I am German. My dad just likes being Irish. . . . I don't know I just never think of myself as being German.

Q: So your dad's father is the one who immigrated?

A: Yes. On his side is Irish for generations. And then my grandmother's name is Dubois, which is French, partly German, partly French, and then the rest of the family is all Irish. So it is only the maternal grandmother who messes up the line. (Waters 1990, p. 10)

Thus in the course of a few questions, this man labeled himself Irish, admitted to being part German but not identifying with it, and then as an afterthought added that he was also part French. This is not an unusual case. With just a little probing, many people will describe a variety of ancestries in their family background, but do not consider these ancestries to be a salient part of their own identities. Thus the 1990 census ancestry question, which estimated that 30 percent of the population is of mixed ancestry, most surely underestimates the degree of mixing among the population. My research, and the research of Richard Alba (1990), shows that many people have already sorted through what they know of their ethnic ancestries and simplified their responses before they ever answer a census or survey question (Waters 1990).

But note that this freedom to include or exclude ancestries in your identification to yourself and others would not be the same for those defined racially in our society. They are constrained to identify with the part of their ancestry that has been socially defined as the "essential" part. African Americans, for example, have been highly socially constrained to identify as Blacks, without other options available to them, even when they know that their forebears included many people of American Indian or European background. Up until the mid-twentieth century, many state governments had specific laws defining one as Black if as little as one-thirty-second of one's ancestors were defined as Black (Davis 1991; Dominguez 1986; Spickard 1989). Even now when the one drop rule[1] has been dropped from our legal codes, there are still strong societal pressures on African Americans to identify in a particular way. Certain ancestries take precedence over others in the societal rules on descent and ancestry reckoning. If one believes one is part English and part German and identifies in a survey as German, one is not in danger of being accused of trying to "pass" as non-English and of being "redefined" English by the interviewer. But if one were part African and part German, one's self identification as German would be highly suspect and probably not accepted if one "looked" Black according to the prevailing social norms.

This is reflected in the ways the census collects race and ethnic identity. While the ethnic ancestry question used in 1980 and 1990 is given to all Americans in the sample regardless of race and allows multiple responses that combine races, the primary source of information on people defined racially in the United States is the census race question or the Hispanic question. Both of these questions require a person to make a choice about an identity. Individuals are not allowed to respond that they are both Black and White, or Japanese and Asian Indian on the race question even if they know that is their background. In fact, people who disobey the instructions to the census race question and check off two races are assigned to the first checked race in the list by the Census Bureau.

In responding to the ancestry question, the comparative latitude that White respondents have does not mean that Whites pick and choose ethnicities out of thin air. For the most part people choose an identity that corresponds with some element of their family tree. However, there are many anecdotal instances of people adopting ethnicities when they marry or move to a strongly identified neighborhood or community. For instance Micaela di Leonardo (1984) reported instances of non-Italian women who married into Italian American families and "became Italian." Karen Leonard (1992) describes a community of Mexican American women who married Punjabi immigrants in California. Some of the Punjabi immigrants and their descendants were said to have "become Mexican" when they joined their wives' kin group and

---

[1] Reference to laws and customs defining a person as Black if he or she had "one drop" of Black blood—that is, any African ancestry at all.

social worlds. Alternatively she describes the community acknowledging that Mexican women made the best curry, as they adapted to life with Indian-origin men.

But what do these identities mean to individuals? Surely an identity that is optional in a number of ways—not legally defined on a passport or birth certificate, not socially consequential in terms of societal discrimination in terms of housing or job access, and not economically limiting in terms of blocking opportunities for social mobility—cannot be the same as an identity that results from and is nurtured by societal exclusion and rejection. The choice to have a symbolic ethnicity is an attractive and widespread one despite its lack of demonstrable content, because having a symbolic ethnicity combines individuality with feelings of community. People reported to me that they liked having an ethnic identity because it gave them a uniqueness and a feeling of being special. They often contrasted their own specialness by virtue of their ethnic identities with "bland" Americanness. Being ethnic makes people feel unique and special and not just "vanilla" as one of my respondents put it. For instance, one woman describes the benefits she feels from being Czech American:

> I work in an office and a lot of people in there always talk about their background. It's weird because it is a big office and people are of all different backgrounds. People are this or that. It is interesting I think to find out. Especially when it is something you do not hear a lot about. Something that is not common like Lithuania or something. That's the good part about being Czech. People think it is something different. (Waters 1990, p. 154)

Because "American" is largely understood by Americans to be a political identity and allegiance and not an ethnic one, the idea of being "American" does not give people the same sense of belonging that their hyphenated American identity does. When I asked people about their dual identities—American and Irish or Italian or whatever—they usually responded in a way that showed how they conceived of the relationship between the two identities. Being an American was their primary identity; but it was so primary that they rarely, if ever, thought about it—most commonly only when they left the country. Being Irish American, on the other hand, was a way they had of differentiating themselves from others whom they interacted with from day to day—in many cases from spouses or in laws. Certain of their traits—being emotional, having a sense of humor, talking with their hands—were understood as stemming from their ethnicity. Yet when asked about their identity as Americans, that identity was both removed from their day-to-day consciousness and understood in terms of loyalty and patriotism. Although they may not think they behave or think in a certain way because they are American, being American is something they are both proud of and committed to.

Symbolic ethnicity is the best of all worlds for these respondents. These White ethnics can claim to be unique and special, while simultaneously finding the community and conformity with others that they also crave. But that "community" is of a type that will not interfere with a person's individuality. It is not as if these people belong to ethnic voluntary organizations or gather as a group in churches or neighborhoods or union halls. They work and reside within the mainstream of American middle-class life, yet they retain the interesting benefits—the "specialness"—of ethnic allegiance, without any of its drawbacks.

It has been suggested by several researchers that this positive value attached to ethnic ancestry, which became popular in the ethnic revival of the 1970s, is the result of assimilation having proceeded to an advanced stage for descendants of White Europeans (Alba 1985; Crispino 1980; Steinberg 1981). Ironically, people celebrate and embrace their ethnic backgrounds precisely because assimilation has proceeded to the point where such identification does not have that much influence on their day-to-day life. Rather than choosing the "least ethnic" and most bland ethnicities, Whites desire the "most ethnic" ones, like the once-stigmatized "Italian," because it is perceived as bringing the most psychic benefits. For instance, when an Italian father is married to an English or a Scottish or a German mother, the likelihood is that the child will be reported to the census with the father's Italian ancestry, rather than the northern European ancestries, which would have been predicted to have a higher social status. Italian is a good ancestry to have, people told me, because they have good food and a warm family life. This change in the social meaning of being Italian American is quite dramatic, given that Italians were subject to discrimination, exclusion, and extreme negative stereotyping in the early part of the twentieth century.

RACE RELATIONS AND SYMBOLIC ETHNICITY

However much symbolic ethnicity is without cost for the individual, there is a cost associated with symbolic ethnicity for the society. That is because symbolic ethnicities of the type described here are confined to White Americans of European origin. Black Americans, Hispanic Americans, Asian Americans, and American Indians do not have the option of a symbolic ethnicity at present in the United States. For all of the ways in which ethnicity does not matter for White Americans, it does matter for non-Whites. Who your ancestors are does affect your choice of spouse, where you live, what job you have, who your friends are, and what your chances are for success in American society, if those ancestors happen not to be from Europe. The reality is that White ethnics have a lot more choice and room for maneuver than they themselves think they do. The situation is very different for members of racial minorities, whose lives are strongly influenced by their race or national origin regardless of how much they may choose not to identify themselves in terms of their ancestries.

When White Americans learn the stories of how their grandparents and great-grandparents triumphed in the United States over adversity, they are usually told in terms of their individual efforts and triumphs. The important role of labor unions and other organized political and economic actors in their social and economic successes are left out of the story in favor of a generational story of individual Americans rising up against communitarian, Old World intolerance and New World resistance. As a result, the "individualized" voluntary, cultural view of ethnicity for Whites is what is remembered.

One important implication of these identities is that they tend to be very individualistic. There is a tendency to view valuing diversity in a pluralist environment as equating all groups. The symbolic ethnic tends to think that all groups are equal; everyone has a background that is their right to celebrate and pass on to their children. This leads to the conclusion that all identities are equal and all identities in some sense are interchangeable—"I'm Italian American, you're Polish American. I'm Irish American, you're African American." The important thing is to treat people as individuals and all equally. However, this assumption ignores the very big difference between an individualistic symbolic ethnic identity and a socially enforced and imposed racial identity.

My favorite example of how this type of thinking can lead to some severe misunderstandings between people of different backgrounds is from the *Dear Abby* advice column. A few years back a person wrote in who had asked an acquaintance of Asian background where his family was from. His acquaintance answered that this was a rude question and he would not reply. The bewildered White asked Abby why it was rude, since he thought it was a sign of respect to wonder where people were from, and he certainly would not mind anyone asking HIM about where his family was from. Abby asked her readers to write in to say whether it was rude to ask about a person's ethnic background. She reported that she got a large response, that most non-Whites thought it was a sign of disrespect, and Whites thought it was flattering:

Dear Abby,

I am 100 percent American and because I am of Asian ancestry I am often asked "What are you?" It's not the personal nature of this question that bothers me, it's the question itself. This query seems to question my very humanity. "What am I? Why I am a person like everyone else!"

Signed, A REAL AMERICAN

Dear Abby,

Why do people resent being asked what they are? The Irish are so proud of being Irish, they tell you before you even ask. Tip O'Neill has never tried to hide his Irish ancestry.

Signed, JIMMY.

In this exchange JIMMY cannot understand why Asians are not as happy to be asked about their ethnicity as he is, because he understands his ethnicity and theirs to be separate but equal. Everyone has to come from somewhere—his family from

Ireland, another's family from Asia—each has a history and each should be proud of it. But the reason he cannot understand the perspective of the Asian American is that all ethnicities are not equal; all are not symbolic, costless, and voluntary. When White Americans equate their own symbolic ethnicities with the socially enforced identities of non-White Americans, they obscure the fact that the experiences of Whites and non-Whites have been qualitatively different in the United States and that the current identities of individuals partly reflect that unequal history.

In the next section I describe how relations between Black and White students on college campuses reflect some of these asymmetries in the understanding of what a racial or ethnic identity means. While I focus on Black and White students in the following discussion, you should be aware that the myriad other groups in the United States—Mexican Americans, American Indians, Japanese Americans—all have some degree of social and individual influences on their identities, which reflect the group's social and economic history and present circumstance.

Relations on College Campuses

Both Black and White students face the task of developing their race and ethnic identities. Sociologists and psychologists note that at the time people leave home and begin to live independently from their parents, often ages eighteen to twenty-two, they report a heightened sense of racial and ethnic identity as they sort through how much of their beliefs and behaviors are idiosyncratic to their families and how much are shared with other people. It is not until one comes in close contact with many people who are different from oneself that individuals realize the ways in which their backgrounds may influence their individual personality. This involves coming into contact with people who are different in terms of their ethnicity, class, religion, region, and race. For White students, the ethnicity they claim is more often than not a symbolic one—with all of the voluntary, enjoyable, and intermittent characteristics I have described.

Black students at the university are also developing identities through interactions with others who are different from them. Their identity development is more complicated than that of Whites because of the added element of racial discrimination and racism, along with the "ethnic" developments of finding others who share their background. Thus Black students have the positive attraction of being around other Black students who share some cultural elements, as well as the need to band together with other students in a reactive and oppositional way in the face of racist incidents on campus.

Colleges and universities across the country have been increasing diversity among their student bodies in the last few decades. This has led in many cases to strained relations among students from different racial and ethnic backgrounds. The 1980s and 1990s produced a great number of racial incidents and high racial tensions on campuses. While there were a number of racial incidents that were due to bigotry, unlawful behavior, and violent or vicious attacks, much of what happens among students on campuses involves a low level of tension and awkwardness in social interactions.

Many Black students experience racism personally for the first time on campus. The upper-middle-class students from White suburbs were often isolated enough that their presence was not threatening to racists in their high schools. Also, their class background was known by their residence and this may have prevented attacks being directed at them. Often Black students at the university who begin talking with other students and recognizing racial slights will remember incidents that happened to them earlier that they might not have thought were related to race.

Black college students across the country experience a sizeable number of incidents that are clearly the result of racism. Many of the most blatant ones that occur between students are the result of drinking. Sometimes late at night, drunken groups of White students coming home from parties will yell slurs at single Black students on the street. The other types of incidents that happen include being singled out for special treatment by employees, such as being followed when shopping at the campus bookstore, or going to the art museum with your class and the guard stops you and asks for your I.D. Others involve impersonal encounters on the street—being called a nigger by a truck driver while crossing the street, or seeing old ladies clutch their pocketbooks and shake in terror as you pass them on the street For the most part these incidents are not specific to the university environment, they are the types of incidents middle-class Blacks face every day throughout American society, and they have been documented by sociologists (Feagin 1991).

In such a climate, however, with students experiencing these types of incidents and talking with each other about them, Black students do experience a tension and a feeling of being singled out. It is unfair that this is part of their college experience and not that of White students. Dealing with incidents like this, or the ever-present threat of such incidents, is an ongoing developmental task for Black students that takes energy, attention, and strength of character. It should be clearly understood that this is an asymmetry in the "college experience" for Black and White students. It is one of the unfair aspects of life that results from living in a society with ongoing racial prejudice and discrimination. It is also very understandable that it makes some students angry at the unfairness of it all, even if there is no one to blame specifically. It is also very troubling because, while most Whites do not create these incidents, some do, and it is never clear until you know someone well whether they are the type of person who could do something like this. So one of the reactions of Black students to these incidents is to band together.

In some sense then, as Blauner (1992) has argued, you can see Black students coming together on campus as both an "ethnic" pull of wanting to be together to share common experiences and community, and a "racial" push of banding together defensively because of perceived rejection and tension from Whites. In this way the ethnic identities of Black students are in some sense similar to, say, Korean students wanting to be together to share experiences. And it is an ethnicity that is generally much stronger than, say, Italian Americans. But for Koreans who come together there is generally a definition of themselves as "different from" Whites. For Blacks reacting to exclusion, there is a tendency for the coming together to involve both being "different from" but also "opposed to" Whites.

The anthropologist John Ogbu (1990) has documented the tendency of minorities in a variety of societies around the world, who have experienced severe blocked mobility for long periods of time, to develop such oppositional identities. An important component of having such an identity is to describe others of your group who do not join in the group solidarity as devaluing and denying their very core identity. This is why it is not common for successful Asians to be accused by others of "acting White" in the United States, but it is quite common for such a term to be used by Blacks and Latinos. The oppositional component of a Black identity also explains how Black people can question whether others are acting "Black enough." On campus, it explains some of the intense pressures felt by Black students who do not make their racial identity central and who choose to hang out primarily with non-Blacks. This pressure from the group, which is partly defining itself by not being White, is exacerbated by the fact that race is a physical marker in American society. No one immediately notices the Jewish students sitting together in the dining hall, or the one Jewish student sitting surrounded by non-Jews, or the Texan sitting with the Californians, but everyone notices the Black student who is or is not at the "Black table" in the cafeteria.

An example of the kinds of misunderstandings that can arise because of different understandings of the meanings and implications of symbolic versus oppositional identities concerns questions students ask one another in the dorms about personal appearances and customs. A very common type of interaction in the dorm concerns questions Whites ask Blacks about their hair. Because Whites tend to know little about Blacks, and Blacks know a lot about Whites, there is a general asymmetry in the level of curiosity people have about one another. Whites, as the numerical majority, have had little contact with Black culture; Blacks, especially those who are in college, have had to develop bicultural skills—knowledge about the social worlds of both Whites and Blacks. Miscommunication and hurt feelings about White students' questions about Black students' hair illustrate this point. One of the things that happens freshman year is that White students are around Black students as they fix their hair. White students are generally quite curious about Black students' hair—they have basic questions such as how often Blacks wash their hair, how they get it straightened or curled, what products they use on their hair, how they comb it, etc. Whites often wonder to themselves whether they should ask these questions. One thought experiment Whites perform is to ask themselves whether a particular question would upset them. Adopting the "do unto others" rule, they ask themselves, "If a Black person was curious about my hair would I get upset?" The answer usually is "No, I would be happy to tell them." Another example is an Italian American student wondering to herself, "Would

I be upset if someone asked me about calamari?" The answer is no, so she asks her Black roommate about collard greens, and the roommate explodes with an angry response such as, "Do you think all Black people eat watermelon too?" Note that if this Italian American knew her friend was Trinidadian American and asked about peas and rice the situation would be more similar and would not necessarily ignite underlying tensions.

Like the debate in *Dear Abby*, these innocent questions are likely to lead to resentment. The issue of stereotypes about Black Americans and the assumption that all Blacks are alike and have the same stereotypical cultural traits has more power to hurt or offend a Black person than vice versa. The innocent questions about Black hair also bring up a number of asymmetries between the Black and White experience. Because Blacks tend to have more knowledge about Whites than vice versa, there is not an even exchange going on, the Black freshman is likely to have fewer basic questions about his White roommate than his White roommate has about him. Because of the differences historically in the group experiences of Blacks and Whites there are some connotations to Black hair that don't exist about White hair. (For instance, is straightening your hair a form of assimilation, do some people distinguish between women having "good hair" and "bad hair" in terms of beauty and how is that related to looking "White"?). Finally, even a Black freshman who cheerfully disregards or is unaware that there are these asymmetries will soon slam into another asymmetry if she willingly answers every innocent question asked of her. In a situation where Blacks make up only 10 percent of the student body, if every non-Black needs to be educated about hair, she will have to explain it to nine other students. As one Black student explained to me, after you've been asked a couple of times about something so personal you begin to feel like you are an attraction in a zoo, that you are at the university for the education of the White students.

Institutional Responses

Our society asks a lot of young people. We ask young people to do something that no one else does as successfully on such a wide scale—that is to live together with people from very different backgrounds, to respect one another, to appreciate one another, and to enjoy and learn from one another. The successes that occur every day in this endeavor are many, and they are too often overlooked. However, the problems and tensions are also real, and they will not vanish on their own. We tend to see pluralism working in the United States in much the same way some people expect capitalism to work. If you put together people with various interests and abilities and resources, the "invisible hand" of capitalism is supposed to make all the parts work together in an economy for the common good.

There is much to be said for such a model—the invisible hand of the market can solve complicated problems of production and distribution better than any "visible hand" of a state plan. However, we have learned that unequal power relations among the actors in the capitalist marketplace, as well as "externalities" that the market cannot account for, such as long-term pollution, or collusion between corporations, or the exploitation of child labor, means that state regulation is often needed. Pluralism and the relations between groups are very similar. There is a lot to be said for the idea that bringing people who belong to different ethnic or racial groups together in institutions with no interference will have good consequences. Students from different backgrounds will make friends if they share a dorm room or corridor, and there is no need for the institution to do any more than provide the locale. But like capitalism, the invisible hand of pluralism does not do well when power relations and externalities are ignored. When you bring together individuals from groups that are differentially valued in the wider society and provide no guidance, there will be problems. In these cases the "invisible hand" of pluralist relations does not work, and tensions and disagreements can arise without any particular individual or group of individuals being "to blame." On college campuses in the 1990s some of the tensions between students are of this sort. They arise from honest misunderstandings, lack of a common background, and very different experiences of what race and ethnicity mean to the individual.

The implications of symbolic ethnicities for thinking about race relations are subtle but consequential. If your understanding of your own ethnicity and its relationship to society and politics is one of individual choice, it becomes harder to understand the need for programs like affirmative action, which recognize the ongoing need for group struggle and group recognition, in order to bring about social change. It also is hard for a White college student to understand the need that minority students feel to band together against discrimination. It also is easy, on the individual level, to expect everyone else to be able to turn their ethnicity on and off at will, the way you are able to, without understanding that ongoing discrimination and societal attention to minority status makes that impossible for individuals from minority groups to do. The paradox of symbolic ethnicity is that it depends upon the ultimate goal of a pluralist society, and at the same time makes it more difficult to achieve that ultimate goal. It is dependent upon the concept that all ethnicities mean the same thing, that enjoying the traditions of one's heritage is an option available to a group or an individual, but that such a heritage should not have any social costs associated with it.

As the Asian Americans who wrote to *Dear Abby* make clear, there are many societal issues and involuntary ascriptions associated with non-White identities. The developments necessary for this to change are not individual but societal in nature. Social mobility and declining racial and ethnic sensitivity are closely associated. The legacy and the present reality of discrimination on the basis of race or ethnicity must be overcome before the ideal of a pluralist society, where all heritages are treated equally and are equally available for individuals to choose or discard at will, is realized.

STUDY QUESTIONS

1. What does Waters mean when she says ethnicity is largely **socially constructed** and not based on biology?

2. What is **symbolic ethnicity** and why does Waters argue that it is only available for white Americans?

3. Waters argues the experiences of students of color (she discusses African Americans specifically) on college campuses are different from those of their white counterparts. Waters believes that, because of this different treatment, students of color have a very different experience with their ethnic **identity** than white students do. Describe, using Waters's article, how the process of forming your ethnic identity is different for students of color and white students. Be sure to talk about both groups.

4. Write an essay or journal entry describing your ethnic identity. Based on what you learned reading this essay, do you think the way you describe yourself presents an accurate picture? Do you wish that you could describe your identity in a more complex—or a simpler—way? Why?

5. Hold a classroom discussion on whether your campus treats whites and people of color differently. Provide evidence or examples for your opinions. How would you describe racial and ethnic relations on your campus?

NADA EL SAWY

Yes, I Follow Islam,
But I'm Not A Terrorist

What does a terrorist look like? Even years after the September 11 terrorist attacks many still believe that most Muslims are terrorists or at the very least religious fanatics. Many Muslim Americans have faced severe **prejudice** and **discrimination**, and some have been victimized by hate crimes just for being Muslim. In this essay, written a month after the attacks, Nada El Sawy tries to educate her readers about her beliefs, and calls upon others to learn about the beauty and peacefulness of Islam. As you read this piece think of the ways that Muslim Americans still face **stereotypes**.

AS AN EGYPTIAN-AMERICAN AND A MUSLIM, I'VE ALWAYS BEEN dismayed by the way Islam has been generally misrepresented in the media and misunderstood by most Americans. Since the tragic events of Sept. 11. Islam has been in the spotlight, and though leaders such as President George W. Bush and New York Mayor Rudolph Giuliani have made a concerted effort to distinguish it from terrorism, some people still aren't getting the message.

I am a graduate student in journalism, often assigned to write articles about current events. The day after the terrorist attacks I headed out to Brooklyn to cover a story about an Islamic school that had been pelted with rocks and bloody pork chops in the hours after the World Trade Center towers collapsed. Whoever committed this act knew enough about Islam to know that pork is forbidden, but apparently little else about Islamic beliefs. "I wish people would stop calling us terrorists," one sixth grader told me.

When I read about Osama bin Laden or groups like the Egyptian Islamic Jihad, I want to tell them, "You're giving Islam a bad name!" I want to show people that the religion I know is one that calls for patience, harmony and understanding.

Islam may be the world's second largest religion, but in the United States, home to about 6 million of its followers, it remains a mystery. Americans seem to believe that backpacking through Europe or keeping up with the news gives them an understanding of everything about the cultures, religions and traditions that differ from their own. While I'm heartened by the sincere curiosity of some, like the stylist who asked me about my beliefs as he trimmed my hair, most people still have a long way to go.

I have yet to meet anyone—who isn't either especially well read, a religion major or a Muslim—who can accurately describe Islamic beliefs. Many people find it fascinating that I worship Allah without understanding that "Allah" is simply the Arabic word for God. Muslims use the word only because the universal teachings of Islam have been preserved in the Arabic language.

I can recall a Thanksgiving dinner with family friends several years ago when the host offered a small prayer. As we all held hands, he started with the customary thanks for the food, family and friends. Then he proceeded to say, "And thank you to God—or whoever else you choose to worship, may it be Allah . . ." He meant well, but I remember flinching. He and his family had traveled to the Middle East, taken pictures of Muslims praying, read about the cultures they were visiting, but none of it had led to a clear understanding of Islam.

I'm not surprised when classmates confront me with the charge that Muslims around the world are killing in the name of religion. I'm careful not to mention the many Muslims who have been killed in places like Kosovo, Indonesia and Palestine. I don't want to respond with that kind of foolish rebuttal because I abhor the senseless murder of all human beings.

The truth is, fanaticism can spring from misguided excess in any religion, and Muslims who kill in the name of their beliefs are not true Muslims. Aggression is not a tenet of our religion, but rather something that is condemned except in self-defense. The Quran states: "Fight in the cause of Allah those who fight you, but commit no aggression; for Allah loves not transgressors" (al-Baqarah 2:190).

If few people understand that Islam is a peaceful religion, even fewer know how beautiful it can be. When I studied in Cairo during my junior year of college, my grandmother had a religion teacher come to her house every week to teach us the Quran. Hearing him chant the verses was like listening to breathtaking music. There is also an element of poetry in a Muslim's everyday life. One says "Allah" or "ma sha'a Allah" ("as God wills") upon seeing something beautiful, like a sunset or a newborn baby. Whenever family members or friends part, one says, "La illah illa Allah" ("there is only one God") and the other responds, "Muhammad rasoul Allah" ("Muhammad is God's prophet").

To me, informing people about these wonderful aspects of Islam is a pleasure, not a burden. There are signs that Americans may be ready to learn. I was moved recently when I saw a woman on the subway reading a book about Islam to her young daughter. She explained that she was teaching herself, as well as her daughter. If more people take that approach, there will come a day when fanaticism is no longer equated with faith, and Muslims aren't seen as terrorists but as human beings.

STUDY QUESTIONS

1. Why does the author think that many non-Muslim Americans are uninformed about the **religion** of Islam?

2. What consequences do Muslim Americans face because of the public's misperceptions of their faith and the assumption that all Muslims are terrorists?

3. Barack Obama's critics and opponents during his campaign in 2008 asserted that he was really a Muslim despite evidence—and his own assertion—that he was a Christian. Regardless of your political views, why do you think opponents used the assertion to hurt Obama's run to become president? What does it mean about how Americans view Muslims if we use religion as a tool to discredit our political opponents?

4. Many people have suggested that because of the terrorist attacks on 9/11 we should aggressively screen Muslims at the airport. The logic here is that, because the hijackers who flew planes into the Twin Towers were all Muslim men, we should assume all Muslims are terrorists. In 1995 Timothy McVeigh blew up a rented moving truck full of explosives in front of the Alfred P. Murrah Federal Building in Oklahoma City, killing 168 people. In 2010 Joseph Stack III flew a plane into a federal Internal Revenue Service building in Austin, Texas, killing two people and injuring many more. Both of these men were white non-Muslims. Discuss whether we should aggressively screen all white, non-Muslim men who rent moving trucks or attempt to fly planes.

BETSY LUCAL

What It Means to Be Gendered Me:
Life on the Boundaries of a
Dichotomous Gender System

Can people tell you are a woman or man just by looking at you? Can you accurately guess the gender of the people around you? How? Many students think masculinity and femininity are *natural*, but as this article will discuss in detail, **gender**, as defined by many sociologists, is not biological. Gender is a **social construction**, constantly defined and redefined. In this article—which echoes Zora Neale Hurston's famous essay on **race**, "How It Feels to Be Colored Me"—Betsy Lucal talks about the performance of gender and the consequences for people who do not fall into the masculinity/femininity binary. As you read think about how you "do your gender" every day.

I UNDERSTOOD THE CONCEPT OF "DOING GENDER" (WEST AND ZIM-merman 1987) long before I became a sociologist. I have been living with the consequences of inappropriate "gender display" (Goffman 1976; West and Zimmerman 1987) for as long as I can remember.

My daily experiences are a testament to the rigidity of gender in our society, to the real implications of "two and only two" when it comes to sex and gender categories (Garfinkel 1967; Kessler and McKenna 1978). Each day, I experience the consequences that our gender system has for my identity and interactions. I am a woman who has been called "Sir" so many times that I no longer even hesitate to assume that it is being

"What It Means To Be Gendered Me: Life On The Boundaries Of A Dichotomous Gender System" by Betsy Lucal from *Gender & Society*, Vol. 13, No. 6, Dec. 1999, pages 781–797. Used by permission of Sage Publications.

directed at me. I am a woman whose use of public rest rooms regularly causes reactions ranging from confused stares to confrontations over what a man is doing in the women's room. I regularly enact a variety of practices either to minimize the need for others to know my gender or to deal with their misattributions.

I am the embodiment of Lorber's (1994) ostensibly paradoxical assertion that the "gender bending" I engage in actually might serve to preserve and perpetuate gender categories. As a feminist who sees gender rebellion as a significant part of her contribution to the dismantling of sexism, I find this possibility disheartening.

In this article, I examine how my experiences both support and contradict Lorber's (1994) argument using my own experiences to illustrate and reflect on the social construction of gender. My analysis offers a discussion of the consequences of gender for people who do not follow the rules as well as an examination of the possible implications of the existence of people like me for the gender system itself. Ultimately, I show how life on the boundaries of gender affects me and how my life, and the lives of others who make similar decisions about their participation in the gender system, has the potential to subvert gender.

Because this article analyzes my experiences as a woman who often is mistaken for a man, my focus is on the social construction of gender for women. My assumption is that, given the gendered nature of the gendering process itself, men's experiences of this phenomenon might well be different from women's.

THE SOCIAL CONSTRUCTION OF GENDER

It is now widely accepted that gender is a social construction, that sex and gender are distinct, and that gender is something all of us "do." This conceptualization of gender can be traced to Garfinkel's (1967) ethnomethodological study of "Agnes."[1] In this analysis, Garfinkel examined the issues facing a male who wished to pass as, and eventually become, a woman. Unlike individuals who perform gender in culturally expected ways, Agnes could not take her gender for granted and always was in danger of failing to pass as a woman (Zimmerman 1992).

This approach was extended by Kessler and McKenna (1978) and codified in the classic "Doing Gender" by West and Zimmerman (1987). The social constructionist approach has been developed most notably by Lorber (1994, 1996). Similar theoretical strains have developed outside of sociology, such as work by Butler (1990) and Weston (1996). Taken as a whole, this work provides a number of insights into the social processes of gender, showing how gender(ing) is, in fact, a process.

We apply gender labels for a variety of reasons; for example, an individual's gender cues our interactions with her or him. Successful social relations require all participants to present, monitor, and interpret gender displays (Martin 1998; West and Zimmerman 1987). We have, according to Lorber, "no social place for a person who is neither woman nor man" (1994, 96); that is, we do not know how to interact with such a person. There is, for example, no way of addressing such a person that does not rely on making an assumption about the person's gender ("Sir" or "Ma'am"). In this context, gender is "omnirelevant" (West and Zimmerman 1987). Also, given the sometimes fractious nature of interactions between men and women, it might be particularly important for women to know the gender of the strangers they encounter; do the women need to be wary, or can they relax (Devor 1989)?

According to Kessler and McKenna (1978), each time we encounter a new person, we make a gender attribution. In most cases, this is not difficult. We learn how to read people's genders by learning which traits culturally signify each gender and by learning rules that enable us to classify individuals with a wide range of gender presentations into two and only two gender categories. As Weston observed, "Gendered traits are called attributes for a reason: People attribute traits to others. No one possesses them. Traits are the product of evaluation" (1996, 21). The fact that most people use the same traits and rules in presenting genders makes it easier for us to attribute genders to them.

We also assume that we can place each individual into one of two mutually exclusive categories in this binary system. As Bem (1993) notes, we have a polarized view of gender; there are two groups that are seen as polar opposites. Although there is "no rule for deciding 'male' or 'female' that will always work" and no attributes "that always and without exception are true of only one gender" (Kessler and McKenna 1978, 158, 1), we operate under the assumption that there are such rules and attributes.

Kessler and McKenna's analysis revealed that the fundamental schema for gender attribution is to "See someone as female only when you cannot see [the person] as male" (1978, 158). Individuals basically are assumed to be male/men until proven otherwise, that is, until some obvious marker of conventional femininity is noted. In other words, the default reading of a nonfeminine person is that she or he is male; people who do not deliberately mark themselves as feminine are taken to be men. Devor attributed this tendency to the operation of gender in a patriarchal context: "Women must mark themselves as 'other,'" whereas on the other hand, "few cues [are required] to identify maleness" (1989, 152). As with language, masculine forms are taken as the generically human; femininity requires that something be added. Femininity "must constantly reassure its audience by a willing demonstration of difference" (Brownmiller 1984, 15).

Patriarchal constructs of gender also devalue the marked category. Devor (1989) found that the women she calls "gender blenders" assumed that femininity was less desirable than masculinity; their gender blending sometimes was a product of their shame about being women. This assumption affects not only our perceptions of other people but also individuals' senses of their own gendered selves.

Not only do we rely on our social skills in attributing genders to others, but we also use our skills to present our own genders to them. The roots of this understanding of how gender operates lie in Goffman's (1959) analysis of the "presentation of self in everyday life," elaborated later in his work on "gender display" (Goffman 1976). From this perspective, gender is a performance, "a stylized repetition of acts" (Butler 1990, 140, emphasis removed). Gender display refers to "conventionalized portrayals" of social correlates of gender (Goffman 1976). These displays are culturally established sets of behaviors, appearances, mannerisms, and other cues that we have learned to associate with members of a particular gender.

In determining the gender of each person we encounter and in presenting our genders to others, we rely extensively on these gender displays. Our bodies and their adornments provide us with "texts" for reading a person's gender (Bordo 1993). As Lorber noted, "Without the deliberate use of gendered clothing, hairstyles, jewelry, and cosmetics, women and men would look far more alike" (1994, 18–19). Myhre summarized the markers of femininity as "having longish hair; wearing makeup, skirts, jewelry, and high heels; walking with a wiggle; having little or no observable body hair; and being in general soft, rounded (but not too rounded), and sweet-smelling" (1995, 135). (Note that these descriptions comprise a Western conceptualization of gender.) Devor identified "mannerisms, language, facial expressions, dress, and a lack of feminine adornment" (1989, x) as factors that contribute to women being mistaken for men.

A person uses gender display to lead others to make attributions regarding her or his gender, regardless of whether the presented gender corresponds to the person's sex or gender self-identity. Because gender is a social construction, there may be differences among one's sex, gender self-identity (the gender the individual identifies as), presented identity (the gender the person is presenting), and perceived identity (the gender others attribute to the person).[2] For example, a person can be female without being socially identified as a woman, and a male person can appear socially as a woman. Using a feminine gender display, a man can present the identity of a woman and, if the display is successful, be perceived as a woman.

But these processes also mean that a person who fails to establish a gendered appearance that corresponds to the person's gender faces challenges to her or his identity and status. First, the gender nonconformist must find a way in which to construct an identity in a society that denies her or him any legitimacy (Bem 1993). A person is likely to want to define herself or himself as "normal" in the face of cultural evidence to the contrary. Second, the individual also must deal with other people's challenges to identity and status—deciding how to respond, what such reactions to their appearance mean, and so forth.

Because our appearances, mannerisms, and so forth constantly are being read as part of our gender display, we do gender whether we intend to or not. For example, a woman athlete, particularly one participating in a nonfeminine sport such as basketball, might deliberately keep her hair long to show that, despite actions that suggest otherwise, she is a "real" (i.e., feminine) woman. But we also do gender in less conscious ways such as when a man takes up more space when sitting than a woman does. In fact, in a society so clearly organized around gender, as ours is, there is no way in which to not do gender (Lorber 1994).

Given our cultural rules for identifying gender (i.e., that there are only two and that masculinity is assumed in the absence of evidence to the contrary), a person who does not do gender appropriately is placed not into a third category but rather into the one with which her or his gender display seems most closely to fit; that is, if a man appears to be a woman, then he will be categorized as "woman," not as something else. Even if a person does not want to do gender or would like to do a gender other than the two recognized by our society, other people will, in effect, do gender for that person by placing her or him in one and only one of the two available categories. We cannot escape doing gender or, more specifically, doing one of two genders. (There are exceptions in limited contexts such as people doing "drag" [Butler 1990; Lorber 1994].)

People who follow the norms of gender can take their genders for granted. Kessler and McKenna asserted, "Few people besides transsexuals think of their gender as anything other than 'naturally' obvious"; they believe that the risks of not being taken for the gender intended "are minimal for nontranssexuals" (1978, 126). However, such an assertion overlooks the experiences of people such as those women Devor (1989) calls "gender blenders" and those people Lorber (1994) refers to as "gender benders." As West and Zimmerman (1987) pointed out, we all are held accountable for, and might be called on to account for, our genders.

People who, for whatever reasons, do not adhere to the rules, risk gender misattribution and any interactional consequences that might result from this misidentification. What are the consequences of misattribution for social interaction? When must misattribution be minimized? What will one do to minimize such mistakes? In this article, I explore these and related questions using my biography.

For me, the social processes and structures of gender mean that, in the context of our culture, my appearance will be read as masculine. Given the common conflation of sex and gender, I will be assumed to be a male. Because of the two-and-only-two genders rule, I will be classified, perhaps more often than not, as a man—not as an atypical woman, not as a genderless person. I must be one gender or the other; I cannot be neither, nor can I be both. This norm has a variety of mundane and serious consequences for my everyday existence. Like Myhre (1995), I have found that the choice not to participate in femininity is not one made frivolously.

My experiences as a woman who does not do femininity illustrate a paradox of our two-and-only-two gender system. Lorber argued that "bending gender rules and passing between genders does not erode but rather preserves gender boundaries" (1994, 21). Although people who engage in these behaviors and appearances do "demonstrate the social constructedness of sex, sexuality, and gender" (Lorber 1994, 96), they do not actually disrupt gender. Devor made a similar point: "When gender blending females refused to mark themselves by publicly displaying sufficient femininity to be recognized as women, they were in no way challenging patriarchal gender assumptions" (1989, 142). As the following discussion shows, I have found that my own experiences both support and challenge this argument. Before detailing these experiences, I explain my use of my self as data.

MY SELF AS DATA

This analysis is based on my experiences as a person whose appearance and gender/sex are not, in the eyes of many people, congruent. How did my experiences become my data? I began my research "unwittingly" (Krieger 1991). This article is a product of "opportunistic research" in that I am using my "unique biography, life experiences, and/or situational familiarity to understand and explain social life" (Riemer 1988, 121; see also Riemer 1977). It is an analysis of "unplanned personal experience," that is, experiences that were not part of a research project but instead are part of my daily encounters (Reinharz 1992).

This work also is, at least to some extent, an example of Richardson's (1994) notion of writing as a method of inquiry. As a sociologist who specializes in gender, the more I learned, the more I realized that my life could serve as a case study. As I examined my experiences, I found out things—about my experiences and about theory—that I did not know when I started (Richardson 1994).

It also is useful, I think, to consider my analysis an application of Mills's (1959) "sociological imagination." Mills (1959) and Berger (1963) wrote about the importance of seeing the general in the particular. This means that general social patterns can be discerned in the behaviors of particular individuals. In this article, I am examining portions of my biography, situated in U.S. society during the 1990s, to understand the "personal troubles" my gender produces in the context of a two-and-only-two gender system. I am not attempting to generalize my experiences; rather, I am trying to use them to examine and reflect on the processes and structure of gender in our society.

Because my analysis is based on my memories and perceptions of events, it is limited by my ability to recall events and by my interpretation of those events. However, I am not claiming that my experiences provide the truth about gender and how it works. I am claiming that the biography of a person who lives on the margins of our gender system can provide theoretical insights into the processes and social structure of gender. Therefore, after describing my experiences, I examine how they illustrate and extend, as well as contradict, other work on the social construction of gender.

GENDERED ME

Each day, I negotiate the boundaries of gender. Each day, I face the possibility that someone will attribute the "wrong" gender to me based on my physical appearance.

I am six feet tall and large-boned. I have had short hair for most of my life. For the past several years, I have worn a crew cut or flat top. I do not shave or otherwise remove hair from my body (e.g., no eyebrow plucking). I do not wear dresses, skirts, high heels, or makeup. My only jewelry is a class ring, a "men's" watch (my wrists are too large for a "women's" watch), two small earrings (gold hoops, both in my left ear), and (occasionally) a necklace. I wear jeans or shorts, T-shirts, sweaters, polo/golf shirts, button-down collar shirts, and tennis shoes or boots. The jeans are "women's" (I do have hips) but do not look particularly "feminine." The rest of the outer garments are from men's departments. I prefer baggy clothes, so the fact that I have "womanly" breasts often is not obvious (I do not wear a bra). Sometimes, I wear a baseball cap or some other type of hat. I also am white and relatively young (30 years old).[3]

My gender display—what others interpret as my presented identity—regularly leads to the misattribution of my gender. An incongruity exists between my gender self-identity and the gender that others perceive. In my encounters with people I do not know, I sometimes conclude, based on our interactions, that they think I am a man. This does not mean that other people do not think I am a man, just that I have no way of knowing what they think without interacting with them.

Living with It

I have no illusions or delusions about my appearance. I know that my appearance is likely to be read as "masculine" (and male) and that how I see myself is socially irrelevant. Given our two-and-only-two gender structure, I must live with the consequences of my appearance. These consequences fall into two categories: issues of identity and issues of interaction.

My most common experience is being called "Sir" or being referred to by some other masculine linguistic marker (e.g., "he," "man"). This has happened for years, for as long as I can remember, when having encounters with people I do not know.[4] Once, in fact, the same worker at a fast-food restaurant called me "Ma'am" when she took my order and "Sir" when she gave it to me.

Using my credit cards sometimes is a challenge. Some clerks subtly indicate their disbelief, looking from the card to me and back at the card and checking my signature carefully. Others challenge my use of the card, asking whose it is or demanding identification. One cashier asked to see my driver's license and then asked me whether I was the son of the cardholder. Another clerk told me that my signature on the receipt "had better match" the one on the card. Presumably, this was her way of letting me know that she was not convinced it was my credit card.

My identity as a woman also is called into question when I try to use women-only spaces. Encounters in public rest rooms are an adventure. I have been told countless times that "This is the ladies' room." Other women say nothing to me, but their stares and conversations with others let me know what they think. I will hear them say, for example, "There was a man in there." I also get stares when I enter a locker room. However, it seems that women are less concerned about my presence there, perhaps because, given that it is a space for changing clothes, showering, and so forth, they will be able to make sure that I am really a woman. Dressing rooms in department stores also are problematic spaces. I remember shopping with my sister once and being offered a chair outside the room when I began to accompany her into the dressing room.

Women who believe that I am a man do not want me in women-only spaces. For example, one woman would not enter the rest room until I came out, and others have told me that I am in the wrong place. They also might not want to encounter me while they are alone. For example, seeing me walking at night when they are alone might be scary.[5]

I, on the other hand, am not afraid to walk alone, day or night. I do not worry that I will be subjected to the public harassment that many women endure (Gardner 1995). I am not a clear target for a potential rapist. I rely on the fact that a potential attacker would not want to attack a big man by mistake. This is not to say that men never are attacked, just that they are not viewed, and often do not view themselves, as being vulnerable to attack.

Being perceived as a man has made me privy to male-male interactional styles of which most women are not aware. I found out, quite by accident, that many men greet, or acknowledge, people (mostly other men) who make eye contact with them with a single nod. For example, I found that when I walked down the halls of my brother's all-male dormitory making eye contact, men nodded their greetings at me. Oddly enough, these same men did not greet my brother; I had to tell him about making eye contact and nodding as a greeting ritual. Apparently, in this case I was doing masculinity better than he was!

I also believe that I am treated differently, for example, in auto parts stores (staffed almost exclusively by men in most cases) because of the assumption that I am a man. Workers there assume that I know what I need and that my questions are legitimate requests for information. I suspect that I am treated more fairly than a feminine-appearing woman would be. I have not been able to test this proposition. However, Devor's participants did report "being treated more respectfully" (1989, 132) in such situations.

There is, however, a negative side to being assumed to be a man by other men. Once, a friend and I were driving in her car when a man failed to stop at an intersection and nearly crashed into us. As we drove away, I mouthed "stop sign" to him. When we both stopped our cars at the next intersection, he got out of his car and came up to the passenger side of the car, where I was sitting. He yelled obscenities at us and pounded and spit on the car window. Luckily, the windows were closed. I do not think he would have done that if he thought I was a woman. This was the first time I realized that one of the implications of being seen as a man was that I might be called on to defend myself from physical aggression from other men who felt challenged by me. This was a sobering and somewhat frightening thought.

Recently, I was verbally accosted by an older man who did not like where I had parked my car. As I walked down the street to work, he shouted that I should park at the university rather than on a side street nearby. I responded that it was a public street and that I could park there if I chose. He continued to yell, but the only thing I caught was the last part of what he said: "Your tires are going to get cut!" Based on my appearance that day—I was dressed casually and carrying a backpack, and I had my hat on backward—I believe he thought that I was a young male student rather than a female professor. I do not think he would have yelled at a person he thought to be a woman—and perhaps especially not a woman professor.

Given the presumption of heterosexuality that is part of our system of gender, my interactions with women who assume that I am a man also can be viewed from that perspective. For example, once my brother and I were shopping when we were "hit on" by two young women. The encounter ended before I realized what had happened. It was only when we walked away that I told him that I was pretty certain that they had thought both of us were men. A more common experience is realizing that when I am seen in public with one of my women friends, we are likely to be read as a heterosexual dyad. It is likely that if I were to walk through a shopping mall holding hands with a woman, no one would look twice, not because of their open-mindedness toward lesbian couples but rather because of their assumption that I was the male half of a straight couple. Recently, when walking through a mall with a friend and her infant, my observations of others' responses to us led me to believe that many of them assumed that we were a family on an outing, that is, that I was her partner and the father of the child.

Dealing with It

Although I now accept that being mistaken for a man will be a part of my life so long as I choose not to participate in femininity, there have been times when I consciously have tried to appear more feminine. I did this for a while when I was an undergraduate and again recently when I was on the academic job market. The first time, I let my hair grow nearly down to my shoulders and had it permed. I also grew long fingernails and wore nail polish. Much to my chagrin, even then one of my professors, who did not know my name, insistently referred to me in his kinship examples as "the son." Perhaps my first act on the way to my current stance was to point out to this man, politely and after class, that I was a woman.

More recently, I again let my hair grow out for several months, although I did not alter other aspects of my appearance. Once my hair was about two and a half inches long (from its original quarter inch), I realized, based on my encounters with strangers, that I had more or less passed back into the category of "woman." Then, when I returned to wearing a flat top, people again responded to me as if I were a man.

Because of my appearance, much of my negotiation of interactions with strangers involves attempts to anticipate their reactions to me. I need to assess whether they will be likely to assume that I am a man and whether that actually matters in the context of our encounters. Many times, my gender really is irrelevant, and it is just annoying to be misidentified. Other times, particularly when my appearance is coupled with something that identifies me by name (e.g., a check or credit card) without a photo, I might need to do something to ensure that my identity is not questioned. As a result of my experiences, I have developed some techniques to deal with gender misattribution.

In general, in unfamiliar public places, I avoid using the rest room because I know that it is a place where there is a high likelihood of misattribution and where misattribution is socially important. If I must use a public rest room, I try to make myself look as nonthreatening as possible. I do not wear a hat, and I try to rearrange my clothing to make my breasts more obvious. Here, I am trying to use my secondary sex characteristics to make my gender more obvious rather than the usual use of gender to make sex obvious. While in the rest room, I never make eye contact, and I get in and out as quickly as possible. Going in with a woman friend also is helpful; her presence legitimizes my own. People are less likely to think I am entering a space where I do not belong when I am with someone who looks like she does belong.[6]

To those women who verbally challenge my presence in the rest room, I reply, "I know," usually in an annoyed tone. When they stare or talk about me to the women they are with, I simply get out as quickly as possible. In general, I do not wait for someone I am with because there is too much chance of an unpleasant encounter.

I stopped trying on clothes before purchasing them a few years ago because my presence in the changing areas was met with stares and whispers. Exceptions are stores where the dressing rooms are completely private, where there are individual stalls rather than a room with stalls separated by curtains, or where business is slow and no one else is trying on clothes. If I am trying on a garment clearly intended for a woman, then I usually can do so without hassle. I guess the attendants assume that I must be a woman if I have, for example, a women's bathing suit in my hand. But usually, I think it is easier for me to try the clothes on at home and return them, if necessary, rather than risk creating a scene. Similarly, when I am with another woman who is trying on clothes, I just wait outside.

My strategy with credit cards and checks is to anticipate wariness on a clerk's part. When I sense that there is some doubt or when they challenge me, I say, "It's my card." I generally respond courteously to requests for photo ID, realizing that these might be routine checks because of concerns about increasingly widespread fraud. But for the clerk who asked for ID and still did not think it was my card, I had a stronger reaction. When she said that she was sorry for embarrassing me, I told her that I was not embarrassed but that she should be. I also am particularly careful to make sure that my signature is consistent with the back of the card. Faced with such situations, I feel somewhat nervous about signing my name—which, of course, makes me worry that my signature will look different from how it should.

Another strategy I have been experimenting with is wearing nail polish in the dark bright colors currently fashionable. I try to do this when I travel by plane. Given more stringent travel regulations, one always must present a photo ID. But my experiences have shown that my driver's license is not necessarily convincing. Nail polish might be. I also flash my polished nails when I enter airport rest rooms, hoping that they will provide a clue that I am indeed in the right place.

There are other cases in which the issues are less those of identity than of all the norms of interaction that, in our society, are gendered. My most common response to misattribution actually is to appear to ignore it, that is, to go on with the interaction as if nothing out of the ordinary has happened. Unless I feel that there is a good reason to establish my correct gender, I assume the identity others impose on me for the sake of smooth interaction. For example, if someone is selling me a movie ticket, then there is no reason to make sure that the person has accurately discerned my gender. Similarly, if it is clear that the person using "Sir" is talking to me, then I simply respond as appropriate. I accept the designation because it is irrelevant to the situation. It takes enough effort to be alert for misattributions and to decide which of them matter; responding to each one would take more energy than it is worth.

Sometimes, if our interaction involves conversation, my first verbal response is enough to let the other person know that I am actually a woman and not a man. My voice apparently is "feminine" enough to shift people's attributions to the other category. I know when this has happened by the apologies that usually accompany the mistake. I usually respond to the apologies by saying something like "No problem" and/or "It happens all the time." Sometimes, a misattributor will offer an account for the mistake, for example, saying that it was my hair or that they were not being very observant.

These experiences with gender and misattribution provide some theoretical insights into contemporary Western understandings of gender and into the social structure of gender in contemporary society. Although there are a number of ways in which my experiences confirm the work of others, there also are some ways in which my experiences suggest other interpretations and conclusions.

WHAT DOES IT MEAN?

Gender is pervasive in our society. I cannot choose not to participate in it. Even if I try not to do gender, other people will do it for me. That is, given our two-and-only-two rule, they must attribute one of two genders to me. Still, although I cannot choose not to participate in gender, I can choose not to participate in femininity (as I have), at least with respect to physical appearance.

That is where the problems begin. Without the decorations of femininity, I do not look like a woman. That is, I do not look like what many people's commonsense understanding of gender tells them a woman looks like. How I see myself, even how I might wish others would see me, is socially irrelevant. It is the gender that I *appear* to be (my "perceived gender") that is most relevant to my social identity and interactions with others. The major consequence of this fact is that I must be continually aware of which gender I "give off" as well as which gender I "give" (Goffman 1959).

Because my gender self-identity is "not displayed obviously, immediately, and consistently" (Devor 1989, 58), I am somewhat of a failure in social terms with respect to gender. Causing people to be uncertain or wrong about one's gender is a violation of taken-for-granted rules that leads to embarrassment and discomfort; it means that something has gone wrong with the interaction (Garfinkel 1967; Kessler and McKenna 1978). This means that my nonresponse to misattribution is the more socially appropriate response; I am allowing others to maintain face (Goffman 1959, 1967). By not calling attention to their mistakes, I uphold their images of themselves as competent social actors. I also maintain my own image as competent by letting them assume that I am the gender I appear to them to be.

But I still have discreditable status; I carry a stigma (Goffman 1963). Because I have failed to participate appropriately in the creation of meaning with respect to gender (Devor 1989), I can be called on to account for my appearance. If discredited, I show myself to be an incompetent social actor. I am the one not following the rules, and I will pay the price for not providing people with the appropriate cues for placing me in the gender category to which I really belong.

I do think that it is, in many cases, safer to be read as a man than as some sort of deviant woman. "Man" is an acceptable category; it fits properly into people's gender worldview. Passing as a man often is the "path of least resistance" (Devor 1989; Johnson 1997). For example, in situations where gender does not matter, letting people take me as a man is easier than correcting them.

Conversely, as Butler noted, "We regularly punish those who fail to do their gender right" (1990, 140). Feinberg maintained, "Masculine girls and women face terrible condemnation and brutality—including sexual violence—for crossing the boundary of what is 'acceptable' female expression" (1996, 114). People are more likely to harass me when they perceive me to be a woman who looks like a man. For example, when a group of teenagers realized that I was not a man because one of their mothers identified me correctly, they began to make derogatory comments when I passed them. One asked, for example, "Does she have a penis?"

Because of the assumption that a "masculine" woman is a lesbian, there is the risk of homophobic reactions (Gardner 1995; Lucal 1997). Perhaps surprisingly, I find that I am much more likely to be taken for a man than for a lesbian, at least based on my interactions with people and their reactions to me. This might be because people are less likely to reveal that they have taken me for a lesbian because it is less relevant to an encounter or because they believe this would be unacceptable. But I think it is more

likely a product of the strength of our two-and-only-two system. I give enough masculine cues that I am seen not as a deviant woman but rather as a man, at least in most
cases. The problem seems not to be that people are uncertain about my gender, which
might lead them to conclude that I was a lesbian once they realized I was a woman.
Rather, I seem to fit easily into a gender category—just not the one with which I
identify.

In fact, because men represent the dominant gender in our society, being mistaken for a man can protect me from other types of gendered harassment. Because
men can move around in public spaces safely (at least relative to women), a "masculine" woman also can enjoy this freedom (Devor 1989).

On the other hand, my use of particular spaces—those designated as for women
only—may be challenged. Feinberg provided an intriguing analysis of the public rest
room experience. She characterized women's reactions to a masculine person in a
public rest room as "an example of genderphobia" (1996, 117), viewing such women
as policing gender boundaries rather than believing that there really is a man in the
women's rest room. She argued that women who truly believed that there was a man in
their midst would react differently. Although this is an interesting perspective on her
experiences, my experiences do not lead to the same conclusion.[7] Enough people have
said to me that "This is the ladies' room" or have said to their companions that "There
was a man in there" that I take their reactions at face value.

Still, if the two-and-only-two gender system is to be maintained, participants
must be involved in policing the categories and their attendant identities and spaces.
Even if policing boundaries is not explicitly intended, boundary maintenance is the
effect of such responses to people's gender displays.

Boundaries and margins are an important component of both my experiences of
gender and our theoretical understanding of gendering processes. I am, in effect, both
woman and not-woman. As a woman who often is a social man but who also is a
woman living in a patriarchal society, I am in a unique position to see and act. I sometimes receive privileges usually limited to men, and I sometimes am oppressed by my
status as a deviant woman. I am, in a sense, an outsider-within (Collins 1991). Posi-
tioned on the boundaries of gender categories, I have developed a consciousness that I
hope will prove transformative (Anzaldúa 1987).

In fact, one of the reasons why I decided to continue my nonparticipation in femininity was that my sociological training suggested that this could be one of my contributions to the eventual dismantling of patriarchal gender constructs. It would be my
way of making the personal political. I accepted being taken for a man as the price I
would pay to help subvert patriarchy. I believed that all of the inconveniences I was
enduring meant that I actually was doing something to bring down the gender structures that entangled all of us.

Then, I read Lorber's (1994) *Paradoxes of Gender* and found out, much to my dis-
may, that I might not actually be challenging gender after all. Because of the way in
which doing gender works in our two-and-only-two system, gender displays are simply

read as evidence of one of the two categories. Therefore, gender bending, blending, and passing between the categories do not question the categories themselves. If one's social gender and personal (true) gender do not correspond, then this is irrelevant unless someone notices the lack of congruence.

This reality brings me to a paradox of my experiences. First, not only do others assume that I am one gender or the other, but I also insist that I *really am* a member of one of the two gender categories. That is, I am female; I self-identify as a woman. I do not claim to be some other gender or to have no gender at all. I simply place myself in the wrong category according to stereotypes and cultural standards; the gender I present, or that some people perceive me to be presenting, is inconsistent with the gender with which I identify myself as well as with the gender I could be "proven" to be. Socially, I display the wrong gender; personally, I identify as the proper gender.

Second, although I ultimately would like to see the destruction of our current gender structure, I am not to the point of personally abandoning gender. Right now, I do not want people to see me as genderless as much as I want them to see me as a woman. That is, I would like to expand the category of "woman" to include people like me. I, too, am deeply embedded in our gender system, even though I do not play by many of its rules. For me, as for most people in our society, gender is a substantial part of my personal identity (Howard and Hollander 1997). Socially, the problem is that I do not present a gender display that is consistently read as feminine. In fact, I consciously do not participate in the trappings of femininity. However, I do identify myself as a woman, not as a man or as someone outside of the two-and-only-two categories.

Yet, I do believe, as Lorber (1994) does, that the purpose of gender, as it currently is constructed, is to oppress women. Lorber analyzed gender as a "process of creating distinguishable social statuses for the assignment of rights and responsibilities" that ends up putting women in a devalued and oppressed position (1994, 32). As Martin put it, "Bodies that clearly delineate gender status facilitate the maintenance of the gender hierarchy" (1998, 495).

For society, gender means difference (Lorber 1994). The erosion of the boundaries would problematize that structure. Therefore, for gender to operate as it currently does, the category "woman" *cannot* be expanded to include people like me. The maintenance of the gender structure is dependent on the creation of a few categories that are mutually exclusive, the members of which are as different as possible (Lorber 1994). It is the clarity of the boundaries between the categories that allows gender to be used to assign rights and responsibilities as well as resources and rewards.

It is that part of gender—what it is used for—that is most problematic. Indeed, is it not *patriarchal*—or, even more specifically, *heteropatriarchal*—constructions of gender that are actually the problem? It is not the differences between men and women, or the categories themselves, so much as the meanings ascribed to the categories and, even more important, the hierarchical nature of gender under patriarchy that is the problem (Johnson 1997). Therefore, I am rebelling not against my femaleness or even my womanhood; instead, I am protesting contemporary constructions of femininity and, at least indirectly, masculinity under patriarchy. We do not, in fact, know what gender would look like if it were not constructed around heterosexuality in the context of patriarchy.

Although it is possible that the end of patriarchy would mean the end of gender, it is at least conceivable that something like what we now call gender could exist in a postpatriarchal future. The two-and-only-two categorization might well disappear, there being no hierarchy for it to justify. But I do not think that we should make the assumption that gender and patriarchy are synonymous.

Theoretically, this analysis points to some similarities and differences between the work of Lorber (1994) and the works of Butler (1990), Goffman (1976, 1977), and West and Zimmerman (1987). Lorber (1994) conceptualized gender as social structure, whereas the others focused more on the interactive and processual nature of gender. Butler (1990) and Goffman (1976, 1977) view gender as a performance, and West and Zimmerman (1987) examined it as something all of us do. One result of this difference in approach is that in Lorber's (1994) work, gender comes across as something that we are caught in—something that, despite any attempts to the contrary, we cannot break out of. This conclusion is particularly apparent in Lorber's argument that gender rebellion, in the context of our two-and-only-two system, ends up supporting what it purports to subvert. Yet, my own experiences suggest an alternative possibility that is more in line with the view of gender offered by West and Zimmerman (1987): If gender is a product of interaction, and if it is produced in a particular context, then it can be changed if we change our performances. However, the effects of a performance linger, and gender ends up being institutionalized. It is institutionalized, in our society, in a way that perpetuates inequality, as Lorber's (1994) work shows. So, it seems that a combination of these two approaches is needed.

In fact, Lorber's (1994) work seems to suggest that effective gender rebellion requires a more blatant approach—bearded men in dresses, perhaps, or more active responses to misattribution. For example, if I corrected every person who called me "Sir," and if I insisted on my right to be addressed appropriately and granted access to women-only spaces, then perhaps I could start to break down gender norms. If I asserted my right to use public facilities without being harassed, and if I challenged each person who gave me "the look," then perhaps I would be contributing to the demise of gender as we know it. It seems that the key would be to provide visible evidence of the nonmutual exclusivity of the categories. Would *this* break down the patriarchal components of gender? Perhaps it would, but it also would be exhausting.

Perhaps there is another possibility. In a recent book, *The Gender Knot*, Johnson (1997) argued that when it comes to gender and patriarchy, most of us follow the paths of least resistance; we "go along to get along," allowing our actions to be shaped by the gender system. Collectively, our actions help patriarchy maintain and perpetuate a system of oppression and privilege. Thus, by withdrawing our support from this system by choosing paths of greater resistance, we can start to chip away at it. Many people participate in gender because they cannot imagine any alternatives. In my classroom, and in my interactions and encounters with strangers, my presence can make it difficult for people not to see that there *are* other paths. In other words, following from West and Zimmerman (1987), I can subvert gender by doing it differently.

For example, I think it is true that my existence does not have an effect on strangers who assume that I am a man and never learn otherwise. For them, I do uphold the two-and-only-two system. But there are other cases in which my existence can have an effect. For example, when people initially take me for a man but then find out that I actually am a woman, at least for that moment, the naturalness of gender may be called into question. In these cases, my presence can provoke a "category crisis" (Garber 1992, 16) because it challenges the sex/gender binary system.

The subversive potential of my gender might be strongest in my classrooms. When I teach about the sociology of gender, my students can see me as the embodiment of the social construction of gender. Not all of my students have transformative experiences as a result of taking a course with me; there is the chance that some of them see me as a "freak" or as an exception. Still, after listening to stories about my experiences with gender and reading literature on the subject, many students begin to see how and why gender is a social product. I can disentangle sex, gender, and sexuality in the contemporary United States for them. Students can begin to see the connection between biographical experiences and the structure of society. As one of my students noted, I clearly live the material I am teaching. If that helps me to get my point across, then perhaps I am subverting the binary gender system after all. Although my gendered presence and my way of doing gender might make others—and sometimes even me—uncomfortable, no one ever said that dismantling patriarchy was going to be easy.

NOTES

1. Ethnomethodology has been described as "the study of commonsense practical reasoning" (Collins 1988, 274). It examines how people make sense of their everyday experiences. Ethnomethodology is particularly useful in studying gender because it helps to uncover the assumptions on which our understandings of sex and gender are based.
2. I thank an anonymous reviewer for suggesting that I use these distinctions among the parts of a person's gender.
3. I obviously have left much out by not examining my gendered experiences in the context of race, age, class, sexuality, region, and so forth. Such a project clearly is more complex. As Weston pointed out, gender presentations are complicated by other statuses of their presenters: "What it takes to kick a person over into another gendered category can differ with race, class, religion, and time" (1996, 168). Furthermore, I am well aware that my whiteness allows me to assume that my experiences are simply a product of gender (see, e.g., hooks 1981; Lucal 1996; Spelman 1988; West and Fenstermaker 1995). For now, suffice it to

say that it is my privileged position on some of these axes and my more disadvantaged position on others that combine to delineate my overall experience.

4. In fact, such experiences are not always limited to encounters with strangers. My grandmother, who does not see me often, twice has mistaken me for either my brother-in-law or some unknown man.

5. My experiences in rest rooms and other public spaces might be very different if I were, say, African American rather than white. Given the stereotypes of African American men, I think that white women would react very differently to encountering me (see, e.g., Staples [1986] 1993).

6. I also have noticed that there are certain types of rest rooms in which I will not be verbally challenged; the higher the social status of the place, the less likely I will be harassed. For example, when I go to the theater, I might get stared at, but my presence never has been challenged.

7. An anonymous reviewer offered one possible explanation for this. Women see women's rest rooms as their space; they feel safe, and even empowered, there. Instead of fearing men in such space, they might instead pose a threat to any man who might intrude. Their invulnerability in this situation is, of course, not physically based but rather socially constructed. I thank the reviewer for this suggestion.

REFERENCES

Anzaldua, G. 1987. *Borderlands/La frontera*. San Francisco: Aunt Lute Books.

Bem, S. L. 1993. *The lenses of gender*. New Haven, CT: Yale University Press.

Berger, P. 1963. *Invitation to sociology*. New York: Anchor.

Bordo, S. 1993. *Unbearable weight*. Berkeley: University of California Press.

Brownmiller, C. 1984. *Femininity*. New York: Fawcett.

Butler, J. 1990. *Gender trouble*. New York: Routledge.

Collins, P. H. 1991. *Black feminist thought*. New York: Routledge.

Collins, R. 1988. *Theoretical sociology*. San Diego: Harcourt Brace Jovanovich.

Devor, H. 1989. *Gender blending: Confronting the limits of duality*. Bloomington: Indiana University Press.

Feinberg, L. 1996. *Transgender warriors*. Boston: Beacon.

Garber, M. 1992. *Vested interests: Cross-dressing and cultural anxiety*. New York: HarperPerennial.

Gardner, C. B. 1995. *Passing by: Gender and public harassment*. Berkeley: University of California.

Garfinkel, H. 1967. *Studies in ethnomethodology*. Englewood Cliffs, NJ: Prentice Hall.

Goffman, E. 1959. *The presentation of self in everyday life*. Garden City, NY: Doubleday.

———. 1963. *Stigma*. Englewood Cliffs, NJ: Prentice Hall.

———. 1967. *Interaction ritual*. New York: Anchor/Doubleday.

———. 1976. Gender display. *Studies in the Anthropology of Visual Communication* 3:69–77.

———. 1977. The arrangement between the sexes. *Theory and Society* 4:301–31.

hooks, b. 1981. *Ain't I a woman: Black women and feminism*. Boston: South End Press.

Howard, J. A., and J. Hollander. 1997. *Gendered situations, gendered selves*. Thousand Oaks, CA: Sage.

Kessler, S. J., and W. McKenna. 1978. *Gender: An ethnomethodological approach*. New York: John Wiley.

Krieger, S. 1991. *Social science and the self*. New Brunswick, NJ: Rutgers University Press.

Johnson, A. G. 1997. *The gender knot: Unraveling our patriarchal legacy*. Philadelphia: Temple University Press.

Lorber, J. 1994. *Paradoxes of gender*. New Haven, CT: Yale University Press.

———. 1996. Beyond the binaries: Depolarizing the categories of sex, sexuality, and gender. *Sociological Inquiry* 66:143–59.

Lucal, B. 1996. Oppression and privilege: Toward a relational conceptualization of race. *Teaching Sociology* 24:245–55.

———. 1997. "Hey, this is the ladies' room!": Gender misattribution and public harassment. *Perspectives on Social Problems* 9:43–57.

Martin, K. A. 1998. Becoming a gendered body: Practices of preschools. *American Sociological Review* 63:494–511.

Mills, C. W. 1959. *The sociological imagination*. London: Oxford University Press.

Myhre, J.R.M. 1995. One bad hair day too many, or the hairstory of an androgynous young feminist. In *Listen up: Voices from the next feminist generation*, edited by B. Findlen. Seattle, WA: Seal Press.

Reinharz, S. 1992. *Feminist methods in social research*. New York: Oxford University Press.

Richardson, L. 1994. Writing: A method of inquiry. In *Handbook of Qualitative Research*, edited by N. K. Denzin and Y. S. Lincoln. Thousand Oaks, CA: Sage.

Riemer, J. W. 1977. Varieties of opportunistic research. *Urban Life* 5:467–77.

———. 1988. Work and self. In *Personal sociology*, edited by P. C. Higgins and J. M. Johnson. New York: Praeger.

Spelman, E. V. 1988. *Inessential woman: Problems of exclusion in feminist thought*. Boston: Beacon.

Staples, B. 1993. Just walk on by. In *Experiencing race, class, and gender in the United States*, edited by V. Cyrus. Mountain View, CA: Mayfield. (Originally published 1986)

West, C., and S. Fenstermaker. 1995. Doing difference. *Gender & Society* 9:8–37.

West, C., and D. H. Zimmerman. 1987. Doing gender. *Gender & Society* 1:125–51.

Weston, K. 1996. *Render me, gender me*. New York: Columbia University Press.

Zimmerman, D. H. 1992. They were all doing gender, but they weren't all passing: Comment on Rogers. *Gender & Society* 6:192–98.

STUDY QUESTIONS

1. Provide detailed examples of how Lucal is treated differently from most women.

2. Lucal says, "I know my appearance is likely to be read as 'masculine' (and male) and that how I see myself is socially irrelevant." Discuss whether each of us defines our own **gender**.

3. How do you "do gender"? That is, what do you say, do, wear, and where do you go to perform your masculinity, femininity, or your unique gender expression? How would you cope if, like Lucal, you didn't fit neatly into our two-and-only-two system?

4. Lucal argues that binary (either/or) gender expressions limit people whose gender expression does not neatly fall into the masculine or feminine category. Multiple cultures today have more than two gender categories. What social, cultural, and physical changes would have to happen to make the United States a more gender diverse society? Sure, we'll need new bathroom arrangements, but dig deeper in your answer—how might language have to change, for example, or fashion?

C. J. PASCOE

Dude, You're a Fag: Adolescent Male Homophobia

From Dude, You're a Fag: Masculinity and Sexuality in High School

---

urn on the TV, listen to the radio, or just eavesdrop, and before long, you're bound to hear a guy use a phrase like, "You're such a fag!" "No homo," or "That's gay." But while this casual **homophobia** is rampant, Americans increasingly support same-sex **marriage** and sexual-orientation equality. What can explain this disconnect? In this article, C. J. Pascoe sets out to discover why homophobic terms are so common and what they actually mean to the young men who use them.

THE SUN SHONE BRIGHT AND CLEAR OVER RIVER HIGH'S ANNUAL Creative and Performing Arts Happening, or CAPA. During CAPA the school's various art programs displayed students' work in a fairlike atmosphere. The front quad sported student-generated computer programs. Colorful and ornate chalk art covered the cement sidewalks. Tables lined with student-crafted pottery were set up on the grass. Tall displays of students' paintings divided the rear quad. To the left of the paintings a television blared student-directed music videos. At the rear of the back quad, a square, roped-off area of cement served as a makeshift stage for drama, choir, and dance performances. Teachers released students from class to wander around the quads, watch performances, and look at the art. This freedom from class time lent the day an air of excitement because students were rarely allowed to roam the campus without a hall pass, an office summons, or a parent/faculty escort. In honor of CAPA, the school district bussed in elementary school students from the surrounding grammar schools to participate in the day's festivities.

Running through the rear quad, Brian, a senior, yelled to a group of boys visiting from the elementary schools, "There's a faggot over there! There's a faggot over there! Come look!" Following Brian, the ten-year-olds dashed down a hallway. At the end of the hallway Brian's friend Dan pursed his lips and began sashaying toward the little boys. As he minced, he swung his hips exaggeratedly and wildly waved his arms. To the boys Brian yelled, "Look at the faggot! Watch out! He'll get you!" In response, the ten-year-olds raced back down the hallway screaming in terror. Brian and Dan repeated this drama throughout the following half hour, each time with a new group of young boys.

Making jokes like these about faggots was central to social life at River High. Indeed, boys learned long before adolescence that faggots were simultaneously predatory and passive and that they were, at all costs, to be avoided. Older boys repeatedly impressed upon younger ones through these types of homophobic rituals that whatever they did, whatever they became, however they talked, they had to avoid becoming a faggot.

Feminist scholars of masculinity have documented the centrality of homophobic insults and attitudes to masculinity (Kimmel 2001; Lehne 1998), especially in school settings (Burn 2000; Kimmel 2003; Messner 2005; Plummer 2001; G. Smith 1998; Wood 1984). They argue that homophobic teasing often characterizes masculinity in adolescence and early adulthood and that antigay slurs tend to be directed primarily at gay boys. This chapter both expands on and challenges these accounts of relationships between homophobia and masculinity. Homophobia is indeed a central mechanism in the making of contemporary American adolescent masculinity. A close analysis of the way boys at River High invoke the faggot as a disciplinary mechanism makes clear that something more than simple homophobia is at play in adolescent masculinity. The use of the word *fag* by boys at River High points to the limits of an argument that focuses centrally on homophobia. Fag is not only an identity linked to homosexual boys but an identity that can temporarily adhere to heterosexual boys as well. The fag trope is also a racialized disciplinary mechanism.

Homophobia is too facile a term with which to describe the deployment of *fag* as an epithet. By calling the use of the word *fag* homophobia—and letting the argument stop there—previous research has obscured the gendered nature of sexualized insults (Plummer 2001). Invoking homophobia to describe the ways boys aggressively tease each other overlooks the powerful relationship between masculinity and this sort of insult. Instead, it seems incidental, in this conventional line of argument, that girls do not harass each other and are not harassed in this same manner. This framing naturalizes the relationship between masculinity and homophobia, thus obscuring that such harassment is central to the formation of a gendered identity for boys in a way that it is not for girls.

Fag is not necessarily a static identity attached to a particular (homosexual) boy. Fag talk and fag imitations serve as a discourse with which boys discipline themselves and each other through joking relationships. Any boy can temporarily become a fag in a given social space or interaction. This does not mean that boys who identify as or are perceived to be homosexual aren't subject to intense harassment. Many are. But becoming a fag has as much to do with failing at the masculine tasks of competence, heterosexual prowess, and strength or in any way revealing weakness or femininity as it does with a sexual identity. This fluidity of the fag identity is what makes the specter of the fag such a powerful disciplinary mechanism. It is fluid enough that boys police their behaviors out of fear of having the fag identity permanently adhere and definitive enough so that boys recognize a fag behavior and strive to avoid it.

An analysis of the fag discourse also indicates ways in which gendered power works through racialized selves. The fag discourse is invoked differently by and in relation to white boys' bodies than it is by and in relation to African American boys' bodies. While certain behaviors put all boys at risk for becoming temporarily a fag, some behaviors can be enacted by African American boys without putting them at risk of receiving the label. The racialized meanings of the fag discourse suggest that something more than simple homophobia is involved in these sorts of interactions. It is not that gendered homophobia does not exist in African American communities. Indeed, making fun of "negro faggotry seems to be a rite of passage among contemporary black male rappers and filmmakers" (Riggs 1991, 253). However, the fact that "white women and men, gay and straight, have more or less colonized cultural debates about sexual representation" (Julien and Mercer 1991, 167) obscures varied systems of sexualized meanings among different racialized ethnic groups (Almaguer 1991). Thus far male homophobia has primarily been written about as a racially neutral phenomenon. However, as D. L. King's (2004) recent work on African American men and same-sex desire pointed out, homophobia is characterized by racial identities as well as sexual and gendered ones.

WHAT IS A FAG? GENDERED MEANINGS

"Since you were little boys you've been told, 'Hey, don't be a little faggot,'" explained Darnell, a football player of mixed African American and white heritage, as we sat on a bench next to the athletic field. Indeed, both the boys and girls I interviewed told me that *fag* was the worst epithet one guy could direct at another. Jeff, a slight white sophomore, explained to me that boys call each other fag because "gay people aren't really liked over here and stuff." Jeremy, a Latino junior, told me that this insult literally reduced a boy to nothing, "To call someone *gay* or *fag* is like the lowest thing you can call someone. Because that's like saying that you're nothing."

Most guys explained their or others' dislike of fags by claiming that homophobia was synonymous with being a guy. For instance, Keith, a white soccer-playing senior, explained, "I think guys are just homophobic." However, boys were not equal-opportunity homophobes. Several students told me that these homophobic insults applied only to boys and not to girls. For example, while Jake, a handsome white senior, told me that he didn't like gay people, he quickly added, "Lesbians, okay, that's *good.*" Similarly Cathy, a popular white cheerleader, told me, "Being a lesbian is accepted because guys think, 'Oh that's cool.'" Darnell, after telling me that boys were warned about becoming faggots, said, "They [guys] are fine with girls. I think it's the guy part that they're like ewwww." In this sense it was not strictly homophobia but a gendered homophobia that constituted adolescent masculinity in the culture of River High. It is clear, according to these comments, that lesbians were "good" because of their place in heterosexual male fantasy, not necessarily because of some enlightened approach to same-sex relationships. A popular trope in heterosexual por-nography depicts two women engaging in sexual acts for the purpose of male titilla-tion. The boys at River High are not unique in making this distinction; adolescent boys in general dislike gay men more than they dislike lesbians (Baker and Fishbein 1998). The fetishizing of sex acts between women indicates that using only the term *homophobia* to describe boys' repeated use of the word *fag* might be a bit simplistic and misleading.

Girls at River High rarely deployed the word *fag* and were never called fags. I recorded girls uttering *fag* only three times during my research. In one instance, Angela, a Latina cheerleader, teased Jeremy, a well-liked white senior involved in stu-dent government, for not ditching school with her: "You wouldn't 'cause you're a fag-got." However, girls did not use this word as part of their regular lexicon. The sort of gendered homophobia that constituted adolescent masculinity did not constitute adolescent femininity. Girls were not called dykes or lesbians in any sort of regular or systematic way. Students did tell me that *slut* was the worst thing a girl could be called. However, my field notes indicate that the word *slut* (or its synonym *ho*) appeared one time for every eight times the word *fag* appeared.

Highlighting the difference between the deployment of *gay* and *fag* as insults brings the gendered nature of this homophobia into focus. For boys and girls at River High *gay* was a fairly common synonym for "stupid." While this word shared the sex-ual origins of *fag*, it didn't *consistently* have the skew of gender-loaded meaning. Girls and boys often used *gay* as an adjective referring to inanimate objects and male or female people, whereas they used *fag* as a noun that denoted only unmasculine males. Students used *gay* to describe anything from someone's clothes to a new school rule that they didn't like. For instance, one day in auto shop, Arnie pulled out a large older version of a black laptop computer and placed it on his desk. Behind him Nick cried, "That's a gay laptop! It's five inches thick!" The rest of the boys in the class laughed at Arnie's outdated laptop. A laptop can be gay, a movie can be gay, or a group of people can be gay. Boys used *gay* and *fag* interchangeably when they referred to other boys, but *fag* didn't have the gender-neutral attributes that *gay* frequently invoked.

Surprisingly, some boys took pains to say that the term *fag* did not imply sexuality. Darnell told me, "It doesn't even have anything to do with being gay." Similarly, J. L., a white sophomore at Hillside High (River High's cross-town rival), asserted, "*Fag*, seriously, it has nothing to do with sexual preference at all. You could just be calling somebody an idiot, you know?" I asked Ben, a quiet, white sophomore who wore heavy-metal T-shirts to auto shop each day, "What kind of things do guys get called a fag for?" Ben answered, "Anything . . . literally, anything. Like you were trying to turn a wrench the wrong way, 'Dude, you're a fag.' Even if a piece of meat drops out of your sandwich, 'You fag!'" Each time Ben said, "You fag," his voice deepened as if he were imitating a more masculine boy. While Ben might rightly *feel* that a guy could be called a fag for "anything . . . literally, anything," there were actually specific behaviors that, when enacted by most boys, could render them more vulnerable to a *fag* epithet. In this instance Ben's comment highlights the use of *fag* as a generic insult for incompetence, which in the world of River High, was central to a masculine identity. A boy could get called a fag for exhibiting any sort of behavior defined as unmasculine (although not necessarily behaviors aligned with femininity): being stupid or incompetent, dancing, caring too much about clothing, being too emotional, or expressing interest (sexual or platonic) in other guys. However, given the extent of its deployment and the laundry list of behaviors that could get a boy in trouble, it is no wonder that Ben felt a boy could be called fag for "anything." These nonsexual meanings didn't replace sexual meanings but rather existed alongside them.

One-third (thirteen) of the boys I interviewed told me that, while they might liberally insult each other with the term, they would not direct it at a homosexual peer. Jabes, a Filipino senior, told me, "I actually say it [*fag*] quite a lot, except for when I'm in the company of an actual homosexual person. Then I try not to say it at all. But when I'm just hanging out with my friends I'll be like, 'Shut up, I don't want to hear you any more, you stupid fag.'" Similarly J. L. compared homosexuality to a disability, saying there was "no way" he'd call an actually gay guy a fag because "there's people who are the retarded people who nobody wants to associate with. I'll be so nice to those guys, and I hate it when people make fun of them. It's like, 'Bro do you realize that they can't help that?' And then there's gay people. They were born that way." According to this group of boys, gay was a legitimate, or at least biological, identity.

There was a possibility, however slight, that a boy could be gay and masculine (Connell 1995). David, a handsome white senior dressed smartly in khaki pants and a white button-down shirt, told me, "Being gay is just a lifestyle. It's someone you choose to sleep with. You can still throw around a football and be gay." It was as if David was justifying the use of the word *fag* by arguing that gay men could be men if they tried but that if they failed at it (i.e., if they couldn't throw a football) then they deserved to be called a fag. In other words, to be a fag was, by definition, the opposite of masculine, whether the word was deployed with sexualized or nonsexualized meanings. In explaining this to me, Jamaal, an African American junior, cited the explanation of the popular rap artist Eminem: "Although I don't like Eminem, he had a good definition of it. It's like taking away your title. In an interview they were like, 'You're always capping on gays, but then you sing with Elton John.' He was like 'I don't mean gay as in gay.'" This is what Riki Wilchins (2003) calls the "Eminem Exception. Eminem explains that he doesn't call people 'faggot' because of their sexual orientation but because they're weak and unmanly" (72). This is precisely the way boys at River High used the term *faggot*. While it was not necessarily acceptable to be gay, at least a man who was gay could do other things that would render him acceptably masculine. A fag, by the very definition of the word, could not be masculine.

This distinction between fag as an unmasculine and problematic identity and gay as a possibly masculine, although marginalized, sexual identity is not limited to a teenage lexicon; it is reflected in both psychological discourses and gay and lesbian activism. Eve Sedgwick (1995) argues that in contemporary psychological literature homosexuality is no longer a problem for men so long as the homosexual man is of the right age and gender orientation. In this literature a homosexual male must be an adult and must be masculine. Male homosexuality is not pathologized, but gay male *effeminacy* is. The lack of masculinity is the problem, not the sexual practice or orientation. Indeed, the edition of the *Diagnostic and Statistical Manual of Mental Disorders* (a key document in the mental health field) that erased homosexuality as a diagnosis in the 1970s added a new diagnosis in its wake: Gender Identity Disorder. According to Sedgwick, the criteria for diagnosis are different for girls and boys. A girl has to actually assert that she is a boy, indicating a psychotic disconnection with reality, whereas a boy need only display a preoccupation with female activities. The policing of boys' gender orientation and of a strict masculine identity for gay men is also reflected in gay culture itself. The war against fags as the specter of unmasculine manhood appears in gay male personal ads in which men look for "straight-appearing, straight-acting men." This concern with both straight and gay men's masculinity not only reflects teenage boys' obsession with hypermasculinity but also points to the conflict at the heart of the contemporary "crisis of masculinity" being played out in popular, scientific, and educational arenas.

BECOMING A FAG: FAG FLUIDITY

"The ubiquity of the word *faggot* speaks to the reach of its discrediting capacity" (Corbett 2001, 4). It's almost as if boys cannot help shouting it out on a regular basis—in the hallway, in class, or across campus as a greeting. In my fieldwork I was amazed by the way the word seemed to pop uncontrollably out of boys' mouths in all kinds of situations. To quote just one of many instances from my field notes: two boys walked out of the PE locker room, and one yelled, "Fucking faggot!" at no one in particular. None of the other students paid them any mind, since this sort of thing happened so frequently. Similar spontaneous yelling of some variation of the word *fag*, seemingly apropos of nothing, happened repeatedly among boys throughout the school. This and repeated imitations of fags constitute what I refer to as a "fag discourse."

Fag discourse is central to boys' joking relationships. Joking cements relationships among boys (Kehily and Nayak 1997; Lyman 1998) and helps to manage anxiety and discomfort (Freud 1905). Boys both connect with one another and manage the anxiety around this sort of relationship through joking about fags. Boys invoked the specter of the fag in two ways: through humorous imitation and through lobbing the epithet at one another. Boys at River High imitated the fag by acting out an exaggerated "femininity" and/or by pretending to sexually desire other boys. As indicated by the introductory vignette in which an older boy imitated a predatory fag to threaten little boys, male students at River High linked these performative scenarios with a fag identity. They also lobbed the *fag* epithet at each other in a verbal game of hot potato, each careful to deflect the insult quickly by hurling it toward someone else. These games and imitations made up a fag discourse that highlighted the fag not as a static but rather as a fluid identity that boys constantly struggled to avoid.

In imitative performances the fag discourse functioned as a constant reiteration of the fag's existence, affirming that the fag was out there; boys reminded themselves and each other that at any moment they could become fags if they were not sufficiently masculine. At the same time these performances demonstrated that the boy who was invoking the fag was *not* a fag. Emir, a tall, thin African American boy, frequently imitated fags to draw laughs from other students in his introductory drama class. One day Mr. McNally, the drama teacher, disturbed by the noise outside the classroom, turned to the open door, saying, "We'll shut this unless anyone really wants to watch sweaty boys playing basketball." Emir lisped, "I wanna watch the boys play!" The rest of the class cracked up at his imitation. No one in the class actually thought Emir was gay, as he purposefully mocked both same-sex sexual desire (through pretending to admire the boys playing basketball) and an effeminate gender identity (through speaking with a lisp and in a high-pitched voice). Had he said this in all seriousness, the class most likely would have responded in stunned silence. Instead, Emir reminded them he was masculine by immediately dropping the fag act. After imitating a fag, boys assure others that they are not a fag by instantly becoming masculine again after the performance. They mock their own performed femininity and/or same-sex desire, assuring themselves and others that such an identity deserves derisive laughter.

Boys consistently tried to force others into the fag position by lobbing the *fag* epithet at each other. One day in auto shop, Jay was rummaging through a junk-filled car in the parking lot. He poked his head out of the trunk and asked, "Where are Craig and Brian?" Neil responded with "I think they're over there," pointing, then thrusting his hips and pulling his arms back and forth to indicate that Craig and Brian might be having sex. The boys in auto shop laughed. This sort of joke temporarily labeled both Craig and Brian as faggots. Because the fag discourse was so familiar, the other boys immediately understood that Neil was indicating that Craig and Brian were having sex. However, these were not necessarily identities that stuck. Nobody actually thought Craig and Brian were homosexuals. Rather, the fag identity was fluid— certainly an identity that no boy wanted but that most boys could escape, usually by engaging in some sort of discursive contest to turn another boy into a fag.

In this way the fag became a hot potato that no boy wanted to be left holding. One of the best ways to move out of the fag position was to thrust another boy into that position. For instance, soon after Neil made the joke about Brian having sex with Craig, Brian lobbed the *fag* epithet at someone else, deflecting it from himself, by initiating a round of a favorite game in auto shop, the "cock game." Brain said quietly, looking at Josh, "Josh loves the cock," then slightly louder, "Josh loves the cock." He continued saying this until he was yelling, "JOSH LOVES THE COCK!" The rest of the boys laughed hysterically as Josh slunk away, saying, "I have a bigger dick than all you motherfuckers!" These two instances show how the fag could be mapped, for a moment, onto one boy's body and how he, in turn, could attach it to another boy, thus deflecting it from himself. In the first instance Neil made fun of Craig and Brian for simply hanging out together. In the second instance Brian went from being a fag to making Josh into a fag through the "cock game." Through joking interactions boys moved in and out of the fag identity by discursively creating another as a fag.

Given the pervasiveness of fag jokes and the fluidity of the fag identity, it is difficult for boys to consistently avoid the brand. As Ben stated, it almost seemed that a boy could get called a fag for "anything." But most readily acknowledged that there were spaces, behaviors, and bodily comportments that made one more likely to be subject to the fag discourse, such as bodily practices involving clothing and dancing.

According to boys at River, fags cared about the style of their clothes, wore tighter clothes, and cared about cleanliness. Nils explained to me that he could tell that a guy was a fag by the way he dressed: "Most guys wear loose-fitting clothing, just kind of baggy. They [fags] wear more tight clothes. More fashionable, I guess." Similarly, nonfags were not supposed to care about dirtying their clothes. Auto shop was a telling example of this. Given that the boys spent two hours working with greasy car parts, they frequently ended up smudged and rumpled by the end of class. While in the front of the classroom there was a room boys could change in, most of them opted not to change out of their school clothes, with a few modifying their outfits by taking their shirts off and walking around in their "beaters." These tank tops were banned at River High because of their association with gang membership. Auto shop was the one place on campus where boys could wear them with impunity. Like most of the boys in auto shop, Ben never changed out of his jeans or heavy-metal T-shirts. After working on a particularly oily engine he walked in to the classroom with grease stains covering his pants. He looked down at them, made a face, and walked toward me laughing, waving his hands around with limp wrists, and lisping in a high-pitched singsong voice, "I got my good panths all dirty!" Ben's imitation indicated that only a fag would actually care about getting his clothes dirty. "Real" guys didn't care about their appearance; thus it didn't matter if they were covered in grease stains. Of course, to not care about one's clothes, or to make fun of those who care about their clothes, ironically, is to also care about one's appearance. In this sense, masculinity became the carefully crafted appearance of not caring about appearance.

Indeed, the boys' approach to clothing and cleanliness mirrored trends in larger society and the ascendance of the "metrosexual." *Metrosexual* is the recently coined label for straight men who care about their appearance, meticulously piecing together outfits, using product in their hair, and even making manicure appointments (for clear polish, of course). Because these sorts of grooming practices are associated with gay men, straight men developed a new moniker to differentiate themselves from other straight men and from gay men.

Dancing was another practice that put a boy at risk of being labeled a fag. Often boys would jokingly dance together to diffuse the sexualized and feminized meanings embedded in dancing. At dances white boys frequently held their female dates tightly, locking their hips together. The boys never danced with one another unless they were joking or trying to embarrass one another. The examples of boys jokingly dancing together are too numerous to discuss, but the following example was particularly memorable. Lindy danced behind her date, Chris. Chris's friend Matt walked up and nudged Lindy aside, imitating her dance moves behind Chris. As Matt rubbed his hands up and down Chris's back, Chris turned around and jumped back, startled to see Matt there instead of Lindy. Matt cracked up as Chris turned red and swore at his friend.

A similar thing happened at CAPA as two of the boys from the band listened to another band play swing music. These two boys walked toward each other and began to ballroom-dance. Within a second or two they keeled over in laughter, hitting each other and moving away. This ritualized dance, moving closer and then apart, happened again and again when music played at River High. Boys participated in this ritualized exchange to emphasize that indeed they weren't fags.

When boys were forced to dance with one another, as in classroom activities, this sort of joking escalated. In the drama class Mr. McNally walked the students through an exercise that required them to stand so close to each other that most parts of their bodies touched. He instructed the students to stand in two circles on the stage, with each person on the outer circle directly behind someone in the inner circle. He began to play a haunting instrumental song with no vocals. As the song continued Mr. McNally told the students in the inner circle to close their eyes and let their bodies go limp, while still standing. He instructed the students in the outer circle to move the person in front through an interpretive dance, following his lead as he moved the student in front of him. As the music continued, most of the students in the outer circle watched Mr. McNally's movements intently, trying their best to mirror his actions. The result was an intimate and beautiful puppet-and-puppeteer-like dance with the student in back moving the student in front through slow, fluid poses. Instead of following Mr. McNally's movements like the rest of the class, one pair of white sophomores, Liam and Jacob, barely touched. Jacob stood in back of Liam and, instead of gently holding Liam's wrist with their full arms touching as the other students did, picked up Liam's wrist with two fingers as if picking up something repulsive and flung Liam's hand to its destination. He made jokes with Liam's arm, repeatedly flinging it up against Liam's chest in a movement that indicated Liam was "retarded." The jokes continued as the students switched places, so that the inner circle became the outer circle, with Liam now "in control" of Jacob. Liam placed Jacob's hand against his forehead as if saluting, made his arms flap like birds, and used Jacob's finger to poke at his eyes, all the while, unlike the other students, never letting the majority of his body touch Jacob's. At the end of the exercise Mr. McNally asked for the students' feedback. One of the girls said, a little embarrassed, "I hate to say it, but it was almost sexual." To which Mr. McNally responded, "Yeah, it's full physical contact," at which point Liam and Jacob took two steps apart from one another. Even though the entire class was assigned to touch one another simultaneously, Jacob and Liam had a hard time following the instructions because it was so dangerous to actually "dance" together like this. Even in a class situation, in the most nonsuspect of interactions, the fag discourse ran deep, forbidding boys to touch one another.

The constant threat of the fag regulated boys' attitudes toward their bodies in terms of clothing, dancing, and touching. Boys constantly engaged in repudiatory rituals to avoid permanently inhabiting the fag position. Boys' interactions were composed of competitive joking through which they interactionally created the constitutive outside and affirmed their positions as subjects.

* * *

REFRAMING HOMOPHOBIA

Homophobia is central to contemporary definitions of adolescent masculinity. Unpacking multilayered meanings that boys deploy through their uses of homophobic language and joking rituals makes clear that it is not just homophobia but a gendered and racialized homophobia. By attending to these meanings, I reframe the discussion as a fag discourse rather than simply labeling it as homophobia. The fag is an "abject" (Butler 1993) position, a position outside masculinity that actually constitutes masculinity. Thus masculinity, in part, becomes the daily interactional work of repudiating the threatening specter of the fag.

The fag extends beyond a static sexual identity attached to a gay boy. Few boys are permanently identified as fags; most move in and out of fag positions. Looking at fag as a discourse in addition to a static identity reveals that the term can be invested with different meanings in different social spaces. *Fag* may be used as a weapon with which to temporarily assert one's masculinity by denying it to others. Thus the fag becomes a symbol around which contests of masculinity take place.

* * *

The *fag* epithet, when hurled at other boys, may or may not have explicit sexual meanings, but it always has gendered meanings. When a boy calls another boy a fag, it means he is not a man but not necessarily that he is a homosexual. The boys at River High knew that they were not supposed to call homosexual boys fags because that was mean. This, then, has been the limited success of the mainstream gay rights movement. The message absorbed by some of these teenage boys was that "gay men can be masculine, just like you." Instead of challenging gender inequality, this particular discourse of gay rights has reinscribed it. Thus we need to begin to think about how gay men may be in a unique position to challenge gendered as well as sexual norms. The boys in the drama performances show an alternative way to be teenage boys, which is about playing with gender, not just enforcing gender duality based on sexual meanings.

STUDY QUESTIONS

1. Why does Pascoe doubt the word "fag," as used by the high school men she studies, is based solely in **homophobia**?

2. What role does "the fag" serve in the social construction of **gender**? As an abject social position, how does "the fag" define masculinity and enforce gender normativity?

3. How are the words "fag," "gay," and "homo" used in your social circles? Do you notice differences in the use of such terms when students who identify as gay or lesbian are present?

4. Watch Dalton Conley's interview with C. J. Pascoe on the Norton Sociology YouTube channel (http://bit.ly/cjpascoe). Describe the policy recommendations Pascoe makes; how might they reduce homophobic harassment in high schools and on university campuses?

PATRICIA HILL COLLINS

Race, Class, and Gender
as Categories of Analysis
and Connection

t's easy to see how women are oppressed—if you're a woman. It's easy to
see how blacks are oppressed—if you're African American. It's much harder,
however, for us to see how we might oppress people different from ourselves. In this selection, influential **sociologist** Patricia Hill Collins argues that
we need a new conception of **race**, **class**, and **gender** that is not based on
either/or dichotomies or on hierarchies of oppression.

* * * WHILE MANY OF US HAVE LITTLE DIFFICULTY ASSESSING OUR
own victimization within some major system of oppression, whether it be by race,
social class, religion, sexual orientation, ethnicity, age or gender, we typically fail to
see how our thoughts and actions uphold someone else's subordination. Thus, white
feminists routinely point with confidence to their oppression as women but resist
seeing how much their white skin privileges them. African-Americans who possess
eloquent analyses of racism often persist in viewing poor White women as symbols
of white power. The radical left fares little better. "If only people of color and women
could see their true class interests," they argue, "class solidarity would eliminate racism and sexism." In essence, each group identifies the type of oppression with which
it feels most comfortable as being fundamental and classifies all other types as being
of lesser importance.

Oppression is full of such contradictions. Errors in political judgment that we make concerning how we teach our courses, what we tell our children, and which organizations are worthy of our time, talents and financial support flow smoothly from errors in theoretical analysis about the nature of oppression and activism. Once we realize that there are few pure victims or oppressors, and that each one of us derives varying amounts of penalty and privilege from the multiple systems of oppression that frame our lives, then we will be in a position to see the need for new ways of thought and action.

To get at that "piece of the oppressor which is planted deep within each of us," we need at least two things. First, we need new visions of what oppression is, new categories of analysis that are inclusive of race, class, and gender as distinctive yet interlocking structures of oppression. Adhering to a stance of comparing and ranking oppressions—the proverbial, "I'm more oppressed than you"—locks us all into a dangerous dance of competing for attention, resources, and theoretical supremacy. Instead, I suggest that we examine our different experiences within the more fundamental relationship of damnation and subordination. To focus on the particular arrangements that race or class or gender take in our time and place without seeing these structures as sometimes parallel and sometimes interlocking dimensions of the more fundamental relationship of domination and subordination may temporarily ease our consciences. But while such thinking may lead to short term social reforms, it is simply inadequate for the task of bringing about long term social transformation.

While race, class and gender as categories of analysis are essential in helping us understand the structural bases of domination and subordination, new ways of thinking that are not accompanied by new ways of acting offer incomplete prospects for change. To get at that "piece of the oppressor which is planted deep within each of us," we also need to change our daily behavior. Currently, we are all enmeshed in a complex web of problematic relationships that grant our minor images full human subjectivity while stereotyping and objectifying those most different than ourselves. We often assume that the people we work with, teach, send our children to school with, and sit next to in conferences such as this, will act and feel in prescribed ways because they belong to given race, social class or gender categories. These judgments by category must be replaced with fully human relationships that transcend the legitimate differences created by race, class and gender as categories of analysis. We require new categories of connection, new visions of what our relationships with one another can be.

Our task is immense. We must first recognize race, class and gender as interlocking categories of analysis that together cultivate profound differences in our personal biographies. But then we must transcend those very differences by reconceptualizing race, class and gender in order to create new categories of connection.

My presentation today addresses this need for new patterns of thought and action. I focus on two basic questions. First, how can we reconceptualize race, class and gender as categories of analysis? Second, how can we transcend the barriers created by our experiences with race, class and gender oppression in order to build the types of coalitions essential for social exchange? To address these questions I contend that we must acquire both new theories of how race, class and gender have shaped the experiences not just of women of color, but of all groups. Moreover, we must see the connections between these categories of analysis and the personal issues in our everyday lives, particularly our scholarship, our teaching and our relationships with our colleagues and students. As Audre Lorde points out, change starts with self, and relationships that we have with those around us must always be the primary site for social change.

HOW CAN WE RECONCEPTUALIZE RACE, CLASS, AND GENDER AS CATEGORIES OF ANALYSIS?

To me, we must shift our discourse away from additive analyses of oppression (Spelman 1982; Collins 1989). Such approaches are typically based on two key premises. First, they depend on either/or, dichotomous thinking. Persons, things and ideas are conceptualized in terms of their opposites. For example, Black/White, man/woman, thought/feeling, and fact/opinion are defined in oppositional terms. Thought and feeling are not seen as two different and interconnected ways of approaching truth that can coexist in scholarship and teaching. Instead, feeling is defined as antithetical to reason, as its opposite. In spite of the fact that we all have "both/and" identities, (I am both a college professor and a mother—I don't stop being a mother when I drop my child off at school, or forget everything I learned while scrubbing the toilet), we persist in trying to classify each other in either/or categories. I live each day as an African-American woman—a race/gender specific experience. And I am not alone. Everyone in this room has a race/gender/class specific identity. Either/or, dichotomous thinking is especially troublesome when applied to theories of oppression because every individual must be classified as being either oppressed or not oppressed. The both/and position of simultaneously being oppressed and oppressor becomes conceptually impossible.

A second premise of additive analyses of oppression is that these dichotomous differences must be ranked. One side of the dichotomy is typically labeled dominant and the other subordinate. Thus, Whites rule Blacks, men are deemed superior to women, and reason is seen as being preferable to emotion. Applying this premise to discussions of oppression leads to the assumption that oppression can be quantified, and that some groups are oppressed more than others. I am frequently asked, "Which has been most oppressive to you, your status as a Black person or your status as a woman?" What I am really being asked to do is divide myself into little boxes and rank my various statuses. If I experience oppression as a both/and phenomenon, why should I analyze it any differently?

Additive analyses of oppression rest squarely on the twin pillars of either/or thinking and the necessity to quantify and rank all relationships in order to know where one stands. Such approaches typically see African-American women as being more oppressed than everyone else because the majority of Black women experience the negative effects of race, class and gender oppression simultaneously. In essence, if you add together separate oppressions, you are left with a grand oppression greater than the sum of its parts.

I am not denying that specific groups experience oppression more harshly than others—lynching is certainly objectively worse than being held up as a sex object. But we must be careful not to confuse this issue of the saliency of one type of oppression in people's lives with a theoretical stance positing the interlocking nature of oppression. Race, class and gender may all structure a situation but may not be equally visible and/ or important in people's self-definitions. In certain contexts, such as the antebellum American South and contemporary South America, racial oppression is more visibly salient, while in other contexts, such as Haiti, El Salvador and Nicaragua, social class oppression may be more apparent. For middle class White women, gender may assume experiential primacy unavailable to poor Hispanic women struggling with the ongoing issues of low paid jobs and the frustrations of the welfare bureaucracy. This recognition that one category may have salience over another for a given time and place does not minimize the theoretical importance of assuming that race, class and gender as categories of analysis structure all relationships.

In order to move toward new visions of what oppression is, I think that we need to ask new questions. How are relationships of domination and subordination structured and maintained in the American political economy? How do race, class and gender function as parallel and interlocking systems that shape this basic relationship of domination and subordination? Questions such as these promise to move us away from futile theoretical struggles concerned with ranking oppressions and towards analyses that assume race, class and gender are all present in any given setting, even if one appears more visible and salient than the others. Our task becomes redefined as one of reconceptualizing oppression by uncovering the connections among race, class and gender as categories of analysis.

Institutional Dimension of Oppression

Sandra Harding's contention that gender oppression is structured along three main dimensions—the institutional, the symbolic, and the individual—offers a useful model for a more comprehensive analysis encompassing race, class and gender oppression (Harding 1989). Systemic relationships of domination and subordination structured through social institutions such as schools, businesses, hospitals, the work place, and government agencies represent the institutional dimension of oppression. Racism, sexism and elitism all have concrete institutional locations. Even though the workings of the institutional dimension of oppression are often obscured with ideologies claiming equality of opportunity, in actuality, race, class and gender place Asian-American women, Native American men, White men, African-American women, and other groups in distinct institutional niches with varying degrees of penalty and privilege.

* * * Let us assume that the institutions of American society discriminate, whether by design or by accident. While many of us are familiar with how race, gender and class operate separately to structure inequality, I want to focus on how these three systems interlock in structuring the institutional dimension of oppression. To get at the interlocking nature of race, class and gender, I want you to think about the antebellum plantation as a guiding metaphor for a variety of American social institutions. Even though slavery is typically analyzed as a racist institution, and occasionally as a class institution, I suggest that slavery was a race, class, gender specific institution. Removing any one piece from our analysis diminishes our understanding of the true nature of relations of domination and subordination under slavery.

Slavery was a profoundly patriarchal institution. It rested on the dual tenets of White male authority and White male property, a joining of the political and the economic within the institution of the family. Heterosexism was assumed and all Whites were expected to marry. Control over affluent White women's sexuality remained key to slavery's survival because property was to be passed on to the legitimate heirs of the slave owner. Ensuring affluent White women's virginity and chastity was deeply intertwined with maintenance of property relations.

Under slavery, we see varying levels of institutional protection given to affluent White women, working class and poor White women, and enslaved African women. Poor White women enjoyed few of the protections held out to their upper class sisters. Moreover, the devalued status of Black women was key in keeping all White women in their assigned places. Controlling Black women's fertility was also key to the continuation of slavery, for children born to slave mothers themselves were slaves.

African-American women shared the devalued status of chattel with their husbands, fathers and sons. Racism stripped Blacks as a group of legal rights, education, and control over their own persons. African-Americans could be whipped, branded, sold, or killed, not because they were poor, or because they were women, but because they were Black. Racism ensured that Blacks would continue to serve Whites and suffer economic exploitation at the hands of all Whites.

So we have a very interesting chain of command on the plantation—the affluent White master as the reigning patriarch, his White wife helpmate to serve him, help him manage his property and bring up his heirs, his faithful servants whose production and reproduction were tied to the requirements of the capitalist political economy, and largely propertyless, working class White men and women watching from afar. In essence, the foundations for the contemporary roles of elite White women, poor Black women, working class White men, and a series of other groups can be seen in stark relief in this fundamental American social institution. While Blacks experienced the most harsh treatment under slavery, and thus made slavery clearly visible as a racist institution, race, class and gender interlocked in structuring slavery's systemic organization of domination and subordination.

Even today, the plantation remains a compelling metaphor for institutional oppression. Certainly the actual conditions of oppression are not as severe now as they were then. To argue, as some do, that things have not changed all that much denigrates the achievements of those who struggled for social change before us. But the basic relationships among Black men, Black women, elite White women, elite White men, working class White men and working class White women as groups remain essentially intact.

A brief analysis of key American social institutions most controlled by elite White men should convince us of the interlocking nature of race, class and gender in structuring the institutional dimension of oppression. For example, if you are from an American college or university, is your campus a modern plantation? Who controls your university's political economy? Are elite White men over represented among the upper administrators and trustees controlling your university's finances and policies? Are elite White men being joined by growing numbers of elite White women helpmates? What kinds of people are in your classrooms grooming the next generation who will occupy these and other decision-making positions? Who are the support staff that produce the mass mailings, order the supplies, fix the leaky pipes? Do African-Americans, Hispanics or other people of color form the majority of the invisible workers who feed you, wash your dishes, and clean up your offices and libraries after everyone else has gone home?

If your college is anything like mine, you know the answers to these questions. You may be affiliated with an institution that has Hispanic women as vice-presidents for finance, or substantial numbers of Black men among the faculty. If so, you are fortunate. Much more typical are colleges where a modified version of the plantation as a metaphor for the institutional dimension of oppression survives.

The Symbolic Dimension of Oppression

Widespread, societally-sanctioned ideologies used to justify relations of domination and subordination comprise the symbolic dimension of oppression. Central to this process is the use of stereotypical or controlling images of diverse race, class and gender groups. In order to assess the power of this dimension of oppression, I want you to make a list, either on paper or in your head, of "masculine" and "feminine" characteristics. If your list is anything like that compiled by most people, it reflects some variation of the following:

Masculine	Feminine
aggressive	passive
leader	follower
rational	emotional
strong	weak
intellectual	physical

Not only does this list reflect either/or dichotomous thinking and the need to rank both sides of the dichotomy, but ask yourself exactly which men and women you had in mind when compiling these characteristics. This list applies almost exclusively to middle class White men and women. The allegedly "masculine" qualities that you probably listed are only acceptable when exhibited by elite White men, or when used by Black and Hispanic men against each other or against women of color. Aggressive Black and Hispanic men are seen as dangerous, not powerful, and are often penalized when they exhibit any of the allegedly "masculine" characteristics. Working class and poor White men fare slightly better and are also denied the allegedly "masculine" symbols of leadership, intellectual competence, and human rationality. Women of color and working class and poor White women are also not represented on this list, for they have never had the luxury of being "ladies." What appear to be universal categories representing all men and women instead are unmasked as being applicable to only a small group.

It is important to see how the symbolic images applied to different race, class and gender groups interact in maintaining systems of domination and subordination. If I were to ask you to repeat the same assignment, only this time, by making separate lists for Black men, Black women, Hispanic women and Hispanic men, I suspect that your gender symbolism would be quite different. In comparing all of the lists, you might begin to see the interdependence of symbols applied to all groups. For example, the elevated images of White womanhood need devalued images of Black womanhood in order to maintain credibility.

While the above exercise reveals the interlocking nature of race, class and gender in structuring the symbolic dimension of oppression, part of its importance lies in demonstrating how race, class and gender pervade a wide range of what appears to be universal language. Attending to diversity in our scholarship, in our teaching, and in our daily lives provides a new angle of vision on interpretations of reality thought to be natural, normal and "true." Moreover, viewing images of masculinity and femininity as universal gender symbolism, rather than as symbolic images that are race, class and gender specific, renders the experiences of people of color and of non-privileged White women and men invisible. One way to dehumanize an individual or a group is to deny the reality of their experiences. So when we refuse to deal with race or class because they do not appear to be directly relevant to gender, we are actually becoming part of someone else's problem.

Assuming that everyone is affected differently by the same interlocking set of symbolic images allows us to move forward toward new analyses. Women of color and White women have different relationships to White male authority and this difference explains the distinct gender symbolism applied to both groups. Black women encounter controlling images such as the mammy, the matriarch, the mule and the whore, that encourage others to reject us as fully human people. Ironically, the negative nature of these images simultaneously encourages us to reject them. In contrast, White women are offered seductive images, those that promise to reward them for supporting the status quo. And yet seductive images can be equally controlling. Consider, for example, the views of Nancy White, a 73-year old Black woman, concerning images of rejection and seduction:

> My mother used to say that the black woman is the white man's mule and the white woman is his dog. Now, she said that to say this: we do the heavy work and get beat whether we do it well or not. But the white woman is closer to the master and he pats them on the head and lets them sleep in the house, but he ain't gon' treat neither one like he was dealing with a person. (Gwaltney, 148)

Both sets of images stimulate particular political stances. By broadening the analysis beyond the confines of race, we can see the varying levels of rejection and seduction available to each of us due to our race, class and gender identity. Each of us lives with an allotted portion of institutional privilege and penalty, and with varying levels of rejection and seduction inherent in the symbolic images applied to us. This is the context in which we make our choices. Taken together, the institutional and symbolic dimensions of oppression create a structural backdrop against which all of us live our lives.

The Individual Dimension of Oppression

Whether we benefit or not, we all live within institutions that reproduce race, class and gender oppression. Even if we never have any contact with members of other race, class and gender groups, we all encounter images of these groups and are exposed to the symbolic meanings attached to those images. On this dimension of oppression, our individual biographies vary tremendously. As a result of our institutional and symbolic statuses, all of our choices become political acts.

Each of us must come to terms with the multiple ways in which race, class and gender as categories of analysis frame our individual biographies. I have lived my entire life as an African-American woman from a working class family and this basic fact has had a profound impact on my personal biography. Imagine how different your life might be if you had been born Black, or White, or poor, or a different race/class/gender group than the one with which you are most familiar. The institutional treatment you would have received and the symbolic meanings attached to your very existence might differ dramatically from what you now consider to be natural, normal and part of everyday life. You might be the same, but your personal biography might have been quite different.

I believe that each of us carries around the cumulative effect of our lives within multiple structures of oppression. If you want to see how much you have been affected by this whole thing, I ask you one simple question—who are your close friends? Who are the people with whom you can share your hopes, dreams, vulnerabilities, fears and victories? Do they look like you? If they are all the same, circumstance may be the cause. For the first seven years of my life I saw only low income Black people. My friends from those years reflected the composition of my community. But now that I am an adult, can the defense of circumstance explain the patterns of people that I trust as my friends and colleagues? When given other alternatives, if my friends and colleagues reflect the homogeneity of one race, class and gender group, then these categories of analysis have indeed become barriers to connection.

I am not suggesting that people are doomed to follow the paths laid out for them by race, class and gender as categories of analysis. While these three structures certainly frame my opportunity structure, I as an individual always have the choice of accepting things as they are, or trying to change them. As Nikki Giovanni points out, "we've got to live in the real world. If we don't like the world we're living in, change it. And if we can't change it, we change ourselves. We can do something" (Tate 1983, 68). While a piece of the oppressor may be planted deep within each of us, we each have the choice of accepting that piece or challenging it as part of the "true focus of revolutionary change."

*　*　*

REFERENCES

Butler, Johnnella. 1989. "Difficult Dialogues." *The Women's Review of Books* 6, no. 5.

Collins, Patricia Hill. 1989. "The Social Construction of Black Feminist Thought." *Signs*. Summer 1989.

Harding, Sandra. 1986. *The Science Question in Feminism*. Ithaca, New York: Cornell University Press.

Gwaltney, John Langston. 1980. *Drylongso: A Self-Portrait of Black America*. New York: Vintage.

Lorde, Audre. 1984. *Sister Outsider*. Trumansberg, New York: The Crossing Press.

———. 1985 "Sisterhood and Survival." Keynote address, conference on the Black Woman Writer and the Diaspora, Michigan State University.

Jordan, June. 1985. *On Call: Political Essays*. Boston: South End Press.

Spelman, Elizabeth. 1982. "Theories of Race and Gender: The Erasure of Black Women." *Quest* 5: 32–36.

Tate, Claudia, ed. 1983. *Black Women Writers at Work*. New York: Continuum.

STUDY QUESTIONS

1. Why does Collins say that it is dangerous to engage in a comparison of who is more oppressed than whom?

2. How does **slavery** embody the institutional dimension of oppression?

3. What is the difference between "universal gender symbolism" and "symbolic images that are race, class and gender specific"? Why do you think Collins points out this distinction?

4. Take a few moments to list a set of characteristics you think of as "natural" or "normal" to your **race**, your **class**, and your **gender**. Trade your list with someone who differs from you in at least one of those categories. What seems strange to each of you on the other's list? What can you learn from each other?

JONATHAN KOZOL

The Savage Inequalities of Public Education in New York

S ome U.S. students attend school in dilapidated buildings, read tattered, out-of-date textbooks, and have very few opportunities for success. At the same time, other students attend school on beautiful campuses with state-of-the-art resources and limitless opportunities. Students in the United States have very different experiences in their K–12 **education** based on where they live. Students in affluent school districts have far more resources than do their less affluent counterparts. In this essay the author explores the "savage inequalities" in public education.

* * *

IN ORDER TO FIND PUBLIC SCHOOL 261 IN DISTRICT 10, A VISITOR IS told to look for a mortician's office. The funeral home, which faces Jerome Avenue in the North Bronx, is easy to identify by its green awning. The school is next door, in a former roller-skating rink. No sign identifies the building as a school. A metal awning frame without an awning supports a flagpole, but there is no flag.

In the street in front of the school there is an elevated public transit line. Heavy traffic fills the street. The existence of the school is virtually concealed within this crowded city block.

In a vestibule between the outer and inner glass doors of the school there is a sign with these words: "All children are capable of learning."

Beyond the inner doors a guard is seated. The lobby is long and narrow. The ceiling is low. There are no windows. All the teachers that I see at first are middle-aged white women. The principal, who is also a white woman, tells me that the school's "capacity" is 900 but that there are 1,300 children here. The size of classes for fifth and sixth grade children in New York, she says, is "capped" at 32, but she says that class size in the school goes "up to 34." (I later see classes, however, as large as 37.) Classes for younger children, she goes on, are "capped at 25," but a school can go above this limit if it puts an extra adult in the room. Lack of space, she says, prevents the school from operating a pre-kindergarten program.

I ask the principal where her children go to school. They are enrolled in private school, she says.

"Lunchtime is a challenge for us," she explains. "Limited space obliges us to do it in three shifts, 450 children at a time."

Textbooks are scarce and children have to share their social studies books. The principal says there is one full-time pupil counselor and another who is here two days a week: a ratio of 930 children to one counselor. The carpets are patched and sometimes taped together to conceal an open space. "I could use some new rugs," she observes.

To make up for the building's lack of windows and the crowded feeling that results, the staff puts plants and fish tanks in the corridors. Some of the plants are flourishing. Two boys, released from class, are in a corridor beside a tank, their noses pressed against the glass. A school of pinkish fish inside the tank are darting back and forth. Farther down the corridor a small Hispanic girl is watering the plants.

Two first grade classes share a single room without a window, divided only by a blackboard. Four kindergartens and a sixth grade class of Spanish-speaking children have been packed into a single room in which, again, there is no window. A second grade bilingual class of 37 children has its own room but again there is no window.

By eleven o'clock, the lunchroom is already packed with appetite and life. The kids line up to get their meals, then eat them in ten minutes. After that, with no place they can go to play, they sit and wait until it's time to line up and go back to class.

On the second floor I visit four classes taking place within another undivided space. The room has a low ceiling. File cabinets and movable blackboards give a small degree of isolation to each class. Again, there are no windows.

The library is a tiny, windowless and claustrophobic room. I count approximately 700 books. Seeing no reference books, I ask a teacher if encyclopedias and other reference books are kept in classrooms.

"We don't have encyclopedias in classrooms," she replies. "That is for the suburbs."

The school, I am told, has 26 computers for its 1,300 children. There is one small gym and children get one period, and sometimes two, each week. Recess, however, is not possible because there is no playground. "Head Start," the principal says, "scarcely exists in District 10. We have no space."

The school, I am told, is 90 percent black and Hispanic; the other 10 percent are Asian, white or Middle Eastern.

In a sixth grade social studies class the walls are bare of words or decorations. There seems to be no ventilation system, or, if one exists, it isn't working.

The class discusses the Nile River and the Fertile Crescent.

The teacher, in a droning voice: "How is it useful that these civilizations developed close to rivers?"

A child, in a good loud voice: "What kind of question is that?"

In my notes I find these words: "An uncomfortable feeling—being in a building with no windows. There are metal ducts across the room. Do they give air? I feel asphyxiated. . . ."

On the top floor of the school, a sixth grade of 30 children shares a room with 29 bilingual second graders. Because of the high class size there is an assistant with each teacher. This means that 59 children and four grown-ups—63 in all—must share a room that, in a suburban school, would hold no more than 20 children and one teacher. There are, at least, some outside windows in this room—it is the only room with windows in the school—and the room has a high ceiling. It is a relief to see some daylight.

I return to see the kindergarten classes on the ground floor and feel stifled once again by lack of air and the low ceiling. Nearly 120 children and adults are doing what they can to make the best of things: 80 children in four kindergarten classes, 30 children in the sixth grade class, and about eight grown-ups who are aides and teachers. The kindergarten children sitting on the worn rug, which is patched with tape, look up at me and turn their heads to follow me as I walk past them.

As I leave the school, a sixth grade teacher stops to talk. I ask her, "Is there air conditioning in warmer weather?"

Teachers, while inside the building, are reluctant to give answers to this kind of question. Outside, on the sidewalk, she is less constrained: "I had an awful room last year. In the winter it was 56 degrees. In the summer it was up to 90. It was sweltering."

I ask her, "Do the children ever comment on the building?"

"They don't say," she answers, "but they know."

I ask her if they see it as a racial message.

"All these children see TV," she says. "They know what suburban schools are like. Then they look around them at their school. This was a roller-rink, you know. . . . They don't comment on it but you see it in their eyes. They understand."

* * *

Two months later, on a day in May, I visit an elementary school in Riverdale. The dogwoods and magnolias on the lawn in front of P.S. 24 are in full blossom on the day I visit. There is a well-tended park across the street, another larger park three blocks away. To the left of the school is a playground for small children, with an innovative jungle gym, a slide and several climbing toys. Behind the school there are two playing fields for older kids. The grass around the school is neatly trimmed.

The neighborhood around the school, by no means the richest part of Riverdale, is nonetheless expensive and quite beautiful. Residences in the area—some of which are large, free-standing houses, others condominiums in solid red-brick buildings—sell for prices in the region of $400,000; but some of the larger Tudor houses on the winding and tree-shaded streets close to the school can cost up to $1 million. The excellence of P.S. 24, according to the principal, adds to the value of these homes. Advertisements in the *New York Times* will frequently inform prospective buyers that a house is "in the neighborhood of P.S. 24."

The school serves 825 children in the kindergarten through sixth grade. This is approximately half the student population crowded into P.S. 79, where 1,550 children fill a space intended for 1,000, and a great deal smaller than the 1,300 children packed into the former skating rink; but the principal of P.S. 24, a capable and energetic man named David Rothstein, still regards it as excessive for an elementary school.

The school is integrated in the strict sense that the middle- and upper-middle-class white children here do occupy a building that contains some Asian and Hispanic and black children; but there is little integration in the classrooms since the vast majority of the Hispanic and black children are assigned to "special" classes on the basis of evaluations that have classified them "EMR"—"educable mentally retarded"—or else, in the worst of cases, "TMR"—"trainable mentally retarded."

I ask the principal if any of his students qualify for free-lunch programs. "About 130 do," he says. "Perhaps another 35 receive their lunches at reduced price. Most of these kids are in the special classes. They do not come from this neighborhood."

The very few nonwhite children that one sees in mainstream classes tend to be Japanese or else of other Asian origins. Riverdale, I learn, has been the residence of choice for many years to members of the diplomatic corps.

The school therefore contains effectively two separate schools: one of about 130 children, most of whom are poor, Hispanic, black, assigned to one of the 12 special classes; the other of some 700 mainstream students, almost all of whom are white or Asian.

There is a third track also—this one for the students who are labeled "talented" or "gifted." This is termed a "pullout" program since the children who are so identified remain in mainstream classrooms but are taken out for certain periods each week to be provided with intensive and, in my opinion, excellent instruction in some areas of reasoning and logic often known as "higher-order skills" in the contemporary jargon of the public schools. Children identified as "gifted" are admitted to this program in first grade and, in most cases, will remain there for six years. Even here, however, there are two tracks of the gifted. The regular gifted classes are provided with only one semester of this specialized instruction yearly. Those very few children, on the other hand, who are identified as showing the most promise are assigned, beginning in the third grade, to a program that receives a full-year regimen.

In one such class, containing ten intensely verbal and impressive fourth grade children, nine are white and one is Asian. The "special" class I enter first, by way of contrast, has twelve children of whom only one is white and none is Asian. These racial breakdowns prove to be predictive of the schoolwide pattern.

In a classroom for the gifted on the first floor of the school, I ask a child what the class is doing. "Logic and syllogisms," she replies. The room is fitted with a planetarium. The principal says that all the elementary schools in District 10 were given the same planetariums ten years ago but that certain schools, because of overcrowding, have been forced to give them up. At P.S. 261, according to my notes, there was a dome-like space that had been built to hold a planetarium, but the planetarium had been removed to free up space for the small library collection. P.S. 24, in contrast, has a spacious library that holds almost 8,000 books. The windows are decorated with attractive, brightly colored curtains and look out on flowering trees. The principal says that it's inadequate, but it appears spectacular to me after the cubicle that holds a meager 700 books within the former skating rink.

The district can't afford librarians, the principal says, but P.S. 24, unlike the poorer schools of District 10, can draw on educated parent volunteers who staff the room in shifts three days a week. A parent organization also raises independent funds to buy materials, including books, and will soon be running a fund-raiser to enhance the library's collection.

In a large and sunny first grade classroom that I enter next, I see 23 children, all of whom are white or Asian. In another first grade, there are 22 white children and two others who are Japanese. There is a computer in each class. Every classroom also has a modern fitted sink.

In a second grade class of 22 children, there are two black children and three Asian children. Again, there is a sink and a computer. A sixth grade social studies class has only one black child. The children have an in-class research area that holds some up-to-date resources. A set of encyclopedias (World Book, 1985) is in a rack beside a window. The children are doing a Spanish language lesson when I enter. Foreign languages begin in sixth grade at the school, but Spanish is offered also to the kindergarten children. As in every room at P.S. 24, the window shades are clean and new, the floor is neatly tiled in gray and green, and there is not a single light bulb missing.

Walking next into a special class, I see twelve children. One is white. Eleven are black. There are no Asian children. The room is half the size of mainstream classrooms. "Because of overcrowding," says the principal, "we have had to split these rooms in half." There is no computer and no sink.

I enter another special class. Of seven children, five are black, one is Hispanic, one is white. A little black boy with a large head sits in the far corner and is gazing at the ceiling.

"Placement of these kids," the principal explains, "can usually be traced to neurological damage."

In my notes: "How could so many of these children be brain-damaged?"

Next door to the special class is a woodworking shop. "This shop is only for the special classes," says the principal. The children learn to punch in time cards at the door, he says, in order to prepare them for employment.

The fourth grade gifted class, in which I spend the last part of the day, is humming with excitement. "I start with these children in the first grade," says the teacher. "We pull them out of mainstream classes on the basis of their test results and other factors such as the opinion of their teachers. Out of this group, beginning in third grade, I pull out the ones who show the most potential, and they enter classes such as this one."

The curriculum they follow, she explains, "emphasizes critical thinking, reasoning and logic." The planetarium, for instance, is employed not simply for the study of the universe as it exists. "Children also are designing their own galaxies," the teacher says.

A little girl sitting around a table with her classmates speaks with perfect poise: "My name is Susan. We are in the fourth grade gifted program."

I ask them what they're doing and a child says, "My name is Laurie and we're doing problem-solving."

A rather tall, good-natured boy who is half-standing at the table tells me that his name is David. "One thing that we do," he says, "is logical thinking. Some problems, we find, have more than one good answer. We need to learn not simply to be logical in our own thinking but to show respect for someone else's logic even when an answer may be technically incorrect."

When I ask him to explain this, he goes on, "A person who gives an answer that is not 'correct' may nonetheless have done some interesting thinking that we should examine. 'Wrong' answers may be more useful to examine than correct ones."

I ask the children if reasoning and logic are innate or if they're things that you can learn.

"You know some things to start with when you enter school," Susan says. "But we also learn some things that other children don't."

I ask her to explain this.

"We know certain things that other kids don't know because we're *taught* them."

She has braces on her teeth. Her long brown hair falls almost to her waist. Her loose white T-shirt has the word TRI-LOGIC on the front. She tells me that Tri-Logic is her father's firm.

Laurie elaborates on the same point: "Some things you know. Some kinds of logic are inside of you to start with. There are other things that someone needs to teach you."

David expands on what the other two have said: "Everyone can think and speak in logical ways unless they have a mental problem. What this program does is bring us to a higher form of logic."

The class is writing a new "Bill of Rights." The children already know the U.S. Bill of Rights and they explain its first four items to me with precision. What they are examining today, they tell me, is the very *concept* of a "right." Then they will create their own compendium of rights according to their own analysis and definition. Along one wall of the classroom, opposite the planetarium, are seven Apple II computers on which children have developed rather subtle color animations that express the themes—of greed and domination, for example—that they also have described in writing.

"This is an upwardly mobile group," the teacher later says. "They have exposure to whatever New York City has available. Their parents may take them to the theater, to museums...."

In my notes: "Six girls, four boys. Nine white, one Chinese. I am glad they have this class. But what about the others? Aren't there ten black children in the school who could enjoy this also?"

The teacher gives me a newspaper written, edited and computer-printed by her sixth grade gifted class. The children, she tells me, are provided with a link to kids in Europe for transmission of news stories.

A science story by one student asks if scientists have ever falsified their research. "Gregor Mendel," the sixth grader writes, "the Austrian monk who founded the science of genetics, published papers on his work with peas that some experts say were statistically too good to be true. Isaac Newton, who formulated the law of gravitation, relied on unseemly mathematical sleight of hand in his calculations.... Galileo Galilei, founder of modern scientific method, wrote about experiments that were so difficult to duplicate that colleagues doubted he had done them."

Another item in the paper, also by a sixth grade student, is less esoteric: "The Don Cossacks dance company, from Russia, is visiting the United States. The last time it toured America was 1976.... The Don Cossacks will be in New York City for two weeks at the Neil Simon Theater. Don't miss it!"

The tone is breezy—and so confident! That phrase—"Don't miss it!"—speaks a volume about life in Riverdale.

"What makes a good school?" asks the principal when we are talking later on. "The building and teachers are part of it, of course. But it isn't just the building and the teachers. Our kids come from good families and the neighborhood is good. In a three-block area we have a public library, a park, a junior high.... Our typical sixth grader reads at eighth grade level." In a quieter voice he says, "I see how hard my colleagues work in schools like P.S. 79. You have children in those neighborhoods who live in virtual hell. They enter school five years behind. What do they get?" Then, as he spreads his hands out on his desk, he says: "I have to ask myself why there should be an elementary school in District 10 with fifteen hundred children. Why should there be an elementary school within a skating rink? Why should the Board of Ed allow this? This is not the way that things should be."

———

Stark as the inequities in District 10 appear, educators say that they are "mild" in comparison to other situations in the city. Some of the most stunning inequality, according to a report by the Community Service Society, derives from allocations granted by state legislators to school districts where they have political allies. The poorest districts in the city get approximately 90 cents per pupil from these legislative grants, while the richest districts have been given $14 for each pupil.

Newspapers in New York City have reported other instances of the misallocation of resources. "The Board of Education," wrote the *New York Post* during July of 1987, "was hit with bombshell charges yesterday that money earmarked for fighting drug abuse and illiteracy in ghetto schools was funneled instead to schools in wealthy areas."

In receipt of extra legislative funds, according to the *Post*, affluent districts were funded "at a rate 14 times greater than low-income districts." The paper said the city's poorest areas were underfunded "with stunning consistency."

The report by the Community Service Society cites an official of the New York City Board of Education who remarks that there is "no point" in putting further money "into some poor districts" because, in his belief, "new teachers would not stay there." But the report observes that, in an instance where beginning teacher salaries were raised by nearly half, "that problem largely disappeared"—another interesting reminder of the difference money makes when we are willing to invest it. Nonetheless, says the report, "the perception that the poorest districts are beyond help still remains. . . ." Perhaps the worst result of such beliefs, says the report, is the message that resources would be "wasted on poor children." This message "trickles down to districts, schools, and classrooms." Children hear and understand this theme—they are poor investments—and behave accordingly. If society's resources would be wasted on their destinies, perhaps their own determination would be wasted too. "Expectations are a powerful force . . . ," the CSS observes.

Despite the evidence, the CSS report leans over backwards not to fuel the flames of racial indignation. "In the present climate," the report says, "suggestions of racism must be made with caution. However, it is inescapable that these inequities are being perpetrated on [school] districts which are virtually all black and Hispanic. . . ." While the report says, very carefully, that there is no "evidence" of "deliberate individual discrimination," it nonetheless concludes that "those who allocate resources make decisions over and over again which penalize the poorest districts." Analysis of city policy, the study says, "speaks to systemic bias which constitutes a conspiracy of effect. . . . Whether consciously or not, the system writes off its poorest students."

STUDY QUESTIONS

1. Why are the schools Kozol talks about so unequal? Why is there a distinct difference between the amount of money the poorer school has compared to the richer school?

2. The more affluent school couldn't afford a librarian, so how did they handle the librarian's duties? Why didn't the poorer schools use a similar solution? How else does the inequality between the schools go beyond the amount of money spent on each student?

3. Imagine that you attend the poor school described in the essay. Looking around the dilapidated building, what would you think **society** is trying to tell you about yourself?

4. The United States is the only industrialized nation that funds schools in the way that Kozol describes. How could officials make things more fair in your community and across the country? Research online how other countries distribute their educational resources and provide at least one example that you think would work well.

JAMIE LEW

Burden of Acting Neither White nor Black: Asian American Identities and Achievement in Urban Schools

How does your **socioeconomic status** affect the way you view your ethnic identity? In this selection, Jamie Lew compares two groups of Korean American students in New York City. One group attends a highly competitive magnet school while the other is completing GED courses. Lew's findings suggest that our economic **class** affects how we are treated in schools and how we come to understand our racial or ethnic identities. As you read this piece consider how or whether your **culture** was valued by the adults in your high school.

INTRODUCTION

A GROWING BODY OF RESEARCH HAS CHALLENGED OGBU'S THEORY of "burden of acting white"[1] and to what extent cultural explanations account for black students' schooling experience and outcome. Emerging studies show that Ogbu's cultural explanations may be limited when examining variability of school achievement among black and white students, and that other social forces, such as class, peer

[1] John Uzo Ogbu (1939–2003), Nigerian-born American anthropologist known for his theory that some minority students perform worse in school than they might in order to avoid being accused of "acting white" by their peers.

networks, and school context may play a significant role in their schooling aspirations and achievement (Cook & Ludwig, 1998; Downey & Ainsworth-Darnell, 2002; Ferguson, 2001; Tyson, 2002; Tyson, Darity, & Castellino, 2005). In short, variability of school performance among black and white students, for instance, should take into account not only issues of race and culture but how these processes may be fluid and salient depending on the changing social and school contexts.

These studies are important in light of the widening black and white achievement gap and the prevailing cultural discourse often used to explain school achievement. However, in the midst of this on-going debate, there is a limited understanding of how, if at all, the theory of "acting white" plays a role for racial groups other than black and white students. By extending the discussion beyond a black-and-white discourse, researchers may be able to complicate and expand our understanding of the role of culture in school achievement and how it intersects with various structural forces, such as class and schools.

One of the more invisible racial groups discussed in this debate is Asian Americans. Stereotyped as model minorities, Asian American students' negotiation of multiple identities, varied schooling experiences, and racialization process are often ignored (Fong & Shinangawa, 2000; Lee, 1996; Lew, 2006; Espiritu, 1994; Pang & Cheng, 1998; Park, Goodwin, & Lee, 2003). However, Asian American status as model minorities—a stereotype that often conflates them with whiteness—plays an important ideological role in perpetuating ideals of individual meritocracy, especially for poor minority students. Such ideals of "American dream" predicated on cultural explanations place both reward and blame on individuals without adequately taking into account important structural factors, such as race, class, and schools. Therefore, stereotype images of Asian "success" or black "failure" cannot be predicated solely on cultural explanations, but has to take into account the changing social contexts.

In order to address such limitations, this study will examine some of these timely issues by asking the following research questions: How do Asian American students in different social and economic contexts negotiate their racial and ethnic identities, and how does this process impact their academic aspirations and achievement? In what ways do peer networks and race relations in schools affect students' negotiation of identities? How do high-achieving Asian Americans who are typically viewed as model minorities—a portrayal associated with whiteness—negotiate their racial minority status? How is this process similar and different from those Asian American students who are low-achieving or dropping out of high schools? In what ways does this research challenge our understanding of "acting white," and the ways in which students negotiate power relations inherent in the polarized notions of blackness and whiteness?

As a way to answer some of these questions, this study compares experiences of two groups of Korean American students—both high- and low-achieving—in New York City urban schools. I compare experiences of high-achieving middle-class students attending a competitive academic magnet high school with working-class low-achieving high school dropouts attending a community-based GED program. The findings indicate that the two groups of Korean American students experienced their racial minority status and adopted different racial strategies depending on their socio-economic backgrounds, peer networks, and school contexts. For instance, the high-achieving middle-class Korean students, in the school context of academic peer culture attended predominantly by middle-class White and Asian students were more likely to associate and identify with their ethnic backgrounds. Similar to previous studies on Hispanic [students] and children of immigrants, the high-achieving Korean students highlighted their bicultural backgrounds and bilingual ability when noting their experiences as both Korean and American.

On the other hand, the low-achieving Korean American high school dropouts, in the context of urban schools fraught with academic failure and increasing dropout rates that consist predominantly of poor and working-class minorities were more likely to identify themselves as "minorities." As such, the Korean high school dropouts in this study were careful to disassociate themselves from the "wealthy" and "studious" Koreans and other Asian Americans. It is important to note that neither the high- nor the low-achieving students identified themselves with whiteness; however, the two groups negotiated and interpreted their racial minority status and accompanying marginalization differently depending on their given opportunity structure at home and schools.

This research is particularly timely given the on-going debate of Ogbu's theory of "burden of acting white" and the role of culture on school achievement. It argues that academic achievement among Asian American students involves a complex relationship between culture, class, race, and schools. Asian Americans in schools face conflicting messages regarding their racial minority status: On the one hand, as racial minorities, they are often excluded from whiteness, while on the other hand, they are also stereotyped as model minorities that align them with whiteness. Asian Americans in the context of a black and white racial discourse prevalent in our society learn to negotiate their race and ethnic identities differently from black and white students—a process that is largely shaped by changing social contexts. Although neither the high- nor the low-achieving Korean American students aligned themselves with whiteness, the two groups in different economic and school contexts, learned to interpret their minority status and opportunity structure differently. The findings support earlier studies that note the significance of school structure—peer relations, racial and class composition, and academic culture—and show how these structural factors may play an integral role in fulfilling academic aspirations and achievement among minority students. In so doing, it challenges the prevalent stereotype based on cultural discourse to explain Asian "success" and black "failure." It underscores the significance of examining these processes across and within various ethnic and racial groups, while highlighting the salience of race as well as the relational nature of identities in various school and economic contexts.

* * *

RESEARCH SITE AND METHODS

In order to collect information on social processes, such as intergenerational negotiations, racial and ethnic identity construction, and schooling aspirations, the research is based on in-depth interviews and participant observations. This research took place in a New York City public school and a community-based GED program. A total of 72 Korean American students were interviewed: 42 in the academic magnet high school and 30 high school dropouts in the GED program. Both 1.5 (born in Korea but raised in the US) and second-generation (born and raised in the United States) Korean American students were interviewed.

Although most of the students grew up and lived in Queens, New York—the borough with the largest ethnic enclaves of Korean Americans in the New York metropolitan area—they came from different socioeconomic and family backgrounds. Compared to the Korean high school dropouts, the magnet high school students came from higher socioeconomic backgrounds with a greater number of two-parent households. For instance, 36% of the academic students were eligible for reduced and free lunch, compared to 80% of the dropout students. Furthermore, when we consider their schooling context, we see an important distinction.

As a competitive elite high school in New York City, the magnet high school (MH) prides itself on student academic achievement paralleled by few public high schools. According to the annual school report (NYC Board of Assessment, 2002–2003), approximately 2,700 students were enrolled, and since entrance to the school was based on a competitive standardized exam, students commute to the school from all five of New York City's boroughs. Almost half of the students were Asian (46.5%), while 37% were white, 9.1% Hispanic, and 7.4% black. Only about 1% consists of recent immigrants to the US (those who immigrated to the US within the last 3 years).

The Youth Community Center (YCC) is a non-profit community-based organization in Queens, New York. Its education and outreach programs provide students and adults with counseling, tutoring, classes on the Test of English as a Foreign Language (TOEFL), English-as-a-second language (ESL) classes, and preparatory classes for the General Educational Development (GED) exam. All of the Korean students in the GED program had officially dropped out of their respective neighborhood public high schools in New York City and had been referred to the program by teachers, counselors, parents, community members, and peers. The Korean high school dropouts in the GED program came from various public high schools in New York City, most of which had a record of low student academic performance and high school dropout rates, as well as a disproportionate number of poor minority students and recent immigrants.

FINDINGS

Middle-Class and High-Achieving Students: Race, Class, Schools

At MH, one of the most competitive elite public high schools in New York City, the middle-class and high-achieving students were steeped in a competitive college-bound curriculum taught by teachers and administrators who are certified in their fields. The students were also surrounded predominantly by middle-class white and Asian American peers who were immersed in this school culture that fostered academic achievement and excellence; thus, the Korean American students at MH were likely to associate with peers of similar socioeconomic status, education background, and academic expectations. Even for those Korean American students at MH whose families were of lower socioeconomic backgrounds, they were more likely to be exposed to and associate with other students of higher socioeconomic backgrounds.

Moreover, by attending a high school where second-generation Asian Americans represented nearly half (46.5%) of the student population, the Korean American students were likely to reinforce old or establish new friendships with other Asian and Korean American peers who also shared similar experiences growing up as children of immigrant parents. In this respect, institutional characteristics of the school played an important role in providing academic support, as well as strengthening peer relations and helping second-generation youths negotiate their ethnic and racial identities.

According to the high-achieving students in the interview, this regular contact with Korean and Asian Americans in school and community formed the basis for an important set of shared experiences—growing up with immigrant parents and maintaining close ties to ethnic communities at home and school—which reinforced their ethnic identities. Susan explains:

> The Korean community of my age group, everyone knows everyone in some way. Like, either you're friends with someone that knows this other person . . . it's like everything is sort of related into one big circle . . . I started hanging out with Koreans, and then more other Korean friends came along . . . church especially, tae kwon do, neighborhood, they are all part of this big circle.

By being embedded in such networks at home, community, and school, the high-achieving students also reinforced their Korean language skill. For instance, John spoke about the importance of learning to speak Korean, and how bilingual skill is an important part of identifying with and reinforcing their Korean ethnic background:

> How do you identify yourself?

> Korean American. I have a lot of Korean pride. If I see a Korean kid who can't speak Korean at all, I'd just be like, you gotta learn Korean you know, you are Korean.

Helen also highlighted her ethnicity, identifying herself as a Korean American. However, she was careful to point out that she saw herself as both Korean and American. Her comments illustrate that social constructs such as race and ethnic identity are subject to change, contradiction, and variability within specific determinate contexts. When I asked her how she identified herself, she replied:

> Korean American. I was born here, so I am definitely American in some way, but I am, of course, Korean . . . Even if I am born here, I look definitely Asian or Korean or whatever and like the way my parents live and the way we are—we are not Americanized . . . if I compare myself to some of my friends, I am more American. They were born there [Korea] and raised there.

As illustrated, the process of identity construction is relative, filled with contradictions and inconsistencies. However, the students were also keenly aware of their racial minority status and associated becoming American with whiteness. Yet, as Helen noted, in a school context that has such a large number of Asian American students, she takes pride in being identified as "Asian." She continues:

> I would never consider myself just American. Sometimes, if someone teased me or something, I just wanted and would've been happier if I was American, if I looked American. You know how Asians, they look totally different. So I guess if I looked American, no one would tease me and stuff . . . Now, since I am going to this school, and a lot of people are Asians, so I think being Asian is good. I would never want to be like someone else.

If the school context reinforced their ethnic and racial identity, their parents also played an important role. For instance, Beth comments that her parents reminded her that regardless of whether she was born and raised in the United States, most people would not accept her as an American because of her minority racial status:

> When I think of Americans, I think of white people. My parents always told me that even though you are born here and can speak English as well as them, they won't really think of you as American. I don't completely believe that, but I think there is some basis truth in that. I think that if they look at you, they are going to say, you are Asian—and then attach the American thing after. So, the first impression that people will have of me will not be that she is American, but that she is Asian.

As illustrated, despite the students' identification with ethnic backgrounds, the high-achieving Korean American students at MH were also painfully aware of how their racial minority status may be used to label them as foreigners or non-American by outsiders, despite their having been born and raised in the US. Therefore as much as the students identified with their ethnicity, this process is also framed by exclusion and marginalization.

According to the students, in order to address such marginalization, their parents emphasized the importance of using education to compensate for their racial barriers. Underlying this advice was a firm belief that to compensate for their racial-minority status, they had to work even harder and excel in school. Therefore, embedded in strong social support at home, communities, and school, the high-achieving Korean students learned to use education as a means to, in part, withstand the stigma accompanying their racial minority status. Yun Shin at MH reiterated her mother's advice:

> My mom would want me to be Americanized and get education, since there is so much racism against Asians and stuff, but she wants me to keep my Korean culture. Being American never entered my mind. It's not that I don't want to be, but it's just that I've never been accepted as one, never been considered one, so I never thought of myself as one. Because I am always surrounded by Asians, being American never entered my mind. You know, if I say, "I am American," they would say, "No, you are not. You are Asian."

The students' responses also echo findings from earlier studies that have shown how children of immigrants who maintain close ties to their ethnic communities are more likely to reinforce their ethnic identity toward excelling in school (Caplan, Choy, & Whitmore, 1991; Gibson, 1988; Lew, 2006, Portes & Rumbaut, 1996; Suárez-Orozco & Suárez-Orozco, 1995, 2001; Zhou and Bankston, 1996, 1998). Gibson (1988) describes this as a strategy of accommodation or selective assimilation—a process whereby the children in Punjabi community learned skills necessary to be competitive in American society but resisted assimilating with the lower-socioeconomic white community in which they resided. Other studies on Southeast Asian refugee students also indicate that their academic success was primarily attributable to their close ties to their first-generation parental ethnic networks, and their ability to resist downward assimilation into their surrounding poor minority communities (Zhou and Bankston, 1996, 1998).

Poor and Working-Class High School Dropouts: Race, Class, Schools

Expanding on Ogbu's (1987) theory of oppositional cultural frame of reference and "acting white," an increasing number of studies have complicated the dichotomy of voluntary and involuntary groups' experiences by illustrating how members of both groups learn to adopt oppositional cultural frames of reference (Portes and Rumbaut, 1996, 2001; Waters, 1994, 1999). These studies show that children of immigrants who live in poor, isolated neighborhoods without the protection of strong immigrant networks and social capital are likely to assimilate the cultures and norms of their poor minority peers and adopt an oppositional cultural frame of reference that may not be conducive to schooling success.

The working-class Korean American dropouts not only struggled financially at home, but faced limited support in school. These urban schools, mostly populated by poor minorities and recent immigrants, were fraught with violence and high dropout rates. In this school context, the low-income Korean American dropouts rarely came into contact with wealthy Asian Americans or whites. Rather, most of their peers were working-class and poor Asians, blacks, and Hispanics. The racial and economic isolation of these youngsters, therefore, perpetuated their distrust of and alienation from wealthy whites and Asian Americans.

Henry who was born in Korea but raised in the US explained that he and his friends had very little contact with wealthy whites, either in school or in their neighborhoods, and that they saw whites largely through an oppositional lens:

> I feel closer to blacks and Hispanics than whites. I think most Koreans are closer to black culture. It's not like I hate whites, but I don't like them either. When I see a white person, I don't see them as just a person. I see them as a white person. When I see them, I think, "I don't know you, I don't know what you do, and I don't want to get to know you." My friends don't like whites either 'cause we sometimes get into fights with whites and the way they talk about white people. When I see a white person, the first thing I think about is that they are rich and educated, and most of Koreans like me are not educated and rich. So when I see them, I think they are from another planet.

Interestingly enough, however, my informants also distinguished themselves from the "wealthy" Korean and other Asian Americans who grew up in middle-class homes and privileged neighborhoods. For instance, Emily explained how such "wealthy" Korean Americans from better neighborhoods would not understand her experience and struggles of growing up in housing projects populated by poor blacks and Hispanics:

> This Korean girl I know at church was brought up in Bayside, which is mostly white and Asian. If she was brought up in Philadelphia, it would be different. For me, where I lived, majority of the people were Hispanics and blacks. She doesn't know the environment I grew up in. I know their culture and the way they work. She only knows what she knows. It's mixed, but they are wealthier, and they live in houses. We struggled, and she grew up more comfortable. You know, where I grew up, everybody worked to make a living, the houses were dirty, lived in one bedroom with four people in it. You know, that's how I lived. One bedroom with my mother, father, brother, and me.

Emily continued to explain that her low social and economic status represented a kind of collective "minority" experience that distinguished her from the wealthier and privileged whites and Asians:

> We went through a lot living in that environment. She [wealthy Korean American friend] doesn't know a lot about that. She is more to the whites and Asians, and I am more to the blacks and Hispanics, more toward the minority.

Similarly, Lee (2004) in her study of second-generation Korean American adults in New York City also found that middle-class Koreans touted their ethnicity and model minority status as reasons for their achievement. However, working-class Koreans interpreted their experiences as shaped largely by their class position. In the context of an ethnic community that is predominantly middle-class and socially mobile, the working-class Korean Americans, in order to "save face" from being "looked down" upon, tend to distance themselves somewhat from Korean communities at large and downplay their ethnicity (2004).

Interestingly enough, as the Korean American high school dropouts distinguished themselves from their co-ethnic peers along class lines, they also distinguished themselves from more educated or "studious" Koreans. Ken explained that he had many Korean American friends whom he had met in Korean churches, clubs, or schools. But he carefully distinguished himself from the high-achieving "studious" Koreans. He noted that while his Korean American friends "hang out" after church, the "studious" Koreans go home after school with their family:

> I don't hang out with anyone else but Koreans. I used to hang out at the Elmhurst Park a lot. I used to play basketball there, and when you play sports there you meet people, and then you meet their friends. The basketball thing was always after the [church] service. Those kinds of people, you know, the studious people who don't go out much, would leave right after the service. So, you know who they are.

Ken continued to explain how he aligned "studious" and "wealthy" Koreans with whiteness because of the way they spoke, dressed, and succeeded in school:

> They [studious Koreans] live a different world. Totally different. When I look at them, I never had a friend like them, so I don't know. When I see them, it's like I am seeing a white person. They never cut school, they use a different language, they use proper language, and I use slangs. They dress more simple; some try to show off, but they don't care what other people think. Their hairstyles are different. Most of them are like whites because they don't know this kind of life, and they hang out with whites, and most of the time they don't hang out anyway.

The findings show that in addition to distinguishing themselves from wealthy whites, the low-status dropouts also distinguished themselves from socially mobile Koreans and other Asians whom they deemed "wealthy and studious"—attributes of "success" they associated with whiteness. In the process, most of the dropouts aligned their shared experiences of racism and low socioeconomic status with those of their low-income minority peers—blacks, Hispanics, and Asians (Lew, 2004, 2006).

In a society based on a polarized discourse of success and failure, rich and poor, and black and white, it is no surprise that students struggled to make sense of their distinctive experience, one marked by low socioeconomic and racial-minority status. Their comments represent their negotiation within a polarized racial discourse that tolerates Asians as either "near-whites" or invisible minorities, and whose experiences are often de-racialized and de-contextualized. Within the black and white racial paradigm, Asians, American Indians, and Latinos are defined in relation to acting either white or black. As Okihiro (1994) notes, racial paradigm of being "near-whites" or "just like blacks" is historically and socially constructed, where Asian Americans have been marginalized throughout US history, as the labels of "near-blacks" in the past or "near-whites" in the present demonstrate.

Meanwhile, embedded in students' comments is also the implicit marginalization they experience *within* the Korean community (Lew, 2005, 2006). To be poor and uneducated within a community that is predominantly middle-class, college edu-cated, and upwardly mobile also means looked down on and being excluded. As a means of developing survival strategies to endure and resist such marginalization within their own co-ethnic communities, as well as withstand institutional barriers such as inferior schooling, economic limitation, and racial discrimination within the larger society, the working-class Korean American high school dropouts formed cultural frames of reference and social identities in opposition to the dominant society.

CONCLUSION

To summarize, both groups of Korean students negotiated their racial and ethnic identities differently according to the changing social and economic context. The high-achieving Korean American students in the context of an academic high school with a significant number of middle-class white and Asian student body, were more likely to identify with their ethnicity. They often described themselves as both Korean and American noting the varied ways in which this process is filled with contradictions.

Despite the fluidity of identities, however, the students also saw their racial identities ascribed to them in the form of exclusionary stereotypes and false constructs of homogeneity. As illustrated, the high-achieving Korean American students typically associated being "American" with whiteness and pointed out that because of their racial minority status, they would not be accepted as "American" despite being born and raised in the US.

In order to resist this racial minority status and marginalization that accompanies it, the middle-class and high-achieving students are more likely to use education as a racial strategy. That is, they firmly uphold the belief that as racial minorities, they would have to work even harder in school to obtain the economic parity with white Americans. This predicament highlights multiple and situational meanings associated with being American, the salience of race, as well as the integral and complex relationship between race and class in the United States.

On the other hand, the Korean high school dropouts in the context of poor urban schools fraught with academic failure and populated by poor minority students, adopted different mode of adaptation. The Korean dropouts were less likely to identify with their ethnicity. By distinguishing themselves from wealthy and educated Koreans and Asians who symbolically represent whiteness, they identified themselves with other "minorities"—a collective term symbolizing downward mobility and struggles with racism and poverty. In order to negotiate and resist such institutional barriers in their homes, schools, and communities, these low-income Korean American students dropped out of high school and adopted behaviors that were not conducive to school achievement.

The findings poignantly illustrate how social class intersects with identity and school achievement. It shows how middle-class high-achieving students, compared to the poor and working-class high school dropouts, have greater access to educational resources and social capital at their respective schools and ethnic communities—institutional resources that are pivotal for students to achieve academically (Lew, 2004, 2006, in press). The middle-class Korean students in the study, compared to poor and working-class Korean students, are more likely to gain access to teachers, counselors, and peers who can provide important schooling resources toward achieving in school. Therefore, even though both groups of Korean American students bring with them their distinct cultural capital and forge important relationships with fellow peers in schools and communities, the social and cultural resources available to middle-class high-achieving students are more likely to be rewarded by the mainstream school system.

Moreover, the findings point to the importance of noting class variability within ethnic communities and the implications this may have in negotiation of racial and ethnic identities. For instance, as beneficial as ethnic networks can be, depending on the background of the member, it can also serve to exclude: that is, in the context of an ethnic community that is predominantly middle-class and socially mobile, the middle-class and high-achieving Korean Americans are more likely to benefit from their ethnic communities and align themselves with their ethnic backgrounds. However, the poor and working-class high school dropouts, often facing exclusion from their own ethnic communities, are less likely to benefit from their ethnic communities and disassociate themselves from their ethnic backgrounds.

The findings also complicate earlier understandings of oppositional cultural frames of reference and "acting white": In the context of a binary black and white racial discourse, as well as the prevalent model minority stereotype that conflates Asian Americans with whiteness, the findings in this study illustrate how Asian American students in different social and economic contexts negotiate their racial minority status and social class backgrounds. To that end, it is important to distinguish variability of social class and peer relations, highlight the fluidity of multiple identities, and examine institutional factors and schooling contexts when accounting for students' negotiation of identities and interpretation of opportunity structure.

The stereotype of Asian "success" much like black "failure" cannot be explained solely on their cultural orientation. Although race and cultures play an important role in students' outlook and negotiations of their opportunity structure, this process changes and adapts to given social and school contexts. Through expanding the current debate across and within racial/ethnic lines, this research shows that culture is significant and race remains salient; however, in order to examine academic aspirations and achievement among minority students, researchers may benefit by examining race relations beyond a black and white discourse, and how students' racial and ethnic identities intersect with culture, class, race, and school context.

REFERENCES

Ainsworth-Darnell, J. W., & Downey, D. B. (1998). Assessing the oppositional culture explanation for racial/ethnic differences in school performance. *American Sociological Review.* 63(4), 536–553.

Caplan, N., Choy, M. H., & Whitmore, J. K. (1991). *Children of the boat people: A study of educational success.* Ann Arbor, MI: University of Michigan Press.

Carter, P. (2003). "Black" cultural capital, status positioning, and schooling conflicts for low-income African American youth. *Social Problems, 50*(1), 136–155.

Cook, P. J., & Ludwig, J. (1998). The Burden of acting white: Do black adolescents disparage academic achievement. In Jencks, C., & Phillips, M. (Eds.), *The black-white test score gap* (pp. 375–400). Washington, DC: Brookings Institute Press.

Downey, D. B., & Ainsworth-Darnell, J. W. (2002). The search for oppositional culture among black students. *American Sociological Review, 67*(1), 156–164.

Espiritu, Y. L. (1994). The intersection of race, ethnicity, and class: The multiple identities of second-generation Filipinos. *Identities, 9,* 249–273.

Ferguson, R. (2001). A diagnostic analysis of black-white GPA disparities in Shaker Heights, Ohio. In Ravitch, D. (Ed.), *Brookings paper on education policy 2001* (pp. 347–414). Washington, DC: Brookings Institute Press.

Fong, T. P., & Shinangawa, L. H. (2000). *Asian Americans: Experiences and Perspectives.* Upper Saddle River, NJ: Prentice-Hall.

Flores-Gonzales, N. (1999). Puerto Rican high achievers: An example of ethnic and academic identity compatibility. *Anthropology and Education Quarterly, 30*(3), 343–362.

Fordham, S., & Ogbu, J. U. (1986). Black student's school success: Coping with the "burden of 'acting white'." *The Urban Review, 18,* 176–204.

Gibson, M. A. (1988). *Accommodation without assimilation.* Ithaca, NY: Cornell University.

Lee, S. (2004). Class matters: Racial and ethnic identities of working- and middle-class second-generation Korean Americans in New York City. In Kasinitz, P., Mollenkopf, J. H., & Waters, M. C. (Eds.), *Becoming New Yorkers. Ethnographies of the New Second Generation* (pp. 154–196). New York: Russell Sage Foundation.

Lee, S. J. (1996). *Unraveling the "model minority" stereotype: Listening to Asian American youth.* New York: Teachers College Press.

Lew, J. (2004). The "other" story of model minorities: Korean American high school dropouts in an urban context. *Anthropology and Education Quarterly, 35*(3), 297–311.

Lew, J. (2006). *Asian Americans in class: Charting the achievement gap among Korean American youth.* New York: Teachers College Press.

Lew, J. (in press). A Structural Analysis of High- and Low-Achieving Korean American Youths: Class, Social Capital, Parental Strategies. *Teachers College Record 109*(2), 2007.

Ogbu, J. U. (1987). Variability in minority school performance: A problem in search of an explanation. *Anthropology & Education Quarterly, 18,* 312–334.

Ogbu, J. U. (1994). Racial stratification and education in the United States: Why inequality persists. *Teachers College Record, 96*(2), 264–298.

Ogbu, J. U. (2004). Collective identity and the burden of "acting white" in black history, community, and education. *The Urban Review, 36*(1), 1–35.

Ogbu, J. U., & Matute-Bianchi, M. E. (1986). Understanding sociocultural factors: Knowledge, identity, and school adjustment. In *Beyond language: Social and cultural factors in schooling language minority students.* Los Angeles: Evaluation, Dissemination, and Assessment Center, California State University.

Okihiro, G. (1994). *Margins and mainstreams: Asians in American history and culture.* Seattle, WA: University of Washington Press.

Pang, V. O., & Cheng, L. L. (Eds.) (1998). *Struggling to be heard: The unmet needs of Asian Pacific American children.* New York: SUNY Press.

Park, C. C., Lin Goodwin, A., & Lee, S. J., (Eds.) (2003). *Research on the education of Asian Pacific Americans, Vol. II.* Greenwich: Information Age Publishing, Inc.

Portes, A., & Rumbaut, R. G. (1996). *Immigrant America: A portrait.* Berkeley: University of California Press.

Portes, A., & Rumbaut, R. G. (2001). *Legacies: The story of the immigrant second-generation.* Berkeley: University of California Press.

Portes, A., & Zhou, M. (1993). The new second generation: Segmented assimilation and its variants. *Annals of the American Academy, 530,* 74–96.

Suárez-Orozco, C, & Suárez-Orozco, M. (1995). *Transformations: Immigration, family, life, and achievement motivation among Latino adolescents.* Stanford, CA: Stanford University Press.

Suárez-Orozco, C., & Suárez-Orozco, M. (2001). *Children of immigration.* Cambridge, MA: Harvard University Press.

Tyson, K. (2002). Weighing in: Elementary-age students and the debate on attitudes toward school among black students. *Social Forces, 80*(4), 1157–1189.

Tyson, K., Darity, W. Jr., & Castellino, D. R. (2005). It's not "a black thing": Understanding the burden of acting white and other dilemmas of high achievement. *American Sociological Review, 70*(4), 582–605.

Waters, M. C. (1999). *Black identities: West Indian immigrant dreams and American realities.* Cambridge, MA: Harvard University Press.

Zhou, M., & Bankston, C. L. III (1996). Social capital and the adaptation of the second generation: The case of Vietnamese youth in New Orleans. In Portes, A. (Ed.), *The new second generation* (pp. 197–220). New York: Russell Sage Foundation.

Zhou, M., & Bankston, C. L. III (1998). *Growing up American: How Vietnamese children adapt to life in the United States.* New York: Russell Sage Foundation.

STUDY QUESTIONS

1. How did the high-income, high-achieving Korean American students view their racial or ethnic identity?

2. Why did working-class Korean Americans tend to distance themselves from the rest of the Korean community?

3. Central to Lew's argument is the idea that schools reward some types of cultural standards (such as speaking "proper English") and neglect or are hostile toward other forms (such as "unprofessional" clothing styles). What types of cultural standards were rewarded when you were in high school and what cultural standards were not?

4. Watch Dalton Conley's interview with Jennifer Lee on YouTube (http://bit.ly/ jenniferlee_ethnicity). How do the students from Lew's study fit into the framework of Lee's distinction between **race** and **ethnicity**? What do you make of the lower income Korean students' identifying themselves as closer to black and the higher income Korean students' not associating their racial ethnic identity with being black? What role does class play in how these students perceive and understand their racial or ethnic identities?

KATHERINE NEWMAN AND CHAUNCY LENNON

The Job Ghetto

n this reading, Katherine Newman and Chauncy Lennon discuss fast-food restaurant jobs in central Harlem (New York City) as an unrealistic venue for improving the **economic** success of welfare recipients. The implications of their findings are time tested and speak volumes about the continuing struggles and lack of jobs available to residents of poor neighborhoods, particularly in **inner-city** areas. As you read, think about your first job—how you found it, how you got it, and what your experiences were as a paid worker.

TO FIX THE WELFARE MESS, CONSERVATIVES SAY, WE SHOULD stop making life on the dole so comfortable, cut benefits, and force over-indulged welfare moms to go out and find honest jobs. Unskilled foreigners can find work, so why can't AFDC recipients? With unemployment rates down, these expectations sound reasonable, particularly to middle-class Americans with stagnating incomes. The premise that jobs are available for those willing to take them is a great comfort to politicians with budget axes in hand and to conservative commentators calling on them to slash benefits. After all, they can claim they're not really casting poor women and children into the streets; they're just upholding the American work ethic.

But can just any warm body find a job? For the past two years, we have studied the low-wage labor market in Harlem, focusing on minimum-wage jobs in the fast-food industry, which are typical of the employment opportunities many reformers have in mind for welfare recipients. After all, these jobs presumably demand little skill, education, or prior work experience—or so the public believes.

The fast-food industry is growing more rapidly than almost any other service business and now employs more than 2.3 million workers. One in 15 Americans working today found their first job at McDonald's—not including Burger King and the rest. As a gateway to employment, fast-food establishments are gaining on the armed forces, which have long functioned as a national job-training factory. No wonder the average citizen believes these jobs are wide open! Yet, in inner cities, the picture looks different. With manufacturing gone, fast-food jobs have become the object of fierce competition.

DOWNWARD PRESSURES

Between 1992 and 1994, we tracked the work histories of 200 people working in fast-food restaurants in central Harlem, where according to official data about 18 percent of the population are unemployed and about 40 percent live below the poverty line. These numbers are typical of the communities where many long-term recipients of public assistance will have to look for work if their benefits are cut off. Some 29 percent of the households in Harlem receive public assistance.

Although the 200 workers in our study receive only the minimum wage, they are actually the victors in an intense competition to find work in a community with relatively few jobs to offer. At the restaurants where they work, the ratio of applicants to hires is approximately 14 to 1. Among those people who applied but were rejected for fast-food work in early 1993, 73 percent had not found work of any kind a year later, despite considerable effort. Even the youngest job-hunters in our study (16- to 18-year-olds) had applied for four or five positions before they came looking for these fast-food jobs. The oldest applicants (over 25) had applied for an average of seven or eight jobs.

The oversupply of job-seekers causes a creeping credentialism in the ghetto's low-wage service industries. Older workers in their twenties, who are more often high school graduates, now dominate jobs once taken by school dropouts or other young people first starting out. Long-term welfare recipients will have a tough time beating out their competition even for these low-wage jobs. They will be joining an inner-city labor market that is already saturated with better educated and more experienced workers who are preferred by employers.

WINNERS AND LOSERS

We tracked nearly 100 people who applied for these minimum-wage jobs but were turned down, and compared them to the fortunate ones who got jobs. The comparison is instructive. Even in Harlem, African Americans are at a disadvantage in hiring compared to Latinos and others. Employers, including black employers, favor applicants who are not African American. Blacks are not shut out of the low-wage labor market; indeed, they represent about 70 percent of the new hires in these jobs. But they are rejected at a much higher rate than applicants from other ethnic groups with the same educational qualifications.

Employers also seem to favor job applicants who commute from more distant neighborhoods. The rejection rate for local applicants is higher than the rate for similarly educated individuals who live farther away. This pattern holds even for people of the same race, sex, and age. Other studies in the warehouse and dockyard industries report the same results. These findings suggest that residents of poor neighborhoods such as central Harlem are at a distinct disadvantage in finding minimum-wage jobs near home.

Mothers of young children face particular problems if they can't find jobs close to home. The costs and logistical complexities of commuting (and paying for longer child care hours to accommodate it) are a big burden.

In searching for jobs, "who you know" makes a big difference. Friends and family members who already have jobs help people get work even in the fast-food industry; those isolated from such networks are less likely to get hired. Personal contacts have long been recognized as crucial for getting higher-skilled employment. This research suggests that contacts are important at the bottom of the job ladder, too.

Native-born applicants are at a disadvantage compared to legal immigrants in securing entry-level work. In fact, even though central Harlem residents are nearly all African American, recent immigrants have a higher probability of being hired for Harlem's fast-food jobs than anyone else. Interviews with employers suggest that they believe immigrants are easier to manage in part because they come from countries where $4.25 an hour represents a king's ransom. Whether or not employers are right about the tractability of immigrants, such attitudes make it harder for the native-born to obtain low-wage jobs.

The people who succeed in getting these minimum-wage jobs are not new to the labor market. More than half of the new hires over the age of 18 found their first jobs when they were younger than 15 years of age. Even the people rejected for the minimum-wage positions had some prior job experience. Half of them also began working before they were 15 years old. Welfare recipients with no prior job experience, or no recent job experience, are going to be at a disadvantage in the competition.

"THEY EXPECT TOO MUCH"

One explanation often advanced for low employment in poor communities is that the poor have unrealistic expectations. In this view, they are reluctant to seek (or take) jobs that fall below a "reservation wage," which is supposedly far above the minimum. We asked job-seekers who were refused these entry-level jobs what they were hoping for and what wages they would accept. Their desires were modest: $4.59 per hour on average, which is quite close to the minimum wage. The younger the job seeker, the lower was the expectation.

These job seekers were willing to accept even more modest wages. On average the lowest they would take was $4.17 per hour, which is less than the minimum level legally permitted for adult workers. It is striking that many applicants previously had higher salaries; the average wage for the best job they had ever held was $6.79 per hour. Many of central Harlem's job hunters are suffering from downward mobility, falling into the minimum-wage market even though they have done better in the past.

Comparing job-seekers to jobholders shows the intensity of employment competition in the inner city, but it doesn't tell us how welfare recipients will fare. What assets do welfare recipients bring to the competition compared to other job hunters? The news is grim.

Nationally, one-third of the long-term welfare recipients have received high school diplomas. Recently hired fast-food workers in central Harlem have completed high school at a higher rate—54 percent. Almost 40 percent of welfare recipients have not held jobs in the year preceding their enrollment in welfare. Yet even the central Harlem applicants rejected for fast-food jobs have had more job experience. They have held an average of more than three jobs before applying for these positions.

In short, it is simply not the case that anyone who wants a low-wage job can get one. As is true for almost any glutted labor market, there is a queue of applicants, and employers can be fairly choosy. When conservatives point to the success of immigrants as proof that jobs are available for welfare moms, they are ignoring the realities of the inner city. Ethnic minorities of all kinds are already locked into a fierce struggle for scarce opportunities at the bottom.

When they go looking for jobs, welfare recipients go to the back of a long line. Policymakers should neither fool nor comfort themselves with the notion that welfare mothers can simply go out and get jobs. Investment in public employment and tax incentives for private employers will be needed on a massive scale if anything like that rosy scenario is to come about. Even then, the competitive hurdles facing the very poor will be high and many better-qualified people will be out there looking to leap over them.

1. Why do the authors believe that long-term welfare recipients will have a hard time getting fast-food jobs?

2. What are the implications for mothers of young children that employers tend to favor job applicants who commute from distant neighborhoods?

3. Have you ever worked at a fast-food restaurant? Why or why not? Please discuss.

4. Access the mySkillsmyFuture website (www.myskillsmyfuture.org). Try entering a variety of your past jobs to determine the different career paths available.

DOUGLAS S. MASSEY AND NANCY A. DENTON

How to Build an Underclass

From *American Apartheid: Segregation and
the Making of the Underclass*

I f you set out to create a "ghetto," how would you go about it? In this selection from their important work *American Apartheid*, sociologists Douglas
Massey and Nancy Denton vividly describe the ways that U.S. **society** has
fostered conditions detrimental to minority populations and effectively created such ghetto neighborhoods. Although no mastermind takes credit for
having created an **underclass** in the United States, the authors argue that it
can feel that way. Read on for a new understanding of the ostracism caused
by **segregation**, poverty, and political marginalization.

HOW TO BUILD AN UNDERCLASS

HOW TO CONSTRUCT AN URBAN UNDERCLASS: TO BEGIN, CHOOSE
a minority group whose members are somehow identifiably different from the
majority.

Once the group has been selected, the next step in creating an underclass is
to confine its members to a small number of contiguous residential areas, and then
to impose on them stringent barriers to residential mobility. These barriers are
effectively created through discrimination buttressed by prejudice. Those who

Reprinted by permission of the publisher from "The Perpetuation of the Underclass" in AMERICAN
APARTHEID: SEGREGATION AND THE MAKING OF THE UNDERCLASS by Douglas S. Massey
and Nancy A. Denton, pp. 182–185, 275, Cambridge, Mass.: Harvard University Press, Copyright ©
1993 by the President and Fellows of Harvard College.

attempt to leave the enclave are systematically steered away from majority neighborhoods and back to minority or racially mixed areas. If they inquire about homes in other areas, they are treated brusquely and told none are available, and if they insist on seeing an advertised unit, little information is provided about it and no other units are shown. If these deceptions are overcome and a minority homebuyer succeeds in making an offer on a home in a majority neighborhood, the sales agent provides as little information as possible about the options for financing the sale and makes no effort to assist the customer in obtaining a mortgage. At the same time, the seller is discouraged from coming down in price to meet the offer that has been made.

If, despite these efforts, a minority family succeeds in having its offer to buy a majority home accepted, financial institutions take over the task of enforcing the barriers to residential mobility by attempting to deny the family's application for a mortgage, either on the basis of "objective" criteria such as the applicant's income, employment, or family history or because of more subjective concerns about neighborhood "quality" or "stability." Through whatever means, minority loan applications are rejected at a rate several times that of majority applications.

If the foregoing barriers are still somehow overcome and a minority family actually succeeds in moving into a majority neighborhood, then the fallback mechanisms of prejudice come into play. The minority family is systematically harassed by threatening phone calls, rocks thrown through windows, property vandalism, burning crosses, and if these crass measures are unacceptable, through more genteel mechanisms of social ostracism. If acts of prejudice do not succeed in dislodging the family, the ultimate weapon is the avoidance by majority members of the neighborhood. Those in the immediate area seek to leave as soon as they are able and no potential majority homebuyers are shown properties in the area. As a result, the neighborhood rapidly turns from a majority to a minority population.

Through the systematic application of these principles, areas where members of the minority manage to gain entry can be restricted in number and confined largely to locations adjacent to existing minority neighborhoods, thereby maintaining the residential structure of the ghetto. Moreover, prejudice and discrimination applied in the manner just discussed have the additional effect of undermining minority self-esteem, because they make it very clear that no matter how much money or education a minority person may have, he or she will never be accepted or treated as an equal by majority neighbors.

Once a group's segregation in society has been ensured, the next step in building an underclass is to drive up its rate of poverty. Segregation paradoxically facilitates this task, because policies that harm a highly segregated minority group and its neighborhoods will have few untoward side effects on other racial or ethnic groups. Geographic isolation translates into political isolation, making it difficult for segregated groups to form political coalitions with others to end policies inimical to their self-interests or to promote policies that might advance their welfare. Racial segregation thus makes it politically easy to limit the number of government jobs within the ghetto, to reduce its public services, to keep its schools understaffed and underfunded, to lower the transfer payments on which its poor depend, and to close its hospitals, clinics, employment offices, and other social support institutions.

With the political marginalization of minority members ensured by their segregation, the only thing required to set off a spiral of decay within the ghetto is a first-class economic disaster that removes the means of subsistence from a large share of the population. If the minority migrated to cities largely to take industrial jobs vacated by upwardly mobile majority immigrants, the inner-city manufacturing base provides a particularly opportune point at which to undercut the economic supports of the minority community, thereby bringing about the necessary increases in minority poverty.

Through a combination of corporate disinvestments in older plants and equipment, a decentralization of blue-collar employment from city to suburban areas, the relocation of manufacturing processes to nonmetropolitan areas, the transfer of production jobs to the sunbelt or overseas, and the setting of high real interest rates to produce an overvalued dollar and relatively expensive U.S. products, inner-city manufacturing industries can effectively be driven out of the urban economy. As manufacturing employment falls and employment suburbanizes, thousands of ghetto dwellers, primarily men with little formal education, will be displaced from jobs that pay them relatively high wages and sent into a two-tiered service economy that generates a larger number of menial, low-paying jobs but few high-paying positions for people without education or training.

These inner-city economic dislocations drive up the rate of minority poverty.[1] The additional deprivation created by the economic flux is concentrated geographically within isolated ghetto neighborhoods. As neighborhood poverty concentrations rise, income is withdrawn from minority neighborhoods, and the resulting increase in dilapidation and abandonment sets off physical decay that soon spreads to surrounding stable neighborhoods. If, owing to the constraints of fiscal austerity and the political isolation of these neighborhoods, fire service to ghetto areas is simultaneously reduced, then the process of neighborhood decay will be substantially accelerated. The increase in poverty concentration also brings a sharp constriction of demand density within the ghetto, leading to the collapse of its retail sector and the elimination of most nonessential goods and services.

The interaction of poverty and segregation acts to concentrate a variety of deleterious social and economic characteristics, creating an environment where male joblessness, female welfare dependency, crime, drug abuse, teenage childbearing, and single parenthood are common or even normative. The ghetto comes to house an abundance of negative role models who exemplify attitudes and behaviors detrimental to success in the emerging post-industrial service economy.

Given the lack of opportunity, pervasive poverty, and increasing hopelessness of life in the ghetto, a social-psychological dynamic is set in motion to produce a culture of segregation. Under the structural conditions of segregation, it is difficult for ghetto dwellers to build self-esteem by satisfying the values and ideals of the larger society or to acquire prestige through socially accepted paths. Precisely because the ghetto residents deem themselves failures by the broader standards of society, they evolve a parallel status system defined in opposition to the prevailing majority culture. As new generations are born into conditions of increasing deprivation and deepening racial isolation, however, the oppositional origins of the status system gradually recede and the culture of segregation becomes autonomous and independent.

A sure sign that the culture of segregation is well advanced occurs when the language of the segregated group diverges sharply from the standard dialect spoken in the wider society. Not only will the breakdown in intergroup communications enhance feelings of racial separation between the underclass and the rest of society, but the lack of facility in the standard dialect will undermine the minority group's prospects for success in education and employment.

The emergence of a culture of segregation also limits the number of minority families who aspire to leave the ghetto. As "minority" culture becomes more firmly established and deeply rooted, members of the minority who seek integration within the larger social and economic institutions of the society will come under increasing pressure from others to stop acting like a majority member. Those who succumb to this pressure, or who themselves promote self-segregation in language, culture, and housing, will be unlikely to meet with socioeconomic success in the larger society and will be limited to a life of persistent poverty and deprivation. Through prolonged exposure to life in racially isolated and intensely poor neighborhoods, this poverty will quite likely be passed to children in the next generation. When this point is reached, a well-functioning and efficient social structure for the creation and maintenance of an urban underclass will have been created.

NOTES

1. A series of papers indicates that levels and trends in black poverty are determined by precisely these changes in the urban economy, specifically the suburbanization of employment, the decline of manufacturing, and the rise of a service economy; see Mitchell L. Eggers and Douglas S. Massey, "The Structural Determinants of Urban Poverty: A Comparison of Whites, Blacks, and Hispanics," *Social Science Research* 20 (1991):217–55; and Mitchell L. Eggers and Douglas S. Massey, "A Longitudinal Analysis of Urban Poverty: Blacks in U.S. Metropolitan Areas between 1970 and 1980," *Social Science Research* 21 (1992):175–203.

1. How does **segregation** help increase the poverty rate in a minority group?

2. Do you think the conditions described in this piece are still problems today? If not, what else might account for the continued presence of poverty-stricken, high-crime neighborhoods in a country of relative prosperity?

3. What kind of neighborhood did you grow up in? How does your own background shape your reading of this article?

4. Create a profile of your current neighborhood, describing its **economic** conditions and residents to the best of your knowledge. What conditions might have made your neighborhood the place it is? You might explore the concepts of "**white flight**," "**urban renewal**," and "**gentrification**."

HERBERT KOHL

The Story of Rosa Parks and the Montgomery Bus Boycott Revisited

From *Should we Burn Babar? Essays on Children's Literature and the Power of Stories*

We all think we know about Rosa Parks, but chances are you know only a fraction of her story. By analyzing what aspects of the Rosa Parks story are highlighted and what parts are frequently left out, we can see what the **dominant culture** in **society** values and what it wants to hide. Herbert Kohl examines the common telling of the story of Rosa Parks and the Montgomery Bus Boycott to locate inaccuracies and omissions and then explore what the consequences are for schoolchildren learning this edited history. As you read, compare what you learned about Rosa Parks in school with what you discover here. How could we create a more accurate story for children today?

RACISM, AND THE DIRECT CONFRONTATION BETWEEN AFRICAN American and European American people in the United States, is an issue that is usually considered too sensitive to be dealt with directly in the elementary school classroom. When confrontation between African Americans and European Americans occurs in children's literature, it is routinely described as a problem between individuals that can be worked out on a personal basis. In the few cases where racism is addressed as a social problem, there has to be a happy ending. This is most readily apparent in the biographical treatment of Rosa Parks, one of the two names that most children in the United States associate with the Civil Rights movement in the southern United States during the 1960s; the other is Martin Luther King Jr.

Over the past few years, during visits to schools, I've talked with children about the Civil Rights movement. One of the things I ask the children is what they know of Rosa Parks and her involvement in the Montgomery bus boycott. This focus developed after I observed a play about civil rights in a fourth-grade classroom in southern California several years ago. One scene in the play took place on a bus in Montgomery, Alabama. A tired Rosa Parks got on the bus and sat down. The child portraying Mrs. Parks was dressed in shabby clothes and carried two worn shopping bags. She sat down next to the driver, and other children got on the bus until all the seats in front were filled up. Then a boy got on and asked her to move. She refused, and the bus driver told her he didn't want any trouble. Politely he asked her to move to the back of the bus. She refused again and the scene ended. In the next scene we see a crowd of students, African American and European American, carrying signs saying Don't Ride the Buses, We shall Overcome, and Blacks and Whites Together. One of the students, playing Martin Luther King Jr., addressed the rest of the class, saying something to the effect that African American and European American people in Montgomery got angry because Rosa Parks was arrested for not moving to the back of the bus, and that they were boycotting the buses until all people could ride wherever they wanted. The play ended with a narrator pointing out that the bus problem in Montgomery was solved by people coming together to protest peacefully for justice.

Before talking to the children about their perceptions of Rosa Parks and her motivations, I had a moment to talk with the teacher about a major misrepresentation of facts in the play: there were no European Americans involved in boycotting the buses in Montgomery. The struggle was organized and maintained by the African American community, and to represent it as an interracial struggle was to take the power and credit away from that community. The teacher agreed that the play took some liberty with history but said that since his class was interracial, it was better for all the children to do the play as an integrated struggle. Otherwise, he said, the play might lead to racial strife in the classroom. I disagreed and pointed out that by showing the power of organized African Americans, it might lead all the children to recognize and appreciate the strength oppressed people can show when confronting their oppressors. In addition, the fact that European Americans joined the struggle later on could lead to very interesting discussions about social change and struggles for justice, and could be related to the current situation in South Africa and the resurgence of overt racism in the United States. He disagreed and ended our chat by telling me how hard it was to manage an integrated classroom.

I contented myself with asking the children about Rosa Parks. The girl who played Mrs. Parks, Anna, told me that she imagined "Rosa," as she called Mrs. Parks, to be a poor woman who did tiring and unpleasant work. She added that she imagined Rosa was on her way home to a large family that she had to take care of all by herself when she refused to move to the back of the bus. In other words, Rosa Parks was, in her mind, a poor, single parent with lots of children, and an unskilled worker. I asked her how she got that idea, and she replied that's just the kind of person she felt Rosa Parks must be. She added that nobody had ever told her that her view was wrong, so she never bothered to question it. Her teacher backed her up and claimed that she had made reasonable assumptions about Rosa Parks, ones that he felt were true to the way Rosa Parks was portrayed in the books they had in class. I couldn't argue with that last comment.

I changed the subject and asked Anna why Rosa Parks's arrest led to a boycott. She said she didn't know. Maybe Rosa had a friend who told everybody, or maybe it was in the newspaper. One of the other students suggested that her arrest was on TV and everybody came out to protest because they didn't think it was right to arrest someone just for not moving to the back of the bus. The boycott was, to them, some form of spontaneous action that involved no planning or strategy.

All the children admired Rosa Parks for not moving. Some said she must be a very stubborn person, others that she had to be so angry that she didn't care what happened to her. They agreed that it took a special person to be so courageous and wondered if they would be able to muster such courage. I got the impression that Mrs. Parks's exceptional courage might be an excuse for them to not act.

I decided to push the issue a bit and asked the class why Rosa Parks had to move to the back of the bus anyway. One of the African American children said it was segregated in the South back then, and African Americans and European Americans couldn't do things together. When I asked why there was segregation in those days there was absolute silence. I shifted a bit and asked if the African Americans and European Americans in their classroom could do things together. One of the boys answered, "In school they do, mostly." Since I was just a guest I left it at that. However, it was clear to me that issues of racial conflict were not explicitly discussed in this classroom, and that the play about the Montgomery bus boycott left the children with some vague sense of unity and victory, but with no sense of the risk and courage of the African American people who originated the struggle for civil rights in the United States or of the history and nature of segregation. I have no idea whether there was any racism manifest in the everyday lives of the children in that classroom, but wondered whether they or the teacher were at all prepared to deal with it if it erupted.

The children's visualization of Rosa Parks, whom they felt free to call by her first name, was particularly distressing. As well as poor, they imagined her to be without education or sophistication, a person who acted on impulse and emotion rather than intelligence and moral conviction. There was no sense of her as a community leader or as part of an organized struggle against oppression. I decided to find out how common this view was, and I have been astonished to find that those children's view of Rosa Parks is not at all different from that of most European American adults and almost all the school children I have questioned.

The image of "Rosa the Tired," and the story that goes with it, exists on the level of a national cultural icon in the United States. School textbooks and children's books are major perpetuators of this myth, but none of them I've seen quote sources for their distorted personal information about Mrs. Parks. Yet, most American children's first encounter with the Civil Rights movement comes through these writings. Dozens of children's books and textbooks I've looked at present the same version of Rosa Parks and the Montgomery bus boycott. This version can be reduced to the following generic story, which I fabricated and could be titled:

"ROSA WAS TIRED: THE STORY OF THE MONTGOMERY BUS BOYCOTT"

Rosa Parks was a poor seamstress. She lived in Montgomery, Alabama, during the 1950s. In those days there was still segregation in parts of the United States. That meant that African Americans and European Americans were not allowed to use the same public facilities such as restaurants or swimming pools. It also meant that whenever it was crowded on the city buses African Americans had to give up seats in front to European Americans and move to the back of the bus.

One day on her way home from work Rosa was tired and sat down in the front of the bus. As the bus got crowded she was asked to give up her seat to a European American man, and she refused. The bus driver told her she had to go to the back of the bus, and she still refused to move. It was a hot day, and she was tired and angry, and became very stubborn.

The driver called a policeman, who arrested Rosa.

When other African Americans in Montgomery heard this they became angry too, so they decided to refuse to ride the buses until everyone was allowed to ride together. They boycotted the buses.

The boycott, which was led by Martin Luther King Jr., succeeded. Now African Americans and European Americans can ride the buses together in Montgomery.

Rosa Parks was a very brave person.

This story seems innocent enough. Rosa Parks is treated with respect and dignity and the African American community is given credit for running the boycott and winning the struggle. It reflects the view of Mrs. Parks often found in adult literature as well as writings for children. For example, in the book by eminent psychiatrist Robert Coles, *The Moral Life of Children* (Boston: Houghton Mifflin, 1986), we find the following quote:

> We had come to know . . . a group of poor and poorly educated people, who, nevertheless, acquitted themselves impressively in pursuit of significant ethical objectives. I think of Rosa Parks, a seamstress, whose decision to sit where she pleased on a Montgomery, Alabama, bus in the middle 1950s preceded the emergence of the so-called Civil Rights movement and of Dr. King and Ralph Abernathy as leaders of it. (p. 25)

A more recent example of this can be found in Robert Fulghum's best-selling book, *It Was on Fire When I Lay Down on It.* (Ivy Books, 1988)

> I write this on the first day of December in 1988, the anniversary of a moment when someone sat still and lit the fuse to social dynamite. On this day in 1955, a forty-two-year-old woman was on her way home from work. Getting on a public bus, she paid her fare and sat down on the first vacant seat. It was good to sit down—her feet were tired. As the bus filled with passengers, the driver turned and told her to give up her seat and move on back in the bus. She sat still. The driver got up and shouted, "MOVE IT!" She sat still. Passengers grumbled, cursed her, pushed at her. Still she sat. So the driver got off the bus, called the police, and they came to haul her off to jail and into history.
>
> Rosa Parks. Not an activist or a radical. Just a quiet, conservative, churchgoing woman with a nice family and a decent job as a seamstress. For all the eloquent phrases that have been turned about her place in the flow of history, she did not get on that bus looking for trouble or trying to make a statement. Going home was all she had in mind, like everybody else. She was anchored to her seat by her own dignity. Rosa Parks simply wasn't going to be a "nigger" for anybody anymore. And all she knew to do was to sit still. (pp. 109–10)

And here's a current textbook version of the Montgomery bus boycott story written for elementary school children. It comes from the Heath Social Studies series for elementary school, *Exploring My World* by Jeff Passe and Evangeline Nicholas (Lexington, MA: 1991, D.C. Heath, reproduced on page 188 of the Teachers' Guide) and is similar in content to my generic tale:

> When Rosa Parks rode on a bus, she had to sit all the way in the back. Her city had a law. It said black people could not sit in the front of a bus.
>
> One day Rosa was tired. She sat in the front. The bus driver told her to move. She did not. He called the police. Rosa was put in jail.
>
> Some citizens tried to help. One of them was Martin Luther King Jr. The citizens decided to stop riding buses until the law was changed.
>
> Their plan worked. The law was changed. Soon, many other unfair laws were changed. Rosa Parks led the way!

The Teachers' Guide to this text informs teachers that "Mrs. Parks' single act brought about the desegregation of buses all over the country." In a lesson plan referring to Rosa Parks's being told to move to the back of the bus, it informs teachers to "tell children they will be reading about a woman who became angry when this happened to her. She decided she was not being treated fairly, and she was not going to put up with that kind of treatment anymore. Have children read to find out how the actions of Rosa Parks helped to change the way black people were treated." (p. 188)

This book was published in 1991 and is certainly still in use. It encourages presenting the Montgomery bus boycott as the single act of a person who was tired and angry. Intelligent and passionate opposition to racism is simply not part of the story. In the entire part of the guide dealing with the Montgomery bus boycott, there is no mention of racism at all. Instead the problem is unfairness, a more generic and softer form of abuse that avoids dealing with the fact that the great majority of White people in Montgomery were racist and capable of being violent and cruel to maintain segregation. Thus we have an adequate picture of neither the courage of Rosa Parks nor the intelligence and resolve of the African American community in the face of racism.

Research into the history of the Montgomery bus boycott, however, reveals some distressing characteristics of this generic story, which misrepresents an organized and carefully planned movement for social change as a spontaneous outburst based upon frustration and anger. The following annotations on "Rosa Was Tired" suggest that we need a new story, one more in line with the truth and directed at showing the organizational intelligence and determination of the African American community in Birmingham, as well as the role of the bus boycott in the larger struggle to desegregate Birmingham and the South.

THE ANNOTATED "ROSA WAS TIRED"

Rosa Parks was a seamstress who was poor. She lived in Montgomery, Alabama, during the 1950s.

Rosa Parks was one of the first women in Montgomery to join the NAACP and was its secretary for years. At the NAACP she worked with E. D. Nixon, vice president of the Brotherhood of Sleeping Car Porters, who was president of the Montgomery NAACP, and learned about union struggles from him. She also worked with the youth division of the NAACP, and she took a youth NAACP group to visit the Freedom Train when it came to Montgomery in 1954. The train, which carried the originals of the U.S. Constitution and the Declaration of Independence, was traveling around the United States promoting the virtues of democracy. Since its visit was a federal project, access to the exhibits could not legally be segregated. Mrs. Parks took advantage of that fact to visit the train. There, Rosa Parks and the members of the youth group mingled freely with European Americans from Montgomery who were also looking at the documents. This overt act of crossing the boundaries of segregation did not endear Rosa Parks to the Montgomery political and social establishment.

Her work as a seamstress in a large department store was secondary to her community work. As she says in an interview in *My Soul Is Rested* by Howard Raines (New York: Bantam, 1978, p. 35), she had "almost a life history of being rebellious against being mistreated because of my color." She was well known to all of the African American leaders in Montgomery for her opposition to segregation, her leadership abilities, and her moral strength. Since 1954 and the Supreme Court's *Brown v. Topeka Board of Education* decision, she had been working on the desegregation of the Montgomery schools. In addition, she was good friends with Clifford and Virginia Durr, European Americans who were well known opponents of segregation. She had also attended an interracial meeting at the Highlander Folk School in Tennessee a few months before the boycott. Highlander was known throughout the South as a radical education center that was overtly planning for the total desegregation of the South, and Rosa Parks was aware of that when she attended the meeting. At that meeting, which dealt with plans for school desegregation in the South, she indicated that she intended to become an active participant in other attempts to break down the barriers of segregation. Finally, Rosa Parks had the active support of her mother and her husband in her civil rights activities. To call Rosa Parks a poor, tired seamstress and not talk about her role as a community leader as well is to turn an organized struggle for freedom into a personal act of frustration. It is a thorough misrepresentation of the Civil Rights movement in Montgomery, Alabama, and an insult to Mrs. Parks as well. Here is a more appropriate way of beginning a children's version of the Montgomery bus boycott:

> It was 1955. Everyone in the African American community in Montgomery, Alabama, knew Rosa Parks. She was a community leader, and people admired her courage. All throughout her life she had opposed prejudice, even if it got her into trouble.

In those days there was still segregation in parts of the United States. That meant that African Americans and European Americans were not allowed to use the same public facilities . . .

The existence of legalized segregation in the South during the 1950s is integral to the story of the Montgomery bus boycott, yet it is an embarrassment to many school people and difficult to explain to children without accounting for the moral corruption of the majority of the European American community in the South. The sentence I composed is one way of avoiding direct confrontation with the moral issues of segregation. First it says, "In those days there was still segregation" as if segregation were no longer an issue. However, as recently as July 1, 1990, an article by Ron Rapoport of the *Los Angeles Daily News* (reprinted in the Santa Rosa, CA, *Press Democrat*, July 1, 1990) focused on the current segregation of private golf clubs in Birmingham and other parts of the United States. In the article he says:

> It certainly isn't a secret that Shoal Creek Country Club has no black members because, in the words of its founder, Hall Thompson, "that's just not done in Birmingham."
>
> There are lots of places where it's just not done and not just in the South, either. Many of the golf courses that host PGA (Professional Golfers Association) events are restricted and while it may not often become a public issue, that does not mean people are not aware of it.
>
> As for shame, well, that is a commodity that is in short supply as well.
>
> "The country club is our home," Thompson said, "and we pick and choose who we want."

To this day the club still has only one African American member, who has special status as a guest member. Ironically, in 1994 a young African American golfer won a tournament at the club while other African Americans demonstrated outside its gates protesting the club's segregationist policies.

Locating segregation in the past is a way of avoiding dealing with its current manifestations and implying that racism is no longer a major problem in the United States. This is particularly pernicious at a time when overt racism is once again becoming a common phenomenon and when children have to be helped to understand and eliminate it.

Describing integration passively ("there was still segregation" instead of "European Americans segregated facilities so that African Americans couldn't use them") avoids the issue of activist racist activity on the part of some Whites. Since there was legalized segregation in Alabama, and Mrs. Parks was arrested for a violation of the Alabama state law that institutionalized segregation in public facilities, there must have been racists to have passed those laws. Yet they are absent from the narrative, which doesn't talk overtly about racism. The avoidance of direct discussion of what to do about individuals who are racist is all too characteristic of school programs and children's literature.

This avoidance of dealing directly with racism is also evident in the next sentence, which says that "African Americans and European Americans were not allowed to use the same public facilities." It puts African Americans and European Americans on the same footing, as if there were some symmetry and both were punished by the segregation laws. A more appropriate way of describing the situation would be:

> African American people were prevented by law from using the same public facilities as European Americans. In addition, the African American facilities were vastly inferior to the ones made available to European Americans.

Even this rewriting is too generous given the pervasive, brutal, and absolute nature of segregation in the pre-civil rights South. Perhaps the best analogy that could be used here is apartheid, as legalized segregation in the South hardly differed from South Africa's policy of total separation of the races to ensure White dominance.

I've raised the question with a number of educators, both African American and European American, of how to expose children to the reality of segregation and racism. Most of the European American and a few of the African American educators felt that young children do not need to be exposed to the harsh and violent history of segregation in the United States. They worried about the effects such exposure would have on race relations in their classrooms, and especially about provoking rage on the part of African American students. The other educators felt that, given the resurgence of overt racism in the United States these days, allowing rage and anger to come out was the only way African American and European American children could work from the reality of difference and separation toward a common life. They felt that conflict was a positive thing that could be healing when confronted directly, and that avoiding the horrors of racism was just another way of perpetuating them. I agree with this second group and believe that some recasting of the third and fourth sentences of "Rosa Was Tired" is called for:

> In those days Alabama was legally segregated. That means that African American people were prevented by the state law from using the same swimming pools, schools, and other public facilities as European Americans. There also were separate entrances, toilets, and drinking fountains for African Americans and European Americans in places such as bus and train stations. The facilities African Americans were allowed to use were not only separate from the ones European Americans used but were also very inferior. The reason for this was racism, the belief that European Americans were superior to African Americans and that therefore European Americans deserved better facilities.

. . . whenever it was crowded on the city buses African Americans had to give up seats in front to European Americans and move to the back of the bus.

Actually African Americans were never allowed to sit in the front of the bus in the South in those days. The front seats were *reserved* for European Americans. Between five and ten rows back the "Colored" section began. When the front of the bus filled up, African Americans seated in the "Colored" section had to give up their seats and move toward the back of the bus. Thus, for example, an elderly African American woman would have to give up her seat to a European American teenage male at the peril of being arrested. Consistent with the comments I've been making so far, and with the truth of the experience of segregation, this sentence should be expanded as follows:

> In those days public buses were divided into two sections, one at the front for European Americans, which was supposed to be "for Whites only." From five to ten rows back the section for African Americans began. That part of the bus was called the "Colored" section.
>
> Whenever it was crowded on the city buses African American people were forced to give up seats in the "Colored" section to European Americans and move to the back of the bus. For example, an elderly African American woman would have to give up her seat to a European American teenage male. If she refused she could be arrested for breaking the segregation laws.

One day on her way home from work Rosa was tired and sat down in the front of the bus.

Rosa Parks did not sit in the front of the bus. She sat in the front row of the "Colored" section. When the bus got crowded she refused to give up her seat in the "Colored" section to a European American. It is important to point this out, as it indicates quite clearly that it was not her intent, on that day, to break the segregation laws.

At this point the story lapses into the familiar and refers to Rosa Parks as "Rosa." The question of whether to use the first name for historical characters in a factual story is complicated. One argument in favor of doing so is that young children will more readily identify with characters who are presented in a personalized and familiar way. However, given that it was a sanctioned social practice in the South during the time of the story for European Americans to call African American adults by their first names as a way of reinforcing the African Americans' inferior status (African Americans could never call European Americans by their first names without breaking the social code of segregation), it seems unwise to use that practice in the story.

In addition, it's reasonable to assume that Rosa Parks was not any more tired on that one day than on other days. She worked at an exhausting full-time job and was also active full-time in the community. To emphasize her being tired is another way of saying that her defiance of segregation was an accidental result of her fatigue and consequent short temper on that particular day. However, rage is not a one-day thing, and Rosa Parks acted with full knowledge of what she was doing.

It is more respectful and historically accurate to make these changes:

> December 1, 1955, on her way home from work, Rosa Parks took the bus as usual. She sat down in the front row of the "Colored" section.

As the bus got crowded she was asked to give up her seat to a European American man, and she refused. The bus driver told her she had to go to the back of the bus, and she still refused to move. It was a hot day, and she was tired and angry, and became very stubborn.

The driver called a policeman, who arrested Rosa.

Rosa Parks described her experiences with buses in her own words (*My Soul Is Rested*):

> I had problems with bus drivers over the years because I didn't see fit to pay my money into the front and then go around to the back. Sometimes bus drivers wouldn't permit me to get on the bus, and I had been evicted from the bus. But, as I say, there had been incidents over the years. One of the things that made this . . . (incident) . . . get so much publicity was the fact that the police were called in and I was placed under arrest. See, if I had just been evicted from the bus and he hadn't placed me under arrest or had any charges brought against me, it probably could have been just another incident. (p. 31)

More recently, in *Voices of Freedom* by Henry Hampton and Steve Fayer (New York: Bantam, 1990), she described her thoughts that day in the following way:

> Having to take a certain section [on a bus] because of your race was humiliating, but having to stand up because a particular driver wanted to keep a white person from having to stand was, to my mind, most inhumane.
>
> More than seventy-five, between eighty-five and I think ninety, percent of the patronage of the buses were black people, because more white people could own and drive their own cars than blacks. I happened to be the secretary of the Montgomery branch of the NAACP as well as the NAACP Youth Council adviser. Many cases did come to my attention that nothing came out of because the person that was abused would be too intimidated to sign an affidavit, or to make a statement. Over the years, I had had my own problems with the bus drivers. In fact, some did tell me not to ride their buses if I felt that I was too important to go to the back door to get on. One had evicted me from the bus in 1943, which did not cause anything more than just a passing glance.

On December 1, 1955, I had finished my day's work as a tailor's assistant in the Montgomery Fair department store and I was on my way home. There was one vacant seat on the Cleveland Avenue bus, which I took, alongside a man and two women across the aisle. There were still a few vacant seats in the white section in the front, of course. We went to the next stop without being disturbed. On the third, the front seats were occupied and this one man, a white man, was standing. The driver asked us to stand up and let him have those seats, and when none of us moved at his first words, he said, "You all make it light on yourselves and let me have those seats." And the man who was sitting next to the window stood up, and I made room for him to pass by me. The two women across the aisle stood up and moved out. When the driver saw me still sitting, he asked if I was going to stand up and I said, "No, I'm not."

And he said, "Well, if you don't stand up, I'm going to call the police and have you arrested."

I said, "You may do that."

He did get off the bus, and I still stayed where I was. Two policemen came on the bus. One of the policemen asked me if the bus driver had asked me to stand and I said yes.

He said, "Why don't you stand up?"

And I asked him, "Why do you push us around?"

He said, "I do not know, but the law is the law and you're under arrest." (pp. 19, 20)

Mere anger and stubbornness could not account for the clear resolve with which Rosa Parks acted. Nor was she, as Robert Fulghum says in the selection from his book quoted at the beginning of this issue, "Not an activist or a radical. Just a quiet, conservative, churchgoing woman with a nice family and a decent job as a seamstress." She knew what she was doing, understood the consequences, and was prepared to confront segregation head on at whatever sacrifice she had to make. A more accurate account of the event, taking into consideration Rosa Parks's past history, might be:

As the bus got crowded the driver demanded that she give up her seat to a European American man, and move to the back of the bus. This was not the first time that this had happened to Rosa Parks. In the past she had refused to move, and the driver had simply put her off the bus. Mrs. Parks hated segregation, and along with many other African American people, refused to obey many of its unfair rules. On this day she refused to do what the bus driver demanded.

The bus driver commanded her once more to go to the back of the bus and she stayed in her seat, looking straight ahead and not moving an inch. He got angry at her and became very stubborn. He called a policeman, who arrested Mrs. Parks.

When other African Americans in Montgomery heard this they became angry too, so they decided to refuse to ride the buses until everyone was allowed to ride together. They boycotted the buses.

The connection between Rosa Parks's arrest and the boycott is a mystery in most accounts of what happened in Montgomery. Community support for the boycott is portrayed as being instantaneous and miraculously effective the very day after Mrs. Parks was arrested. Things don't happen that way, and it is an insult to the intelligence and courage of the African American community in Montgomery to turn their planned resistance to segregation into a spontaneous emotional response. The actual situation was more interesting and complex. Not only Rosa Parks had defied the bus segregation laws in the past: According to E. D. Nixon, in the three months preceding Mrs. Parks's arrest at least three other African American people had been arrested in Montgomery for refusing to give up their bus seats to European American people. In each case, Nixon and other people in leadership positions in the African American community in Montgomery investigated the background of the person arrested. They were looking for someone who had the respect of the community and the strength to deal with the racist police force as well as all the publicity that would result from being at the center of a bus boycott. This leads to the most important point left out in popularized accounts of the Montgomery bus boycott: the boycott had been planned and organized before Rosa Parks was arrested. It was an event waiting to take place, and that is why it could be mobilized so quickly. Rosa Parks's arrest brought it about because she was part of the African American leadership in Montgomery and was trusted not to cave in under the pressure everyone knew she would be exposed to, including threats to her life.

But the story goes back even farther than that. There was an African American women's organization in Montgomery called the Women's Political Council (WPC). It was headed those days by Jo Ann Gibson Robinson, who was a professor of English at Alabama State University in Montgomery, an all-African American university. In 1949 Ms. Gibson was put off a bus in Montgomery for refusing to move from her seat in the fifth row of an almost empty bus to the back of the bus. She and other women in Montgomery resolved to do something about bus segregation. As she says in her book *The Montgomery Bus Boycott and the Women Who Started It: The Memoir of Jo Ann Gibson Robinson* (Knoxville: University of Tennessee Press, 1987), "It was during the period of 1949–1955 that the Women's Political Council of Montgomery—founded in 1946 with Dr. Mary Burks as president and headed from 1950 on by me—prepared to stage a bus boycott when the time was ripe and the people were ready. The right time came in 1955." (p. 17)

This story of collective decision making, willed risk, and coordinated action is more dramatic than the story of an angry individual who sparked a demonstration; it has more to teach children who themselves may have to organize and act collectively against oppressive forces in the future. Here's one way to tell this complex story to young children:

> Mrs. Parks was not the first African American person to be arrested in Montgomery for refusing to move to the back of the bus. In the months before her refusal, at least three other people were arrested for the same reason. In fact, African American leaders in Montgomery were planning to overcome segregation. One way they wanted to do this was to have every African American person boycott the buses. Since most of the bus riders in the city were African American, the buses would go broke if they refused to let African Americans and European Americans ride the buses as equals.

From 1949 right up to the day Mrs. Parks refused to move, the Women's Political Council of Montgomery prepared to stage a bus boycott because of how African Americans were treated on the bus. African American people in Montgomery were ready to support the boycott. They were just waiting for the time to be ripe. Nineteen fifty-five was the time.

However, none of the people who were arrested before Mrs. Parks was were leaders. She was a leader, and the day she was arrested the leadership called a meeting at the Dexter Avenue Baptist Church. They decided to begin their refusal to ride the buses the next morning. They knew Mrs. Parks had the courage to deal with the pressure of defying segregation and would not yield even if her life was threatened.

The next day the Montgomery bus boycott began.

The boycott, which was led by Martin Luther King Jr., succeeded. Now African Americans and European Americans can ride the buses together in Montgomery. Rosa Parks was a very brave person.

The boycott was planned by the WPC, E. D. Nixon, and others in Montgomery. Martin Luther King Jr. was a new member of the community. He had just taken over the Dexter Avenue Baptist Church, and when Nixon told him that Rosa Parks's arrest was just what everybody was waiting for to kick off a bus boycott and assault the institution of segregation, King was at first reluctant. However, the community people chose him to lead, and he accepted their call. The boycott lasted 381 inconvenient days, something not usually mentioned in children's books. It did succeed and was one of the events that sparked the entire Civil Rights movement. People who had been planning an overt attack on segregation for years took that victory as a sign that the time was ripe, even though the people involved in the Montgomery boycott did not themselves anticipate such results. Here's one possible way to convey this to children:

There was a young new minister in Montgomery those days. His name was Martin Luther King Jr. People in the community felt that he was a special person and asked him to lead the boycott. At first he wasn't sure. He worried about the violence that might result from the boycott. However, he quickly made up his mind that it was time to destroy segregation and accepted the people's call for him to be their leader.

The Montgomery bus boycott lasted 381 days. For over a year the African American people of Montgomery, Alabama, stayed off the buses. Some walked to work, others rode bicycles or shared car rides. It was very hard for them, but they knew that what they were doing was very important for all African American people in the South.

The boycott succeeded, and by the end of 1956 African Americans and European Americans could ride the buses in Montgomery as equals. However, the struggle for the complete elimination of segregation had just begun.

We all owe a great deal to the courage and intelligence of Rosa Parks and the entire African American community of Montgomery, Alabama. They took risks to make democracy work for all of us.

CONCLUDING THOUGHTS

What remains, then, is to retitle the story. The revised version is still about Rosa Parks, but it is also about the African American people of Montgomery, Alabama. It takes the usual, individualized version of the Rosa Parks tale and puts it in the context of a coherent, community-based social struggle. This does not diminish Rosa Parks in any way. It places her, however, in the midst of a consciously planned movement for social change, and reminds me of the freedom song "We shall not be moved," for it was precisely Rosa Parks's and the community's refusal to be moved that made the boycott possible. For that reason the new title, "She Would Not Be Moved: The Story of Rosa Parks and the Montgomery Bus Boycott" makes sense.

As it turns out, my retelling of the story of Rosa Parks and the Montgomery bus boycott is not the only recent one. In 1990, thirty-five years after the event, we finally have a full, moving, and historically accurate 124-page retelling of the story written for young people. The book, *Rosa Parks: The Movement Organizes* by Kai Friese (Englewood Cliffs, NJ: Silver Burdett, 1990), is one of nine volumes in a series edited by the scholar Eldon Morris entitled *The History of the Civil Rights Movement.* Other volumes in the series, such as those about Ella Baker and Fannie Lou Hamer, also provide a fuller, more accurate look at people's struggles during the Civil Rights movement of the 1960s than has been available to young people until now. These volumes are gifts to all of us from a number of African American scholars who have reclaimed history from the distortions and omissions of years of irresponsible writing for children about the Civil Rights movement. They are models of how history and biography can directly confront racial conflict and illuminate social struggle. This is particularly true of the Rosa Parks volume, which takes us up to date in Mrs. Parks's life and informs us that she remained active over the years, working for social and economic justice in Congressman John Conyer's office in Detroit.

The book, which credits all the people involved in making the Montgomery boycott possible, provides a portrait of a community mobilized for justice. It also leaves us with a sense of the struggle that still needs to be waged to eliminate racism in the United States.

Rosa Parks has also written an autobiography (with Jim Haskins), which presents a more personal version of the story given here.

When the story of the Montgomery bus boycott is told merely as a tale of a single heroic person, it leaves children hanging. Not everyone is a hero or heroine. Of course, the idea that only special people can create change is useful if you want to prevent mass movements and keep change from happening. Not every child can be a Rosa Parks, but everyone can imagine her- or himself as a participant in the boycott. As a tale of a social movement and a community effort to overthrow injustice, the Rosa Parks story as I've tried to rewrite it and as Kai Friese has told it opens the possibility of every child identifying her- or himself as an activist, as someone who can help make justice happen. And it is that kind of empowerment that people in the United States desperately need.

APPENDIX I

The following quotes are taken from recent children's books and school textbooks. The publication date of the earliest of them is 1976; the rest were published in their current form in the 1980s. However, two of the children's books were copyrighted in 1969 and reissued in the 1980s with new illustrations. No attempt was made in these two cases to update the material in the books.

The sample of quotes included is representative of dozens I've read, and cumulatively represents all the different aspects of the Rosa Parks myth I portrayed in "Rosa Was Tired." Some of the other texts and the specific lines that relate to my text are listed at the end of this appendix. The passages quoted more fully here are from the most progressive texts and trade books I've found. I have avoided citing texts no longer in print.

1. From Valerie Schloredt, *Martin Luther King Jr: America's Great Nonviolent Leader in the Struggle for Human Rights* (Harrisburg, PA: Morehouse Publishing, 1990).

> On the evening of Dec. 1, 1955, a black lady named Rosa Parks left the downtown department store where she worked as a seamstress and walked to the bus stop to catch the bus that would take her home.

The book goes on to describe what happened when Mrs. Parks refused to move to the back of the bus:

> Mrs. Parks was tired. She had a long, hard day.... Something snapped in Mrs. Parks at that moment. Perhaps the patience with which she had endured years of subservience and insult.... Mrs. Parks didn't look like a person to challenge the law of Montgomery. She was a quiet looking lady, wearing small steel rimmed spectacles; but like thousands of other black people who rode the buses day after day, she was weary of being treated with such contempt.
>
> Much later she was asked if she had planned her protest. "No," she answered. "I was just plain tired, and my feet hurt."
>
> Mrs. Parks' patience had given way, had she but known it, at the best possible moment. (pp. 19, 20)

2. Here is the Random House version for first- to third-graders from James T. Kay, *Meet Martin Luther King Jr.* (New York: Random House, Step-up Books, 1969), reprinted with new cover in 1989.

On Dec. 1, 1955, a woman named Rosa Parks did something about the Jim Crow buses.

Mrs. Parks was black. She worked in a department store. That evening she climbed the bus and sat down.

Each time the bus stopped, more people got on. Soon no seats were left in the white part of the bus.

At the next stop some white people got on. The driver got up and walked over to Mrs. Parks. He told her to give her seat to a white woman.

But Rosa Parks was tired. She did something she had never done before. She just stayed in her seat. . . .

Black people all over the city heard about Rosa Parks. They were very angry. They were mad at the Jim Crow laws. They were mad at the police. They were mad at the bus company. But what could they do?

Then one man said, "Why don't we boycott the buses?" This meant that all the black people would stop riding the buses. Soon the bus company would lose money. Maybe then the owners would be fair to blacks. (not paged)

3. This selection is from Dharathula H. Millender's *Martin Luther King, Jr.: Young Man with a Dream* (New York: Bobbs-Merrill, 1969; Macmillan, Alladin Books, 1986). It is one of the finest of the older children's books about the Civil Rights movement.

Things came to a head over bus segregation on December 1, 1955. Mrs. Rosa Parks, an attractive negro seamstress, boarded a bus in downtown Montgomery. This was the same bus she had boarded many times after a hard day's work. Today she was tired and eager to get off her aching feet. Accordingly she sat down in the first seat in the Negro section behind the section reserved for white passengers. . . .

At first the driver was surprised (when she refused to move) wondering whether he had heard correctly. When Mrs. Parks clung to her seat, however, and held her head proudly in the air, he realized that he was facing trouble. Accordingly, he stopped his bus, called the police and had her arrested. Her arrest attracted wide attention because she was one of the most respected people in the Negro community. It helped to start a Negro revolt not only in Montgomery but all across the nation. (pp. 148–9)

4. This is from the upper elementary grades social studies textbook *The United States and the Other Americas* by Allan King, Ida Dennis, and Florence Potter, in the Macmillan Social Studies Series (New York: Macmillan, 1982).

In 1955 Rosa Parks, a black, refused to give up her bus seat to a white in Montgomery, Alabama. She was arrested because of this. Other blacks, led by Dr. Martin Luther King Jr., of Atlanta, Georgia, refused to ride the city buses. The following year a federal court ruled that segregated buses were no longer allowed. (p. 141)

In the teachers' edition the following instructions are given to teachers:

Have the pupils read the rest of page 413. Draw their attention to the photograph of Rosa Parks. Explain that on December 1, 1955, Rosa Parks boarded a bus in Montgomery, Alabama. Her arms were full of groceries, so she sat in the front row of the section of the bus in which blacks were permitted to sit. As the bus filled up, more white people got on, and the bus driver told Rosa to give up her seat to a white person. Rosa looked out the window and pretended not to hear him. She refused to give up her seat, and because of this she was arrested. In protest against her arrest, the black people of Montgomery refused to ride the bus. They formed car pools, walked, rode mules and horses and buggies. On April 23, 1956, the Supreme Court declared that state and local laws that required segregation of buses were unconstitutional. (p. 413)

5. This is taken from Allan O. Kownslar and William R. Fielder's *Inquiring About American History* (New York: Holt, Rinehart and Winston, 1976), in the Holt Data-bank System. This is a "modern" series based on inquiry and is considered too liberal for many school districts. It is for upper elementary and junior high students.

> For the black citizens of Montgomery, Alabama, some of the "separate but equal" laws had been changed by 1955. . . . But, in spite of these changes, many people still refused to treat blacks and whites equally. Rosa Parks, a black woman who lived in Montgomery in 1955, had to deal with this problem.
>
> One evening, Rosa Parks was coming home from work on a Montgomery city bus. She had been working hard all day at her job in a downtown department store. Rosa was quite tired. She took a seat toward the back of the bus, where black passengers normally sat. The bus began to fill quickly. As whites got on, they took what seats there were, and soon the bus was full.
>
> Rosa realized that some of the blacks would be asked to give up their seats and move to the back of the bus. They would be asked to stand so that white passengers could sit. She felt that this was unfair. Why should she have to move?
>
> Suddenly the driver turned and asked her, and some other blacks, to move to the rear of the bus. Rosa argued with the driver, but he still insisted that she leave her seat and stand in the back. Rosa paused. She had to make a decision quickly. Should she give up her seat or remain seated?
>
> What would you have done if you had been Rosa Parks? What do you think she did?
>
> Rosa Parks made her choice. She decided to remain seated on the bus. Her action led to the Montgomery Bus Boycott—and eventually, to a Supreme Court ruling against the separation of blacks and whites on all buses. (p. 301)

6. This selection is from another upper elementary text, *The United States and Its Neighbors* by Timothy Helmus, Val Arnsdorf, Edgar Toppin, and Norman Pounds (Morristown, NJ: Silver Burdett, 1984), in the series *The World and Its People*.

> Dr. King gained nationwide fame in Montgomery, Alabama, in 1955. At that time blacks had to sit in the back of public buses. But one day a quiet woman named Rosa Parks decided to sit in the "whites only" part of the bus. She was arrested. Dr. King led a boycott of Montgomery buses to protest her arrest. People who supported Dr. King would not use the buses until anyone could sit wherever she or he pleased. The boycott worked. (p. 248)

Finally, here is a list of quotes from a sampling of texts for all grade levels dealing with Rosa Parks and the Montgomery bus boycott. I've only quoted eighteen of the dozens of books consulted, though I think the unity of their tale comes across quite clearly. The word *racism* was not used in any of them.

1. Karen McAuley et al., *The United States Past to Present,* Teachers Ed. (Lexington, MA: D. C. Heath, 1987), p. 405. Grade 5.

   "It had been a long, hard day and she was tired."

2. Susan Williams McKay, *The World of Mankind* (Chicago: Follet Publishing, 1973), p. 221. Grade 3.

   "Mrs. Parks sat alone. She was tired. She decided not to move."

3. *The United States: Its History and Neighbors,* Teacher's Ed. (Orlando, FL: Harcourt Brace Jovanovich, 1988), p. 507. Grade 5.

   "On Dec. 1, 1955, Rosa Parks sank wearily to her seat on the bus in Montgomery, Alabama. . . .

   "As the bus filled up, Rosa Parks was asked to give up her seat. She refused. The bus driver called the police, and she was taken to jail."

4. Leonard C. Wood et al., *America: Its People and Values,* Teacher's Ed. 1985, p. 721. Junior High.

   "On that day a black seamstress named Rosa Parks refused to give up her seat in the white section of the bus. . . .

   "There as in many other parts of the south, local laws kept public places strictly segregated. Restaurants, businesses, and all forms of public transportation had separate sections for blacks and whites."

5. Allan O. Kownslar et al., *Inquiring About American History* (New York: Holt, Rinehart and Winston, 1976) p. 301. Grade 5.

   "One evening, Rosa Parks was coming home from work on a Montgomery city bus. She had been working hard all day at her job . . . Rosa was quite tired. . . ."

   "Suddenly, the driver turned and asked her, and some other blacks, to move to the rear of the bus. Rosa argued with the driver . . ."

6. JoAnn Cangemi, *Our History,* 1983, pp. 388–89. Grade 5.

   "In 1955, a black woman named Rosa Parks sat down in the front of the bus in Montgomery, Alabama. Parks refused to get up from the seat so that a white person could sit down and she was arrested."

   "Angry about the arrest, Montgomery blacks refused to ride city buses."

   "The bus boycott was led by Dr. Martin Luther King, Jr."

7. Beverly J. Armento et al., *This Is My Country* (Boston: Houghton Mifflin, 1991) p. 98. Grade 4.

   "She was tired and her feet hurt"

   "At that time, black and white people had to sit in separate sections on the bus. Other places were divided too, such as restrooms, waiting rooms, movie theatres and restaurants."

8. Henry F. Graff, *America: The Glorious Republic,* vol. 1, 1985, pp. 717–18. Jr./Sr. High.

   "The next day the 50,000 black citizens of Montgomery began a bus boycott of the city's buses: choosing to walk rather than ride under humiliating conditions."

9. Henry F. Graff, *America: The Glorious Republic*, vol. 2, 1986, pp. 349–50. Jr./Sr. High.

   "... a seamstress named Rosa Parks took a courageous and fateful step."

   "The next day the 50,000 black citizens of Montgomery began a boycott of city buses."

10. John Edward Wiltz, *The Search for Identity: Modern American History* (Philadelphia: J. B. Lippincott, 1973), p. 684. Jr. High.

    "When Mrs. Parks, a small, soft-spoken woman boarded the Cleveland Avenue bus she was tired and her feet hurt."

11. Beverly Jeanne Armento et al., *Living in Our Country* (River Forest, IL: Laidlaw Brothers, 1988) pp. 417–18. Grade 5.

    "In Montgomery, Alabama, a black woman was arrested for using a seat in the front of a bus."

    "For this reason many black people refused to ride the buses in Montgomery."

12. Glen M. Linden et al., *Legacy of Freedom: A History of the United States*, 1986, p. 670. Jr./Sr. High.

    "Tired after a long day's work, Mrs. Parks boarded a bus for home and refused to give up her seat to a white passenger when asked to do so by the bus driver."

    "The leaders of Montgomery's black community were outraged. Almost at once, they organized a boycott of the Mongomery transit system."

13. Ernest R. May, *A Proud Nation,* Teacher's Ed. (Evanston, IL: McDougal, Littell, 1983), p. 691. Jr. High.

    "On Dec. 1, Rosa Parks, a black woman, refused to give up her seat in the front of a bus to a white person. She had simply worked hard all day, Parks said, and her feet hurt."

14. Alma Graham et al., *United States: Our Nation and Neighbors* (New York: McGraw-Hill, 1980, p. 340. Grade 5.

    "The bus boycott was led by Dr. Martin Luther King Jr."

15. George Vuicich et al., *United States*, 1983, p. 322. Grade 5.

    "In 1955, a black woman, Rosa Parks, refused to give up her seat on a bus in Montgomery, Alabama. She was arrested. Some people became determined to do something. Blacks in Montgomery began a boycott of the city's buses."

    "The bus boycott was led by Dr. Martin Luther King, Jr., ..."

16. Henry F. Graff et al., *The Promise of Democracy: The Grand Experiment* (Chicago: Rand McNally, 1978), pp. 365–66, Jr./Sr. High.

    "... in many southern communities, black people had to sit at the back of the city buses."

    "... and she was tired."

17. Roger M. Berg, *Social Studies* (Glenview, IL: Scott, Foresman, 1979), p. 335. Grade 5.

    "In some cities, blacks were forced to ride in separate parts of buses. In 1955, in Montgomery, Alabama, Rosa Parks wanted to sit in a part of a public bus set aside for whites. She was arrested. The black people of Montgomery refused to ride the city buses until they could sit where they wanted."

18. Richard H. Loftin et al., *Our Country's Communities* (Morristown, NJ: Silver Burdett and Ginn), 1988, p. 246, Grade 3.

"One day a black woman named Rosa Parks got on a bus and found the back seats filled. She had been working all day and was tired. She sat down in another seat and was arrested."

"With Dr. King as their leader, the black people of Montgomery refused to ride on the bus until they had the same rights as the other riders."

"They did as he (King) said and finally won out."

APPENDIX II

Here is the complete text of "She Would Not Be Moved: The Story of Rosa Parks and the Montgomery Bus Boycott."

It was 1955. Everyone in the African American community in Montgomery, Alabama, knew Rosa Parks. She was a community leader, and people admired her courage. All throughout her life she had opposed prejudice, even if it got her into trouble with European American people.

In those days Alabama was legally segregated. That means that African American people were prevented by the state law from using the same swimming pools, schools, and other public facilities as European Americans. There also were separate entrances, toilets, and drinking fountains for African Americans and European Americans in places such as bus and train stations.

The facilities African Americans were allowed to use were not only separate from the ones European Americans used but were also very inferior. The reason for this was racism, the belief that European Americans were superior to African Americans and that therefore European Americans deserved better facilities.

In those days public buses were divided into two sections, one at the front for European Americans, which was supposed to be "for Whites only." From five to ten rows back the section for African Americans began. That part of the bus was called the "Colored" section.

Whenever it was crowded on the city buses African American people were forced to give up seats in the "Colored" section to European Americans and move to the back of the bus. For example, an elderly African American woman would have to give up her seat to a European American teenage male. If she refused she could be arrested for breaking the segregation laws.

December 1, 1955 on her way home from work, Rosa Parks took the bus as usual. She sat down in the front row of the "Colored" section. As the bus got crowded the driver demanded that she give up her seat to a European American man, and move to the back of the bus. This was not the first time that this had happened to Rosa Parks. In the past she had refused to move, and the driver had simply put her off the bus. Mrs.

Parks hated segregation, and along with many other African American people, refused to obey many of its unfair rules. On this day, she refused to do what the bus driver demanded.

The bus driver commanded her once more to go to the back of the bus and she stayed in her seat, looking straight ahead and not moving an inch. It was a hot day and the driver was angry and became very stubborn. He called a policeman, who arrested Mrs. Parks.

Mrs. Parks was not the first African American person to be arrested in Montgomery for refusing to move to the back of the bus. In the months before her refusal, at least three other people were arrested for the same reason. In fact, African American leaders in Montgomery were planning to overcome segregation. One way they wanted to do this was to have every African American person boycott the buses. Since most of the bus riders in the city were African American, the buses would go broke if they refused to let African Americans and European Americans ride the buses as equals.

From 1949 right up to the day Mrs. Parks refused to move, the Women's Political Council of Montgomery prepared to stage a bus boycott because of how African Americans were treated on the bus. They were just waiting for the time to be ripe. Nineteen fifty-five was the time.

However, none of the people who were arrested before Mrs. Parks was were leaders. She was a leader, and the day she was arrested the leadership called a meeting at the Dexter Avenue Baptist Church. They decided to begin their refusal to ride the buses the next morning. They knew Mrs. Parks had the courage to deal with the pressure of defying segregation and would not yield even if her life was threatened.

The next day the Montgomery bus boycott began.

There was a young new minister in Montgomery those days. His name was Martin Luther King, Jr. People in the community felt that he was a special person and asked him to lead the boycott. At first he wasn't sure. He worried about the violence that might result from the boycott. However, he quickly made up his mind that it was time to destroy segregation and accepted the people's call for him to be their leader.

The Montgomery bus boycott lasted 381 days. For over a year the African American people of Montgomery, Alabama, stayed off the buses. Some walked to work, others rode bicycles or shared car rides. It was very inconvenient for them, but they knew that what they were doing was very important for all African American people in the South.

The boycott succeeded, and by the end of 1956 African Americans and European Americans could ride the buses in Montgomery as equals. However, the struggle for the complete elimination of segregation had just begun.

We all owe a great deal to the courage and intelligence of Rosa Parks and the entire African American community of Montgomery, Alabama. They took risks to make democracy work for all of us.

STUDY QUESTIONS

1. Where was Rosa Parks sitting when she was arrested?

2. What are the consequences of telling an inaccurate version of the Rosa Parks story? What do schoolchildren miss?

3. Think back to your K–12 social studies and history **education**. What topics, people, or events in history were either not discussed, discussed inaccurately, or minimized?

4. Go to your public library and peruse the children's picture book section. Flip through books and see if you can find any that teach children about **race**, **class**, or **gender** in a covert or subtle way. That is, your picture book shouldn't directly talk about race, class, or gender. Find one good example and bring this book to class for a discussion.

5. If possible, interview someone under the age of twelve. What does he or she know about Rosa Parks? What is the source of the knowledge? Have things changed since this selection was published in 1995?

BELL HOOKS

Feminism: A Movement to End Sexist Oppression

A re you a feminist? The word *feminist* seems to make people nervous or turn them off even if they support **gender** equality. In this essay bell hooks explores why people are resistant to the label feminist and tries to define exactly what that term means. It's easy for us to say **feminism** means equality between men and women, but hooks delves deeper to ask whether women want to be equal to men of color, poor men, or men without citizenship status. Or do we mean women should be equal to middle-class white men? As you read this piece, consider what the term feminism means to you.

A CENTRAL PROBLEM WITHIN FEMINIST DISCOURSE HAS BEEN our inability to either arrive at a consensus of opinion about what feminism is or accept definition(s) that could serve as points of unification. Without agreed-upon definition(s), we lack a sound foundation on which to construct theory or engage in overall meaningful praxis. Expressing her frustrations with the absence of clear definitions in a recent essay, "Towards a Revolutionary Ethics," Carmen Vazquez comments:

> We can't even agree on what a "Feminist" is, never mind what she would believe in and how she defines the principles that constitute honor among us. In key with the American capitalist obsession for individualism and anything goes so long as it gets you what you want, feminism in America has come to mean anything you like, honey. There are as many definitions of Feminism as there are feminists, some of my sisters say, with a chuckle. I don't think it's funny.

It is not funny. It indicates a growing lack of interest in feminism as a radical political movement. It is a despairing gesture expressive of the belief that solidarity among women is not possible. It is a sign that the political naïveté which has traditionally characterized woman's lot in male-dominated culture abounds.

Most people in the United States think of feminism, or the more commonly used term "women's lib," as a movement that aims to make women the social equals of men. This broad definition, popularized by the media and mainstream segments of the movement, raises problematic questions. Since men are not equals in white suprema-cist, capitalist, patriarchal class structure, which men do women want to be equal to? Do women share a common vision of what equality means? Implicit in this simplistic definition of women's liberation is a dismissal of race and class as factors that, in con-junction with sexism, determine the extent to which an individual will be discrimi-nated against, exploited, or oppressed. Bourgeois white women interested in women's rights issues have been satisfied with simple definitions for obvious reasons. Rhetori-cally placing themselves in the same social category as oppressed women, they are not anxious to call attention to race and class privilege.

Women in lower-class and poor groups, particularly those who are non-white, would not have defined women's liberation as women gaining social equality with men, since they are continually reminded in their everyday lives that all women do not share a common social status. Concurrently, they know that many males in their social groups are exploited and oppressed. Knowing that men in their groups do not have social, political, and economic power, they would not deem it liberatory to share their social status. While they are aware that sexism enables men in their respective groups to have privileges that are denied them, they are more likely to see exaggerated expressions of male chauvinism among their peers as stemming from the male's sense of himself as powerless and ineffectual in relation to ruling male groups, rather than an expression of an overall privileged social status. From the very onset of the wom-en's liberation movement, these women were suspicious of feminism precisely because they recognized the limitations inherent in its definition. They recognized the possi-bility that feminism defined as social equality with men might easily become a move-ment that would primarily affect the social standing of white women in middle- and upper-class groups while affecting only in a very marginal way the social status of working-class and poor women.

* * *

In an article, "Sisters—Under the Skin," in a San Francisco newspaper, columnist Bob Greene commented on the aversion many women apparently have to the term "femi-nism." Greene finds it curious that many women "who obviously believe in everything that proud feminists believe in dismiss the term 'feminist' as something unpleasant; something with which they do not wish to be associated." Even though such women often acknowledge that they have benefited from feminist-generated reform measures that have improved the social status of specific groups of women, they do not wish to be seen as participants in feminist movement:

> There is no getting around it. After all this time, the term "feminist" makes many bright, ambitious, intelligent women embarrassed and uncomfortable. They simply don't want to be associated with it.
>
> It's as if it has an unpleasant connotation that they want no connection with. Chances are if you were to present them with every mainstream feminist belief, they would go along with the beliefs to the letter—and even if they consider themselves feminists, they hasten to say no.

Many women are reluctant to advocate feminism because they are uncertain about the meaning of the term. Other women from exploited and oppressed ethnic groups dismiss the term because they do not wish to be perceived as supporting a racist movement; feminism is often equated with white women's rights efforts. Large numbers of women see feminism as synonymous with lesbianism; their homophobia leads them to reject association with any group identified as pro-lesbian. Some women fear the word "feminism" because they shun identification with any political movement, especially one perceived as radical. Of course there are women who do not wish to be associated with women's rights movement in any form, so they reject and oppose feminist movement. Most women are more familiar with negative perspectives on "women's lib" than with the positive significations of feminism. It is this term's positive political significance and power that we must now struggle to recover and maintain.

Currently feminism seems to be a term without any clear significance. The "anything goes" approach to the definition of the word has rendered it practically meaningless. What is meant by "anything goes" is usually that any woman who wants social equality with men regardless of her political perspective (she can be a conservative right-winger or a nationalist communist) can label herself feminist. Most attempts at defining feminism reflect the class nature of the movement. Definitions are usually liberal in origin and focus on the individual woman's right to freedom and self-determination.

* * *

Feminism defined in political terms that stress collective as well as individual experience challenges women to enter a new domain—to leave behind the apolitical stance sexism decrees is our lot and develop political consciousness. Women know from our everyday lives that many of us rarely discuss politics. Even when women talked about sexist politics in the heyday of contemporary feminism, rather than allow this engagement with serious political matters to lead to complex, in-depth analysis of women's social status, we insisted that men were "the enemy," the cause of all our problems. As a consequence, we examined almost exclusively women's relationship to male supremacy and the ideology of sexism. The focus on "man as enemy" created, as Marlene Dixon emphasizes in her essay "The Rise and Demise of Women's Liberation: A Class

Analysis," a "politics of psychological oppression" that evoked world views that "pit individual against individual and mystify the social basis of exploitation." By repudiating the popular notion that the focus of feminist movement should be social equality of the sexes and by emphasizing eradication of the cultural basis of group oppression, our own analysis would require an exploration of all aspects of women's political reality. This would mean that race and class oppression would be recognized as feminist issues with as much relevance as sexism.

When feminism is defined in such a way that it calls attention to the diversity of women's social and political reality, it centralizes the experiences of all women, especially the women whose social conditions have been least written about, studied, or changed by political movements. When we cease to focus on the simplistic stance "men are the enemy," we are compelled to examine systems of domination and our role in their maintenance and perpetuation. Lack of adequate definition made it easy for bourgeois women, whether liberal or radical in perspective, to maintain their dominance over the leadership of the movement and its direction. This hegemony continues to exist in most feminist organizations. Exploited and oppressed groups of women are usually encouraged by those in power to feel that their situation is hopeless, that they can do nothing to break the pattern of domination. Given such socialization, these women have often felt that our only response to white, bourgeois, hegemonic dominance of feminist movement is to trash, reject, or dismiss feminism. This reaction is in no way threatening to the women who wish to maintain control over the direction of feminist theory and praxis. They prefer us to be silent, passively accepting their ideas. They prefer us speaking against "them" rather than developing our own ideas about feminist movement.

Feminism is the struggle to end sexist oppression. Its aim is not to benefit solely any specific group of women, any particular race or class of women. It does not privilege women over men. It has the power to transform in a meaningful way all our lives. Most importantly, feminism is neither a lifestyle nor a ready-made identity or role one can step into. Diverting energy from feminist movement that aims to change society, many women concentrate on the development of a counter-culture, a woman-centered world wherein participants have little contact with men. Such attempts do not indicate a respect or concern for the vast majority of women who are unable to integrate their cultural expressions with the visions offered by alternative, woman-centered communities. In *Beyond God the Father*, Mary Daly urged women to give up "the securities offered by the patriarchal system" and create new space that would be woman-centered. Responding to Daly, Jeanne Gross pointed to the contradictions that arise when the focus of feminist movement is on the construction of new space:

> Creating a "counterworld" places an incredible amount of pressure on the women who attempt to embark on such a project. The pressure comes from the belief that the only true resources for such an endeavor are ourselves. The past which is totally patriarchal is viewed as irredeemable . . .

If we go about creating an alternative culture without remaining in dialogue with others (and the historical circumstances that give rise to their identity) we have no reality check for our goals. We run the very real risk that the dominant ideology of the culture is re-duplicated in the feminist movement through cultural imperialism.

Equating feminist struggle with living in a counter-cultural, woman-centered world erected barriers that closed the movement off from most women. Despite sexist discrimination, exploitation, or oppression, many women feel their lives as they live them are important and valuable. Naturally the suggestion that these lives could be simply left or abandoned for an alternative "feminist" lifestyle met with resistance. Feeling their life experiences devalued, deemed solely negative and worthless, many women responded by vehemently attacking feminism. By rejecting the notion of an alternative feminist "lifestyle" that can emerge only when women create a subculture (whether it is living space or even space like women's studies, which on many campuses has become exclusive), and by insisting that feminist struggle can begin wherever an individual woman is, we create a movement that focuses on our collective experience, a movement that is continually mass-based.

Over the past six years, many separatist-oriented communities have been formed by women so that the focus has shifted from the development of woman-centered space towards an emphasis on identity. Once woman-centered space exists, it can be maintained only if women remain convinced that it is the only place where they can be self-realized and free. After assuming a "feminist" identity, women often seek to live the "feminist" lifestyle. These women do not see that it undermines feminist movement to project the assumption that "feminist" is but another pre-packaged role women can now select as they search for identity. The willingness to see feminism as a lifestyle choice rather than a political commitment reflects the class nature of the movement. It is not surprising that the vast majority of women who equate feminism with alternative lifestyle are from middle-class backgrounds, unmarried, college-educated, often students who are without many of the social and economic responsibilities that working-class and poor women who are laborers, parents, homemakers, and wives confront daily. Sometimes lesbians have sought to equate feminism with lifestyle, but for significantly different reasons. Given the prejudice and discrimination against lesbian women in our society, alternative communities that are woman-centered are one means of creating positive, affirming environments. Despite positive reasons for developing woman-centered space (which does not need to be equated with a "feminist" lifestyle), like pleasure, support, and resource-sharing, emphasis on creating a counter-culture has alienated women from feminist movement, for such space can be in churches, kitchens, etc.

Longing for community, connection, a sense of shared purpose, many women found support networks in feminist organizations. Satisfied in a personal way by new relationships generated in what was called a "safe," "supportive" context wherein discussion focused on feminist ideology, they did not question whether masses of women shared the same need for community. Certainly many black women as well as women from other ethnic groups do not feel an absence of community among women in their lives, despite exploitation and oppression. The focus on feminism as a way to develop shared identity and community has little appeal to women who experience community, who seek ways to end exploitation and oppression in the context of their lives. While they may develop an interest in a feminist politic that works to eradicate sexist oppression, they will probably never feel as intense a need for a "feminist" identity and lifestyle.

Often emphasis on identity and lifestyle is appealing because it creates a false sense that one is engaged in praxis. However, praxis within any political movement that aims to have a radical transformative impact on society cannot be solely focused on creating spaces wherein would-be radicals experience safety and support. Feminist movement to end sexist oppression actively engages participants in revolutionary struggle. Struggle is rarely safe or pleasurable.

Focusing on feminism as political commitment, we resist the emphasis on individual identity and lifestyle. (This should not be confused with the very real need to unite theory and practice.) Such resistance engages us in revolutionary praxis. The ethics of Western society informed by imperialism and capitalism are personal rather than social. They teach us that the individual good is more important than the collective good, and consequently that individual change is of greater significance than collective change. This particular form of cultural imperialism has been reproduced in feminist movement in the form of individual women equating the fact that their lives have been changed in a meaningful way by feminism "as is" with a policy that no change need occur in the theory and praxis, even if it has little or no impact on society as a whole, or on masses of women.

To emphasize that engagement with feminist struggle as political commitment, we could avoid using the phrase "I am a feminist" (a linguistic structure designed to refer to some personal aspect of identity and self-definition) and could state, "I advocate feminism." Because there has been undue emphasis placed on feminism as an identity or lifestyle, people usually resort to stereotyped perspectives on feminism. Deflecting attention away from stereotypes is necessary if we are to revise our strategy and direction. I have found that saying "I am a feminist" usually means I am plugged into preconceived notions of identity, role, or behavior. When I say, "I advocate feminism," the response is usually, "What is feminism?" A phrase like "I advocate" does not imply the kind of absolutism that is suggested by "I am." It does not engage us in the either/or dualistic thinking that is the central ideological component of all systems of domination in Western society. It implies that a choice has been made, that commitment to feminism is an act of will. It does not suggest that by committing oneself to feminism, the possibility of supporting other political movements is negated.

As a black woman interested in feminist movement, I am often asked whether being black is more important than being a woman; whether feminist struggle to end sexist oppression is more important than the struggle to end racism or vice versa. All such questions are rooted in competitive either/or thinking, the belief that the self is formed in opposition to an other. Therefore one is a feminist because one is not something else. Most people are socialized to think in terms of opposition rather than compatibility. Rather than seeing anti-racist work as totally compatible with working to end sexist oppression, they often see them as two movements competing for first place. When one is asked, "Are you a feminist?," it appears that an affirmative answer is translated to mean that one is concerned with no political issues other than feminism. When one is black, an affirmative response is likely to be heard as a devaluation of struggle to end racism. Given the fear of being misunderstood, it has been difficult for black women and women in exploited and oppressed ethnic groups to give expression to their interest in feminist concerns. They have been wary of saying "I am a feminist." The shift in expression from "I am a feminist" to "I advocate feminism" could serve as a useful strategy for eliminating the focus on identity and lifestyle. It could serve as a way in which women who are concerned about feminism as well as other political movements could express their support while avoiding linguistic structures that give primacy to one particular group. It would also encourage greater exploration in feminist theory.

The shift in definition away from notions of social equality towards an emphasis on ending sexist oppression leads to a shift in attitudes in regard to the development of theory. Given the class nature of feminist movement so far, as well as racial hierarchies, developing theory (the guiding set of beliefs and principles that becomes the basis for action) has been a task particularly subject to the hegemonic dominance of white academic women. This has led many women outside the privileged race/class group to see the focus on developing theory, even the very use of the term, as a concern that functions only to reinforce the power of the elite group. Such reactions reinforce the sexist/racist/classist notion that developing theory is the domain of the white intellectual. Privileged white women active in feminist movement, whether liberal or radical in perspective, encourage black women to contribute "experiential" work, personal life stories. Personal experiences are important to feminist movement, but they cannot take the place of theory. Charlotte Bunch explains the special significance of theory in her essay "Feminism and Education: Not by Degrees":

> Theory enables us to see immediate needs in terms of long-range goals and an overall perspective on the world. It thus gives us a framework for evaluating various strategies in both the long and the short run and for seeing the types of changes that they are likely to produce. Theory is not just a body of facts or a set of personal opinions. It involves explanations and hypotheses that are based on available knowledge and experience. It is also dependent on conjecture and insight about how to interpret those facts and experiences and their significance.

Since bourgeois white women had defined feminism in such a way as to make it appear that it had no real significance for black women, they could then conclude that black women need not contribute to developing theory. We were to provide the colorful life stories to document and validate the prevailing set of theoretical assumptions. (An interesting discussion of black women's responses to feminist movement may be found in the essay "Challenging Imperial Feminism" by Valerie Amos and Pratibha Parmar.) Focus on social equality with men as a definition of feminism led to an emphasis on discrimination, male attitudes, and legalistic reforms. Feminism as a movement to end sexist oppression directs our attention to systems of domination and the interrelatedness of sex, race, and class oppression. Therefore, it compels us to centralize the experiences and the social predicaments of women who bear the brunt of sexist oppression as a way to understand the collective social status of women in the United States. Defining feminism as a movement to end sexist oppression is crucial for the development of theory because it is a starting point indicating the direction of exploration and analysis.

The foundation of future feminist struggle must be solidly based on a recognition of the need to eradicate the underlying cultural basis and causes of sexism and other forms of group oppression. Without challenging and changing these philosophical structures, no feminist reforms will have a long-range impact. Consequently, it is now necessary for advocates of feminism to collectively acknowledge that our struggle cannot be defined as a movement to gain social equality with men, that terms like "liberal feminist" and "bourgeois feminist" represent contradictions that must be resolved so that feminism will not be continually co-opted to serve the opportunistic ends of special-interest groups.

STUDY QUESTIONS

1. Why does hooks argue that women are resistant to defining themselves as feminists?

2. Why is it harder to define feminism when we consider **race** and **economic class**?

3. What does it mean to you when someone says he or she is a feminist? What do you think about people who define themselves this way? What difference would it make if the person claimed to "advocate feminism" instead?

4. Ask five friends if they support gender equality (i.e., equality between men and women in the generic sense of the term). If they say yes, ask them if they consider themselves a feminist. Regardless of whether they say yes or no, ask them why they answered how they did.